# Mortal Justice

NEW
HORIZON
PRESS

Dear Reader,

We proudly present the newest addition to our internationally acclaimed true crime series of *Real People/Incredible Stories*. These riveting thrillers spotlight men and women who perform extraordinary deeds against tremendous odds: to fight for justice, track down elusive killers, protect the innocent or exonerate the wrongly accused. Their stories, told in their own voices, reveal the untold drama and anguish behind the headlines of those who face horrific realities and find the resiliency to fight back...

*Mortal Justice* follows the shocking trials and gripping tribulations of three lives which unexpectedly intertwine. When Nancy DePriest, a beautiful young woman, was found murdered in her place of employment, there were more questions than answers. Her mother, Jeanette Popp, was relieved when investigators had in custody a suspect who signed a confession and implicated his friend. Then, after years of serving their sentences, another man confessed to being the killer of Nancy DePriest. Now, everything Jeanette's been led to believe is about to be turned upside-down. And one question resonates: If true, how could this have happened?

The next time you want to read a crackling, suspenseful page-turner, which is also a true account of a real-life hero illustrating the resilience of the human spirit – look for the New Horizon Press logo.

Sincerely,

*Joan*

Dr. Joan S. Dunphy
Publisher & Editor-in-Chief

*Real People/Incredible Stories*

# Mortal Justice:

## A True Story of Murder and Vindication

by Jeanette Popp and Wanda Evans

New Horizon Press
Far Hills, NJ

Popp, Jeanette and Evans, Wanda
Mortal Justice: A True Story of Murder and Vindication

Cover design: Robert Aulicino
Interior design: Susan Sanderson

Library of Congress Control Number: 2008925055

ISBN 13: 978-0-88282-338-6
ISBN 10: 0-88282-338-8

New Horizon Press books may be purchased in bulk quantities for educational, business or sales promotional use. For more information please write to:
New Horizon Press Special Sales Department
PO Box 669
Far Hills, NJ 07931
1-800-533-7978
Email: nhp@newhorizonpressbooks.com

www.newhorizonpressbooks.com


Manufactured in the U.S.A.


2013   2012   2011   2010   2009  /  5   4   3   2   1

# Authors' Note

This book is based on the experiences of the authors and reflects their perceptions of the past, present and future. The personalities, events, actions and conversations portrayed within this story have been taken from interviews, research, court documents, letters, personal papers, press accounts and the memories of some participants.

In an effort to safeguard the privacy of certain people, some individuals' names and identifying characteristics have been changed. Events involving the characters happened as described. Only minor details may have been altered.

# Dedication

This book is dedicated to the memory of my beloved daughter, Nancy, and to my equally beloved husband, James Popp, who is my constant supporter, my wise advisor and my best friend.

# Table of Contents

# Prologue

When the man woke up that morning, the only thing on his mind, as he dressed in a dark shirt and pants that could have passed for a uniform of some kind, was how to get some money. Money for food. Money to buy gas for the borrowed, gas-guzzling, beige car he was driving. Money for beer—as important, if not more so, than food. Most important of all, money for the drugs he craved with all his mind and body. And he figured the best way to get the money he needed was to take it from someone else. His business was robbery. When he finished dressing, he put a few hand tools, including a square head screwdriver, in a gym bag, his "tool kit" for the day. Had he called a comrade to join him? Could one man alone commit such savage events as were about to transpire?

Three days earlier, he had scoured the classified section of the newspaper. To his great satisfaction, he had found exactly what he was looking for: a person offering a handgun for sale, no questions asked. That same day, the man took possession of a .22 caliber Ruger semi-automatic pistol. Now, on top of the hand tools in the gym bag, he placed the Ruger.

He had already cased several businesses that might be easy for him to rob, and his target this morning was a family-themed restaurant. When he left his friend's apartment where he had crashed the night before and went out into the beautiful morning, the sun was still low in the east, casting a rosy glow over the city skyline. Oblivious to the beauty of the autumn day, the man drove to the restaurant. He knew it would not be open this early, a little after eight o'clock, but there was a good chance someone would be there, getting ready for the day's business. Parking close to the back door of the building, he got out, took his gym bag from the passenger seat beside him, eased the car door shut and walked the few steps to the door. He rapped sharply and waited a few minutes. When the door opened, he was facing not one, but two men, who eyed him suspiciously.

"I'm here to test your pressurized beverage lines," he said, holding the bag close to his thigh. After a moment's hesitation, the men allowed him inside and both accompanied him to an area where they pointed out the beverage lines. He studied the lines and the various gauges intently, waiting for the employees to go about their work. Only they didn't. Instead, they watched him carefully as he noted the settings on each gauge. He knew he had no chance of getting the pistol out of the bag and getting the drop on them while they were standing so close. Finally, he told the two employees the gauges were working properly and turned to go. Both men followed him to the door and stood in the open doorway, watching him get into his car.

Frustrated and angry, he drove away from the restaurant, headed nowhere.

After a few minutes, he saw a Pizza Hut just ahead, with a small gray car nosed in next to the building. *Maybe I'll have better luck here,* he probably thought, turning into a small parking lot south of the store. Carrying his bag casually in his left hand, he walked around the corner of the building to the west side and knocked loudly on what obviously was the back door.

A young woman—pretty, slim, with curly blonde hair caught up in a ponytail—opened the door. Barefoot, her slender feet encased in taupe colored nylons, she barely came to his chin.

"Can I help you?" she asked in a puzzled tone.

Using the subterfuge he had tried at the previous restaurant, the man explained that he had come to make a safety check on the pressurized beverage lines in the restaurant. Eyeing the bag he carried, she nodded.

"Okay," she said, stepping back to let him enter. She turned and led the way across the restaurant to a far corner, where she pointed out the oxygen tanks and pressurized lines. To his immense relief, she left him to his work. He watched her walk away, admiring the snug fit of her khaki slacks, the way her blue apron, tied securely around her waist, emphasized the lines of her toned body under the knit pullover shirt.

As he watched, the telephone rang and she went behind the counter to answer it, standing with her back to him, talking with great animation to someone, apparently about restaurant-related business. Quickly, he pulled the Ruger from his bag and moved quietly behind the counter, until he could almost touch her back. For the first time, he noticed a low rumbling sound and saw a machine with metal rollers dropping small balls of dough on trays where they were being flattened into pizza shells. A pair of sneakers lay on the floor under the counter, next to where the woman stood at the telephone. When she finished her call, the man put the gun to her back and ordered her to open the safe.

Shock and surprise filled her eyes when she felt the gun pressing into her back.

"Open the safe," he repeated.

"Okay," she said. "I'll do it. Just don't shoot. Be careful with that thing." From memory, she dialed in the code to the safe, opened it and took out two plastic money bags with bank logos on them. She handed him the currency bags, and he motioned to several clear plastic baggies of coins he could see in the safe. With shaking hands, the woman gathered up the baggies and gave them to him as well.

He put the money on the counter and motioned with the gun toward the back of the restaurant. "I want you to turn around and walk slowly into the men's room."

"I gave you the money. Please, just leave now," she pleaded.

He prodded her with the gun. "Do as I say and I won't hurt you."

She nodded and walked ahead of him into the men's room, only a few feet away, down a short hall, casting fearful looks at him over her shoulder. Inside the men's room, the robber told her to put her hands behind her back and he handcuffed them together. "I'm going to take off your clothes and have sex with you," he told her.

She looked at him, her blue eyes wide and frightened. "Please don't do that. Don't hurt me."

Ignoring her plea, the man began to undress her. First, he untied the apron and threw it on the floor. Then he tugged her uniform pants and delicate nylon panties together, down her legs and off, over her feet. He left the knee-high stockings on her lower legs. Wasting no time, he jerked her bra and shirt over her head, leaving them caught on her wrists, since the handcuffs wouldn't allow them to go farther.

The men's room was small and the tile floor hard, so he forced her to a secluded corner of the restaurant. He made her stop at a storage area, where he grabbed a handful of aprons and piled them on the floor to provide a modicum of cushioning. She lay on her back as instructed, and he forced himself into her. It was quick and painful, but she steeled herself not to scream. She didn't struggle, obviously fearing any resistance would earn her blows—or even a bullet—from the gun he still held in his hand.

When he finished, he ordered her back into the men's room and told her to get under the sink counter. "I'm going to cuff you to the pipes so you can't follow me or call the police until I'm gone," he told her.

Possibly believing the worst was over, that her ordeal had ended, she crouched under the counter and turned her head away, because she could no longer bear looking at him. He shot her once in the back of the head and watched her body crumple to the cold, hard floor.

Hurriedly, the killer searched for the ejected shell casing but couldn't find it. He ran his hands over and under her body and through her hair, thinking it might have lodged there, but he didn't feel it. He shook out her clothing, but the shell wasn't there either. He had loaded the gun with his bare hands and knew his prints were on the casing. Frantic now, he couldn't think what to do. Then it came to him. Maybe if he flooded the room, the shell might become dislodged from wherever it was hiding. He stuffed the sink drain with a blue apron and turned on both taps. Then he grabbed the woman's feet, dragged her out into the hall between the men's and women's restrooms and turned her onto her stomach. He took the cuffs off and removed the shirt from her arms, but left the bra hanging loosely around her wrists. Then, roughly, he turned her over onto her back again, leaving her body sprawled awkwardly on the floor that was already wet from the stopped-up sink.

Back in the men's room, although the floor was covered with water, there still was no shell to be found. Reluctant to give up his search, but fearing he might not have much more time, he took a blue bandanna from his pocket and quickly wiped the surfaces he might have touched—the door, the countertops, even the telephone. Then he placed the money he'd taken in his tool bag and snatched a ring of keys from a wall hook. To his relief, one of the keys unlocked the door by which he had entered a brief few minutes earlier, and he hurried out of the building.

Behind him, the noisy rumbling of the pizza dough machine covered the sound of any faint breath left in the young woman sprawled on the floor.

## Chapter 1

# A Stolen Life

The first thing Lester Davis noticed when he unlocked the back door to the Pizza Hut was the rhythmic clatter of the dough machine. *Good. Someone has at least started prep,* he probably thought. *But where was the assistant manager? Why hadn't she answered my calls over the last hour or so?* Then he noticed the water that covered the floor. *Where was that coming from? Why hadn't the manager called someone when she saw she had a problem with the plumbing? What was going on?*

"Hello!" he called, squishing through the food preparation area. "Anybody here?"

No reply. Davis felt a sudden sense of foreboding. Something was terribly wrong. But what could possibly have made one of his managers leave her post? The store manager had been scheduled to open the store that morning, but she had traded shifts with her assistant manager, Nancy DePriest. An area general manager with Pizza Hut, Davis had been transferred to Austin, Texas, only five days earlier. He hadn't had a chance to get to know his managers yet, but he had been briefed about each one. Nancy DePriest had been described to him in glowing terms. She was supposed to be one of his most reliable employees. Surely she would not have left the store, especially with water running everywhere, without notifying him.

Early each morning, it was Davis's habit to call each of the seven stores under his management to gather sales data. He had started calling about eight o'clock, working his way down the list, but when he had called this store, there was no response. One other store had not responded either. Davis had instructed an assistant to find out what was happening at that location and then he had driven here.

His heart pounding, he sloshed through half-inch deep water, past the noisy dough machine, toward the restrooms, which seemed to be the source of the flood. In the hallway, he stopped short. "Oh, my God," he breathed.

Water trickled around the body of a young blonde woman who lay on the floor, naked except for knee-high stockings. Blood-tinged water eddied around her head and neck. Her eyes were wide open, fixed and staring. A dark, pebble-like object protruded from one eye.

"Are you all right?" Davis blurted out, immediately feeling foolish. She certainly was not all right. In fact, she might be dead. He had to get help immediately and, instinctively knowing he shouldn't touch anything so as not to obliterate any evidence, he ran from the building and raced across the street to a gas station.

"Call 911," he yelled at the two attendants behind the counter. Startled, they stood, frozen, staring with open mouths at this madman charging through their door.

"Call the police," he demanded. "A woman's been shot at the Pizza Hut."

It was 9:33 A.M.

It seemed hours, rather than just four minutes, that Davis waited for the police. He paced the parking lot frantically, his eyes constantly scanning the street for emergency vehicles. When Austin police officers Scott Ehlert and Mike Alexander arrived, he told them he had found his assistant manager badly wounded on the floor of the restaurant. When asked, he told them that he had entered the building by the west door. Thinking the intruder must have entered and left by the west door and not wanting to further contaminate the crime scene, they asked him to let them in by the east door, which he unlocked for them. He showed them inside and led them to where the woman lay. Both officers had seen their share of violent death—car crashes, shootings, stabbings—but this scene sickened them. Blood seeped from her head wound and stained the water that trickled around her body. Alexander placed his fingers to her carotid artery and felt a faint flutter beneath his fingertips. She was still alive! He was amazed. EMS had been dispatched when he and Ehlert got the call and an ambulance would be there soon. He tried to talk to the unconscious woman, assuring her help was on the way.

In the meantime, Ehlert called the Austin Police Department's homicide unit and was told detectives were on their way, along with officers from the robbery detail and sex crimes units. Four EMS personnel arrived at 9:40 and instantly knew their patient was in dire distress. Immediately they put her on life support before gently easing her onto a backboard, then onto a gurney and into the ambulance. The driver raced toward Brackenridge Hospital.

Sergeant Hector Polanco was a thirteen-year veteran of the Austin Police Department. He had been a narcotics officer for several years prior to his transfer to the homicide unit. Polanco was known for getting results by nearly any means necessary. He prided himself for being intimidating, tougher than any suspect he ever expected to meet. Working with him that morning was another veteran of the APD, Detective Bruce Boardman, who had been in homicide for two years, although he had been on the force for fifteen. He was very much like Polanco in his zeal to clear cases. Several officers were already at the Pizza Hut when Polanco and Boardman arrived at 10:07. The victim, identified as Nancy DePriest, had already been whisked to the hospital and placed on life support.

Polanco, as lead investigator, took control of the crime scene and began making assignments. A couple of officers were sent to rope off the scene, including the parking lot. Others were sent to canvass the surrounding neighborhood of small businesses and apartment houses to find anyone who might have seen anything suspicious at the restaurant earlier that morning. Had any vehicles stopped at the Pizza Hut? Any persons who acted furtively?

Others began to examine the interior scene. One patrolman discovered the cause of the water everywhere, a stopped up sink. He turned the faucets off and pulled a blue apron, sopping wet, out of the drain and pushed it to the side of the sink. Officer Larry Hall found the shell casing and looked at it, puzzled. For some reason, it was curiously flattened. When he called attention to the misshapen piece of brass, another officer, a sergeant, admitted he may have accidentally stepped on it. Hall gave the casing to Detective Boardman. After that, he diagrammed the scene, to help investigators in the ensuing investigation.

In the back of the store, two blue aprons and a sweater had been spread on the floor and it appeared as if someone had been lying on top of them. Boardman found hairs on top of the clothing, and these were removed and bagged for the Texas Department of Public Safety Crime Laboratory Service. Forensics technicians also found hairs on a yellow bench in the waiting area. Other hairs, soaked in coagulated blood, were discovered under the counter in the men's room. Polanco took swabs of the blood for comparison to Nancy DePriest's.

William Mauldin, of the Austin Police Department's robbery unit, arrived at the scene and was briefed by Boardman and Polanco. Mauldin examined the safe. It was empty and did not appear to have been tampered with. He surmised that someone who knew the combination must have opened it. The open cash register was practically empty, yielding only a few coins.

Four or five feet from the cash register, Mauldin found a set of car keys, a single brass key and a container of pills. DePriest's purse was nearby and it didn't appear to have been opened or searched. In the purse, Boardman found a work phone number for Nancy's husband, Todd DePriest, and called him to tell him what had happened and that his wife was at Brackenridge Hospital by now. Boardman bagged the items and DePriest's clothing, including a bra that he later learned had been wrapped loosely around her wrists.

A short while later, when officer Stephen Baker went outside to secure the east side of the building, he saw a young man coming toward him, looking stunned and disoriented. The man identified himself to Baker as Todd DePriest and wanted to know where his wife was. Baker told him Nancy had been taken to the hospital. DePriest appeared too unnerved to drive, so Baker volunteered to drive him to the hospital.

Clues were few at the crime scene. Since there were no signs of forced entry, Polanco and Boardman suspected that the killer either had a key or knew DePriest. Boardman asked Davis, who had keys to the store, and Davis told him there were two master keys, which opened all the restaurants he supervised. Davis himself had one of the master keys and the district manager had the other one. Otherwise, each store had its own keys, which opened only the doors to that specific building. These keys were given only to shift managers, assistant managers and shift leaders. In addition, various service personnel, such as carpet cleaners and exterminators, had keys.

Davis also said that each restaurant had its own safe, with the combination known only to each store's managers, assistant managers and shift leaders.

Polanco made a note to get someone to start searching for former Pizza Hut employees who might have kept a key.

Eventually, when she returned from her trip that morning, the restaurant manager, Nancy's supervisor, got ready to go to the store.

She found a note on her door to call Lester Davis, who told her what had happened. She arrived at the Pizza Hut, only to find it taped off and she was not allowed to enter. She identified herself to the officer on guard, who went to get Polanco. The sergeant came out to meet her and asked her to come in and give him her assessment of what might have happened. The store seemed disturbingly forlorn, although the only signs of intrusion were the water on the floor and the open safe and cash register. Troubled, she looked around the area to see if she could determine anything that might indicate when Nancy had been attacked. After assessing the work Nancy had done, she said it would have taken anywhere from forty-five minutes to an hour and fifteen minutes to accomplish that much.

Polanco already knew, from information other employees had given him, that Nancy DePriest had called the store's supplier at about 8:30 that morning, asking that paper goods be delivered as soon as possible. The delivery man said he reached the store at about 9:15, although he was not quite sure of the exact time. The door was locked and no one responded to his repeated knocking, although he could hear the phone ringing inside. He called his supervisor, who advised him to hang around for a few minutes and keep trying to get into the store. There was still no response, although he saw two cars, a small gray car and a brown car in the back parking lot. From this information, Polanco surmised that the delivery man had arrived later than 9:15; in fact, probably after Les Davis arrived, because Davis had told them he drove a brown car. Davis could have already discovered the crime and gone across the street to the gas station.

The store manager told police it was company policy to empty paper money from the cash registers every night. Dollar bills were kept in a regular plastic zipper bank bag with the bank's name on it. Coins were kept in a beige cloth bag with a drawstring tie. The change fund, also kept in the safe in clear plastic bags, was one hundred and fifty dollars. It was common knowledge among employees that the money was taken out of the machines and cash register at night.

The store manager told Polanco that some of their aprons were blue and some were black. Employees could wear their choice of either a blue or black apron.

The store manager's description of Nancy's personality and work habits bolstered Polanco's theory that either she knew her killer or the killer had a key to the building. "She would never have let in someone she didn't know," the store manager insisted.

A spokesman for the restaurant chain agreed, saying, "Nancy DePriest had an excellent future with our company. She had previously worked at three other Pizza Huts in Austin. Since she was a real conscientious employee and was a very firm believer in our policies and standards, it is difficult for me to believe that she would let in someone she didn't know."

That assessment was confirmed by co-workers and friends of DePriest.

"She was a very caring and very giving person," said one woman, who usually worked the early morning shift with DePriest. "Nobody had the right to steal her life away like that. She was so young, so in love and so happy. She loved life. It's just so sad."

The woman said DePriest loved her daughter and her husband very much. "She was dedicated to her work and was very happy with what she did." She described DePriest as an understanding supervisor. "It's not that you were working *for* her, you were working *with* her."

Other co-workers said DePriest looked forward to spending the years ahead with her family. She was looking forward to her baby getting older and spoke frequently of wanting to buy her daughter a little motorized car when she was old enough. One employee described DePriest as the type of person who liked to be where there was fun going on. "As a supervisor, she centered everything around the employee. She was the best, I tell you," he said. He echoed what others employees had said about DePriest's undying love for her daughter. "Our whole conversation, all day, would be about her little girl. She was so much into that little girl." He said she had very few interests outside her work and family. "If she didn't have anything to do, she would be on the phone, laughing and talking. She was a real happy person."

An APD fingerprint expert, Charles Dermody, worked the crime scene, processing the fence behind the building, along with other objects outside. Inside, he processed the three entrances, the coolers, the safe area, two telephones and the areas that had not gotten wet in and around the bathrooms.

William Beechinor, an investigator on the robbery detail, was dispatched to Brackenridge Hospital, where he examined Nancy's body for fingerprints, but found none. Afterward, he talked briefly with Todd DePriest, asking him if he would submit to testing for blood, saliva, hair and semen. DePriest agreed to come to the police department for testing.

At the end of the day, with no suspects and few leads to work, Polanco told reporters, "She seems to have been an exceptionally good lady, mother and wife, very supportive of her husband, very supportive of her job."

He told reporters that this was a heinous and cruel crime, hard to understand, hard to rationalize and hard to accept. "But," he said, "we are putting a supreme effort into the investigation."

Chapter 2

# A Daughter
# Taken Away—Again

That Monday was one of the hottest fall days Jeanette Barnes had ever experienced. The temperature hovered around one hundred degrees and her car had no air conditioning, so her job hunt was made miserable by the sticky, steamy, north central Texas air and her inability to find work after quitting her last job as a convenience store manager a few months earlier.

While she was job hunting, she was living out in the country, between Terrell and Mabank, so she could be near her retired father and stepmother, Johnnie and Shirley Stallcup. The cottage was owned by a friend, Doris Barnes, who lived with her son, Freddy, up the hill, behind Jeanette's house.

Freddy Barnes and Jeanette had dated for a while. He suffered horribly from rheumatoid arthritis and he worked when he could, but most of the time, he couldn't work. Many times, he was in so much pain he couldn't walk. Freddy and Jeanette had eventually married, more a marriage of friendship than passion. When she worked, she could put him on her medical insurance so he could get treatment. She helped Doris take care of him when he was too ill to do anything. Sometimes he lived with Jeanette and sometimes he lived with his mother. Their relationship benefitted them both. And it was especially beneficial to Jeanette, now that she had no money coming in, to be able to live in the little house down the hill from the Barneses.

With her experience, she knew she would be able to get a job managing a convenience store, but when she got home at about 3:30 that afternoon from making the rounds, she felt more discouraged than she had at any time in the last few months. Hoping to get some relief from the oppressive heat, she sat for a few minutes under the shade of a huge oak tree in her front yard and played with her dog.

After a few minutes of romping with the dog, she felt better—and definitely in need of a cold drink. She went into the house, got an icy soda out of the fridge and turned on the TV. Just as she settled into her chair, she was surprised to hear Doris Barnes' car coming down the driveway. She knew Doris had not been feeling well. The older woman used oxygen twenty-four hours a day and because of that, she almost never drove. As the sound of the car grew closer, Jeanette could hear the horn blaring, so she ran outside to meet her friend.

"What is it? What's wrong?"

"You have an emergency phone call," Doris gasped. "He sounded really upset."

Jeanette's first thought was that someone was hurt. Or maybe her father was sick. It didn't occur to her the caller was her son-in-law, Todd DePriest. She jumped into the car with Doris and they rushed back to the Barnes family's house.

"Mom? It's Todd."

At those words, Jeanette's heart beat rapidly. Something was horribly wrong. Todd never called her "Mom." In fact, he rarely called her. She began to shake. *The baby! Oh, my God. Something's happened to the baby!*

"Todd! What is it? What's wrong? Has something happened to the baby?"

"No, Mom. It's Nancy." Then he just blurted it out, anguish and fear roughening his voice. "Nancy's been shot."

"Oh, my God! How bad is it?" Jeanette demanded.

Very fast, as if he wouldn't be able to get it out otherwise, Todd told her what had happened. "There was a robbery at the store and they shot her in the head."

Jeanette heard screaming, although she didn't realize the sounds were coming from her own constricted throat. The phone fell from her lifeless fingers and she slumped to the kitchen floor.

Doris Barnes picked up the phone. "Hold on a minute. Hold on a minute," she cried.

"Doris, they shot my baby. They shot my baby," Jeanette moaned and rocked back and forth.

"Calm down. You've got to talk to Todd. Easy now." She handed the phone to Jeanette.

"Todd?" the word was little more than a whisper. "How bad is it?"

"It's bad. Nancy's on life support, and the doctors told me I have to make a decision soon about whether to take her off life support or not."

*Oh, no!* Devastated, Jeanette could only hold the phone and rock back and forth. Finally, when she could speak, she begged her son-in-law, through scalding tears, "Todd, please don't make any decisions like that until I get there."

"Okay," he agreed quickly, tears evident in his own voice. He choked out the name of the hospital where Nancy was. She assured him she would get there as soon as possible. Even after the call ended, Jeanette remained on the floor, clutching the phone to her breast.

During the conversation, Freddy Barnes had come into the kitchen and now he helped her to a chair. "What can we do to help?" he asked kindly.

"I've got to find her brother," Jeanette whispered. "I don't know where he is."

Doris offered to call the Red Cross, knowing that was, perhaps, the quickest way to find Nancy's brother. She made that call immediately. Then Jeanette called her mother. When Edith Sparks heard her granddaughter had been shot, she dropped the phone and Jeanette heard only silence on the line. She never knew if her mother fainted or what happened, but Jeanette's stepfather, Larry, came to the phone, wanting to know what was wrong.

Jeanette explained that there had been a robbery at the Pizza Hut where Nancy worked and Nancy had been shot. Then she told him the name of the Austin hospital where Nancy was on life support. Larry promised that he and Edith would leave their home in Fort Worth and get to Austin as soon as they could. Jeanette asked him if he would call her sisters, so she wouldn't have to repeat the horror story over and over again. He agreed.

Then Jeanette called her father in Mabank. Johnnie Stallcup loved his granddaughter Nancy even more than he loved his own daughters, if that was possible, and the two were extremely close. Todd had joined the Air Force soon after he and Nancy married, and Nancy had stayed with the Stallcups while her husband was in boot camp. Jeanette's heart broke all over again when her father broke down sobbing and was forced to give the phone to his wife. When Jeanette's stepmother Shirley heard the story, she told Jeanette she would drive her to Austin when she was ready to go. Jeanette said she would come over and they could leave from the Stallcups' home.

Sensing she couldn't manage alone, Freddy drove Jeanette back down the hill to her house. Feeling as if her body weighed 5,000 pounds, Jeanette sank into her rocking chair, unable to move, unable to speak. Freddy told her he would go back to his mother's, to see if the Red Cross had located Nancy's brother.

Jeanette, dazed, was completely unaware of the passage of time, but she was vaguely cognizant that over the next few hours Freddy and

Doris were in and out of the house. She simply sat in the rocking chair, unmoving, completely silent, for hours, aware somewhere deep in the center of her being that she should be on her way to the hospital where her daughter lay dying. Then she started screaming and sobbing. At that moment she felt as if someone had literally put their hand inside of her and pulled part of her out. Freddy knelt beside the chair to comfort her.

"Let me give you a sedative and put you to bed," Doris said, but Jeanette refused. She knew she couldn't go to sleep. There was something she was supposed to do.

Finally, she was able to rouse herself and put a few things in a bag. At about 3:30 in the morning, she arrived at the home of her father and stepmother. Jeanette and Shirley left immediately for Austin, mournful silence heavy in the car around them. Shirley apparently didn't know what to say, and Jeanette was lost in her own anguished thoughts and memories of her daughter. As if through a hazy mirror, her mind spun back to glimpses of Nancy and their time together and of her own life apart from her daughter.

Jeanette had given birth to Nancy when Jeanette was eighteen, but mothering her—the ability to love, nurture, protect—did not emerge until many years later. It was both a hard-won ability and a hard-won joy.

Jeanette's own mother hadn't been able to offer her a role model for motherhood. Jeanette was one of five daughters Edith had when she was very young. Her life became about survival, an all-consuming effort to keep her family fed and sheltered. Edith remarried several times in an attempt to put herself and the girls on secure footing, but the men—the husbands and the stepfathers—came and went.

Jeanette was an intelligent child, always reading, always speaking her mind with great articulation. But there was no one and nothing in her world to suggest a more rewarding path when, at age twelve, she began dating the boy next door; on the contrary, when he and Jeanette were still dating at fourteen, her mother insisted they get married. Although Jeanette was stubborn and outspoken, her mother was the one person who could intimidate her, the one person she couldn't tell "no." By age fifteen, Jeanette had married, dropped out of junior high school and given birth to a baby daughter. Neither marriage nor motherhood went well. The birth of a child only magnified the challenges of a teenage marriage and, at sixteen, Jeanette and her husband divorced and their child was placed in the permanent care of his mother. At age eighteen, Jeanette met a handsome Air Force sergeant in Fort Worth and they married quickly. Soon she was pregnant again and gave birth to Nancy and then a little boy fourteen months later.

When Nancy was four and her brother was three, the family lived off the military base in Spokane, Washington. Jeanette felt her husband seemed to be spending an inordinate amount of time in Japan—"On duty," he said. Then Jeanette learned that a woman, who turned out to be her husband's mistress, was stationed in Japan. In a blaze of anger and humiliation, Jeanette packed her bags and drove down the coast to where her father was living in California. She had promised her children she would be back for them as soon as she found a job and an apartment. When she got back to Spokane, her husband had filed for divorce and transferred to Japan, taking the children with him. She tried to find him, to contact her children, but got no cooperation from the Air Force. It would be long, lonely years before she saw her children again.

Then, when Nancy was fifteen, *she* found her mother. Jeanette was living in Graham, Texas, a small, charming town just northwest of Possum Kingdom Lake, a popular resort community where Jeanette's grandparents lived. Jeanette immediately saw that Nancy was in need of mothering as much as she needed to be her mother. From that moment, Jeanette reveled in the relationship with her daughter. Jeanette felt that Nancy grounded her, gave her something special to hold onto. Nancy became the entire focus of Jeanette's attention; her daughter *became* her life.

Although Jeanette was working, she could barely make ends meet for her own self, much less support a child. Nancy insisted on helping out around the house and financially, so she went to work, first as a waitress and then as assistant manager at the local Pizza Hut. They didn't have much money, but Nancy never complained.

Jeanette was Nancy's mother first and a friend second, but it is hard to imagine a mother and daughter who had more fun. They did everything together, behaving like pals; they dressed alike and wore their long blonde curls alike. When they cruised the courthouse square in Jeanette's sleek pickup, people thought they were sisters. Blue jeans and a shirt were all Nancy needed, and there was no doubt she looked good in them.

Mother and daughter even had "their" song, "It's You and Me Against the World." As Jeanette and her stepmother drove through the dark night, Jeanette recalled the words and tears came to her eyes: *Sometimes it feels like you and me against the world / When one of us is gone and one of us is left to carry on / Our memories will have to do.* At the end of the song, a little girl says, *"I love you, Mommy."* And the mommy says, *"I love you, too."*

Every time she and Nancy heard it, Nancy would high-five her daughter and say, "That's our song. You and me against the world." The idea that the worst possible thing in the world that could happen, that her daughter would die first, never occurred to her. It was just impossible.

During Nancy's senior year in high school, on Valentine's Day, at the local skating rink, where all the kids hung out—Nancy met Todd DePriest, a rancher who was a year older than Nancy. He was manly, good looking in a rugged way. He didn't talk much and when he did, he spoke with a slow drawl. However, his cowboy charm and soft words enchanted Nancy.

Nancy fell immediately, deeply in love with Todd and nothing Jeanette said could persuade her daughter differently. Todd and Nancy had known each other only a few weeks when they decided to get married. Jeanette wasn't ready to face losing her daughter to marriage, so soon after their reunion following years of separation. And she didn't want Nancy to make the mistakes she had made, of marrying too young and not finishing her education. Jeanette tried to persuade Nancy to finish her senior year in high school, at least. "If he loves you now, he'll love you in two months, when you graduate," Jeanette told her daughter. "If he loves you now, he will love you in a year, if you want to go to college."

But on Nancy's eighteenth birthday, she and Todd ran away together. Two months later, they got married. Jeanette was very unhappy.

"First, her daddy took her away from me. Then Todd took her away from me," she mourned. She cried for weeks, but in her heart she acknowledged that Nancy adored Todd, and she knew that if she wanted a relationship with her daughter, she would have to accept her daughter's husband. Jeanette had reconciled herself to the marriage and she and Todd were cordial but not close. The distance between them was magnified by geographical distance when Todd joined the Air Force and was stationed in Austin, Texas, where he and Nancy had lived ever since.

By the time Jeanette and Shirley reached Austin, it was about 7:30 Tuesday morning, almost a full day since Nancy had been shot. Her daughter had been pronounced brain dead the previous night, a little more than twelve hours after she had been found battered, bound and left for dead on the restaurant floor.

First, Shirley drove to Todd and Nancy's apartment, because Jeanette wanted to ask Todd to go to the hospital with her. At the apartment, they found Todd, his mother, the baby and a friend. Todd told her he couldn't go to the hospital, because he had an important doctor's appointment that morning, which he couldn't cancel. Jeanette felt upset he couldn't be with her, but she tried not to show it. She held her granddaughter and cuddled the little girl for a while, then she and Shirley went to the hospital.

At Brackenridge Hospital, Jeanette was greeted by kind, sympathetic staff members who immediately whisked her into an elevator, away from a gaggle of reporters who were waiting. On Nancy's floor, Jeanette was shocked to see several police officers, along with her mother, red-eyed and weeping. Her stepfather hovered over Edith protectively, even while she was hugging Jeanette.

Before they went into the room, an organ donor coordinator talked to them, telling Jeanette that Todd had given permission for Nancy's organs to be donated and asked if Jeanette had any objections.

"Absolutely not," she told the woman. "That's what Nancy wanted." Jeanette had an organ donor card when Nancy came to live with her, and when Nancy was fifteen, she said, "Mom, I want one of those cards."

Jeanette had told her she couldn't get one until she was eighteen. On her eighteenth birthday, she got one.

The nurse told Jeanette, trying to comfort her, that had she lived, Nancy would have never known anything, never been conscious, never held her daughter again, because her brain was so damaged. Jeanette knew Nancy wouldn't have wanted to live like that. Actually, they had talked about such situations. They talked about her organ donor card and how they felt about life support and God. Nancy had told her mother, "If I'm not all me, I don't want to be any of me."

Jeanette felt the same way. She would never want to be kept alive artificially and for years, she'd had a living will to that effect.

Nancy believed, as her mother did, that when her body, simply a temple for the spirit, dies, her spirit goes immediately to God for judgment. Jeanette knew in that moment that her daughter went straight to heaven. She had no doubt about that.

Jeanette asked a nurse if she could see Nancy, and the nurse wanted to know if she would be all right. Jeanette assured her she would be fine and went into her daughter's room, accompanied by the nurse along with her mother and stepfather. Nancy appeared to be sleeping in the stark hospital bed, her chest rising and falling to the rhythm of the respirator. "Are you sure, if you turn that machine off, she won't breathe on her own?" Jeanette asked the nurse.

"No, ma'am. She won't breathe."

A patch covered Nancy's right eye, and Jeanette reached to remove it. Larry grabbed her arm and said, "Don't do that."

"Why? What's wrong with her eye?"

He wouldn't tell her, but she found out later that the bullet had entered the back of Nancy's head and had emerged, only partially, through her right eye. It was still there, protruding from her eye, and Larry didn't want Jeanette to see it.

Jeanette's mother and stepfather stayed in the room with her, but they stepped back against the wall, as did the nurse, allowing the mother and daughter a semblance of privacy in this, their last time together. Jeanette held Nancy's hand and stroked her arm. She was relieved that Nancy's skin still felt warm to the touch.

"I love you so much and I will love you always," she murmured. *Her treasure. Her darling girl.* "I'm so sorry I couldn't protect you."

She wept softly, telling herself and her daughter that by keeping Nancy alive in her heart, her daughter would be a part of Jeanette's life forever.

When she stepped back into the hallway, a policewoman asked if Jeanette would talk to her and another officer, as they needed to get as much information as possible but they knew this was a very difficult time. Jeanette was impressed with how kind the police officers were to her, how considerate of her feelings. The two officers took Jeanette to a nearby room and asked her if she knew anyone who would want to hurt her daughter. Jeanette said she could not imagine anyone wanting to hurt Nancy, because everyone loved her. She made friends so easily. When she was a little girl, Jeanette always told her not to talk to strangers. Then, when she was about fifteen, after she had come to live with her mother, Jeanette warned her about it again one day.

Ever logical, Nancy answered, "Mom, if I don't talk to strangers, how am I going to make new friends?"

Jeanette conceded that she had a point. Nancy loved everybody and instinctively made friends wherever she went.

Jeanette began to talk of a time when Nancy was three years old and talking well, when Jeanette took her to a Laundromat. The only other customer was a tall, black gentleman, who was reading a magazine while he waited for his clothes. Nancy walked over to him and tugged at his pants leg. He bent down toward her and she asked, "Are you a chocolate man?"

He smiled and answered, "I might be a chocolate man. Are you a marshmallow?"

"No, I'm not a marshmallow. I'm a girl," Nancy informed him.

Embarrassed, Jeanette scolded her daughter. "Nancy, that's not nice."

The man smiled. "That's a lot nicer than some people have called me," he said and he and Nancy continued their conversation.

*Strange that I should remember that incident now,* she thought. Jeanette told the policewoman she couldn't think of anyone with whom Nancy had a problem and would want to harm her. She asked the officer if they had talked to Todd, and the officer said they had talked to him and that he certainly was not a suspect.

After they talked to the police, Jeanette and her family went back home. Jeanette would live with the memory of Nancy whole and alive and smiling, driving with her around the courthouse square in the pickup.

From that day forward, Jeanette would also have a remembrance of Nancy as she thought of the various people who would live because of her daughter's generous nature, her willingness to pass along the gift of life. She would have an image of a man in Tucson, Arizona, who had become gravely ill the previous Sunday night and that very day would have a new heart—Nancy's heart. At Brackenridge Hospital, one of Nancy's kidneys would be transplanted into a fifty-five-year-old man from Elgin, Texas, and another into a south Austin woman. A liver transplant would be conducted at Presbyterian Memorial Hospital in Pittsburgh, and Jeanette would never know anything more about the recipient, but prayed every day that the transplant was successful.

The coordinator for the Central Texas Organ Program told reporters, "The DePriest family can tell her daughter, 'Your mother died a horrible death, but in her death, she gave her life to others, just like she gave life to you.' Her contributions should also help others realize the importance of organ donation." She said she especially hoped the organ donations might inspire someone to come forward with information about Nancy's assailant.

As Jeanette and her family left Austin after bidding farewell to their daughter and granddaughter, violent images passed through her mind. Had her daughter been tortured? Had she been left for dead on a grimy restaurant floor? Visions of the scene returned to her in nightmares that only magnified in intensity as the years rolled by.

She tried to find acceptance. She tried to find peace. But these things come with truth and there was no truth in sight.

Nancy DePriest's funeral was three days later, in Graham, at the Loving Highway Church of Christ. Jeanette arrived at her grandmother's home in Graham the day before the memorial service so traumatized she hardly knew what was going on, but she was vaguely aware that many people were tracking through the house. All the family was congregating there, although others were staying with local family members and some were staying in hotels. She wasn't sure about the arrangements, but nothing seemed to matter.

In a daze, she submitted to endless hugging, interminable questions from well meaning friends and relatives who wanted to know what they could do for her. A mountain of food seemed to be brought in every day by her grandmother's neighbors, who had known Jeanette since she was a child and who knew Nancy. Potato salad. Chicken. Roast beef and beans and iced tea and rolls. Some of the men were sitting in the kitchen playing dominoes. Women in the kitchen, doing soft, comforting, practical things they do at sad times. Jeanette thought she was holding up really well. She kept thinking that if she fell apart, her father would fall apart. "If I lose it, Daddy won't be able to handle it," she reasoned. "And it would upset Grandma."

In spite of all the commotion, the relatives descending in droves upon the family homestead, the food that had started arriving a day or so earlier, Jeanette's grandmother refused to believe Nancy was dead. She simply could not accept that her beloved great-granddaughter was gone, and she was adamant that she would not go to any funeral services.

Exasperated, Jeanette went into a bedroom and sat down, followed by Freddy Barnes, who hovered over her solicitously, never more than a step or two away from her side. About seven o' clock that evening, a telephone call came from the funeral home, saying Nancy's body was ready for viewing. Jeanette wanted to be the first to see Nancy, and she didn't want anyone with her. Her stepmother and Freddy were so concerned about her fragile emotions, they persuaded her to let them accompany her.

The first person she saw as she walked into the funeral home was Nancy's father with his wife and Nancy's half-brothers and sisters. It had been at least fifteen years since she had seen him, and she hardly recognized him. He recognized her, though, came over and put his arms around her. She accepted his embrace, and he whispered, "She'll always be with us in our hearts."

Trying to smile through her tears, unable to think of a suitable response, she said, "We made good kids, didn't we?"

"Yes, we did." That was the last time they ever talked.

At her first glance at the figure lying in the rosewood casket, Jeanette was shocked. The woman lying there was dressed in a white wedding dress, complete with veil, although she had not worn a wedding dress when she and Todd eloped. Because of the trauma to her face, she looked much older, more like the mother than the daughter. Jeanette told the mortician she wanted the casket closed after the viewing and during the memorial service. Then, she started falling apart.

Freddy took her back to her grandmother's house, to the bedroom where she would stay the night, and they sat on the edge of the bed. Jeanette started screaming and wailing and the pain was so all-consuming that she couldn't hold it in any more. She knew that everyone for blocks around could hear her, but she couldn't help it. And she didn't care. Let them hear her. She couldn't bottle it up any more. She couldn't hold it in any more. Her aunt came to the door, opened it a crack and Freddy said, "I've got her. She'll be all right."

Finally, exhausted, she went to sleep and didn't wake up until morning. In mid-morning, she remembered Nancy's special graduation picture. Not the one Jeanette had bought, but another, almost life-size portrait of Nancy that had graced the photographer's display window for months. He had been asking two hundred and fifty dollars for it and Jeanette just couldn't squeeze that amount out of her skimpy budget. Now, she wondered what had happened to the picture. She called her mother, who was staying with Jeanette's sister and asked if she knew what had happened to the picture. "I wish I had that picture to put on top of the coffin, so people could remember how beautiful she was. I don't want them to see her as she is." Her mother and Jeanette's sister promised they would check with the photographer and see if he still had the negative.

When Jeanette's sister told the photographer they wanted to buy the portrait, he told her it had been in storage, but when he read about Nancy's death in the newspaper, he had gotten the picture out, because he knew someone would be coming for it. He gave them the stunning portrait, refusing any money in payment.

Jeanette's sister, JoAnn, came over to help her dress. The entire family had come to Grandma's to go to the funeral home together. In the living room, Jeanette saw her mother. "Mom, I can't do this."

Her mother took Jeanette's hands and gazed into her eyes.

"You're strong, Jeanette. You are the strongest of all my girls, and you *can* do this."

The funeral home had sent two cars for the family, but to Jeanette they looked more like hearses than limousines. "I can't ride in that car," she told Freddy. Jeanette's sister, always efficient, took care of it, ushering Jeanette, Freddy and her mother into her own car.

Jeanette was getting really shaky by the time they reached the church. A blond young man, whom Jeanette recognized as one of Nancy's old boyfriends, the one, in fact, she had been dating when she met Todd, approached her. "Jeanette, do you remember me?"

"Of course, I do," she said, embracing him. She remembered how much she had liked him when he was seeing Nancy and what a nice young man he had seemed.

"I wish she stayed with me," the man said through tears. "I wish she married me."

Knowing he was grieving, too, Jeanette could only force a sad smile.

Jeanette's former mother-in-law and father-in-law, Nancy's paternal grandparents, were also waiting for her. Jeanette had always liked them and they had seemed fond of her. Now they appeared almost as grief-stricken as she felt.

Finally, Jeanette forced herself to walk down the aisle toward the casket, where she stood for a moment, deathly silent, then leaned over and kissed her daughter on the forehead one last time. A funeral home attendant stood at the end of the casket and Jeanette asked him to lower the lid. She was pleased to see that Nancy's graduation picture was mounted on an easel near the casket. As she found her place between Freddy and her son, a woman Jeanette didn't know came over and introduced herself as a member of the choir. "We're going to do the very best we can," she promised. Jeanette thanked her gratefully.

The a cappella choir sang one of Nancy's favorite songs, "Just As I Am." Nancy's father, now an Episcopal priest, gave a eulogy about her years with him and his wife, but Jeanette was barely aware of his words. She tried to muffle her constant sobbing with a handkerchief. On the way out, she felt as if she would faint and Freddy and her son held her up. Her sister JoAnn, seeing her distress, came toward her and said, "Come on, sis. You can do this. You need to do this."

"God help me, I can't. I just can't do it," Jeanette moaned. As soon as she spoke those words, Jeanette recalled the promise from the Bible that God would not put upon her more than she could bear. She believes it, because after those words came to her, it was as if her mind and spirit disengaged from her body. Later, she didn't remember leaving the church, the ride to the cemetery or anything about the graveside service. She never remembered the ride home. The next thing she knew, Jeanette was back at her grandmother's house and her clothes had been changed.

Later, family members drove her back to the cemetery, because she didn't know where her daughter's grave was. The next day was also a blank. Jeanette knew she must have eaten, slept and talked, but it was washed from her memory by her grief. She didn't remember coming back home, but then, miraculously, she was there.

Freddy said, "I don't know how to help you. I don't know how to make you feel better."

"You can't make me feel better. No one can make me feel better. The best thing you can do is leave me alone. Just go away."

He left and that was, essentially, the end of their relationship.

Chapter 3

# Too Few Clues

While Jeanette was swathed in a cocoon of grief, Austin police were working long hours, trying to unearth clues that might lead them to a suspect in her daughter Nancy DePriest's murder. They would have been grateful for just one piece of evidence, but none seemed forthcoming. They had asked Todd DePriest for samples of saliva, semen and hair to rule him out as his wife's attacker, and he complied readily. On the day following Nancy's death, a spokesman for the police department told the press, "Investigators haven't reached the point yet where optimism is waning, and we're still optimistic," he said.

In an effort to help the police, Pizza Hut company officials offered a five thousand dollar reward for information leading to the arrest and conviction of the person or persons responsible for her death. A spokesman for the group said this was the first time the company had ever offered money for information on a crime at one of its restaurants.

On Thursday, the reward in the case reached ten thousand dollars, when another fast-food restaurant chain matched Pizza Hut's five thousand dollars, in the hope, said the restaurant's officials, that the reward would help solve the slaying. The same restaurant also donated twenty-five hundred dollars to a fund for Nancy DePriest's family, to help defray medical and funeral expenses.

Also on Thursday, Austin police made a public appeal for clues that might solve the rape and slaying. Sergeant Hector Polanco, speaking at a press conference, said, "We've had a lot of responses from the community, but we need more. Officers have received several dozen calls with information about the crime. But we need to talk to more people who were near the restaurant between eight and nine o'clock Monday morning, when we believe the attack took place." Police knew hundreds of university students lived in apartment complexes in the vicinity and routinely caught a bus at a bus stop about a hundred and fifty feet from the restaurant. There were also several other businesses nearby.

"People in the area have been helpful," Polanco went on. "But we just feel that someone saw something else. It may not mean anything to them, but it might mean something to us."

He declined to say if any suspects had been identified. He said police were awaiting results of laboratory tests on evidence taken from the crime scene. He tried to keep Jeanette in the loop as the search went on, but swathed in a tourniquet of grief, Jeanette could think of nothing but her daughter's violent death.

There were only a few more telephone calls in response to Polanco's plea for information. One informant mentioned seeing a yellow or light colored car driving away from the restaurant early Monday morning. The informant had not noted the number on the license plates, however, and efforts to find the car based on such a vague description had so far failed. Another call produced information that a young Austin man was bragging about the crime, although he did not confess that he had killed Nancy. Ostensibly, he was saying another man, a co-worker, was actually implicated in the killing. Investigators found the two men, twenty and thirty-seven years old, at their place of work about 2:30 Thursday afternoon and picked them up for questioning.

District Judge Jon Wisser signed an evidentiary search warrant in connection with the two men. The warrant called for body specimens, including hair, saliva and sperm from both suspects, but it took a few days to get the test results. Police would not disclose any other details regarding the men or further progress of the investigation.

Homicide investigators continued to question the twenty-year-old man overnight, although they released the older man when it became apparent he had no involvement. The next day, police learned from the younger man's employer that he was at work when the assault on Nancy DePriest took place, and he was released.

Other than that, investigators had questioned five people who had been considered suspects during the days since the killing, but all were cleared. "It's kind of an elimination process," Polanco said.

Immediately after the slaying, Polanco had theorized the assailant either had a key or that Nancy knew the man and let him inside, because no sign of a break-in was found. By this time, police had eliminated as suspects former employees who could have had keys.

Polanco had also received the report of the autopsy conducted by Dr. Robert Bayardo, Travis County Medical Examiner, which concluded that Nancy "was shot in the back of the head with a small caliber handgun." Bayardo confirmed the woman had been sexually assaulted before she was shot, but found no other injuries or signs there had been a struggle.

On November 5, Hector Polanco put into motion a plan he had devised, hoping to lure Nancy's killer into the open. Knowing from experience that criminals often return to the scenes of their crimes, he engineered a press conference during which a police spokesman announced they had uncovered some evidence they were following up on. No details about the "evidence" were given.

Following the press conference, Polanco called a meeting of Pizza Hut employees who worked at the location where Nancy had been shot. It had reopened after evidence of the tragedy had been removed and the restaurant cleaned. He told the group he wanted to speak to them about safety precautions and how they could help the police. The company had already hired security guards to patrol the premises at all times.

"There are things you can do to help us and to keep yourselves safe," he explained. "Most important, be on the lookout for anybody whose behavior seems suspicious, because killers sometimes like to return to the scene of their crimes. Sometimes, they like to get involved in the police investigation, calling in tips, asking police for information about the crime. Do not share any information about the crime with curious customers or other employees. Do not share it with *anyone*."

Police were carefully guarding crime scene details. The police knew all too well that unsolved killings brought crazies out of the woodwork. Some people confess to the crime, either to get their fifteen minutes of fame, to experience an interrogation or to see the inside of the police building. For that reason, facts known only to the police and the killer could be used both to screen out any false confessions and to trap the killer. Although he did not give the group any specifics about how the crime was committed, Polanco did tell them a small caliber weapon was used, without specifying the caliber. He mentioned the plugged sink but didn't tell them what was used to plug it. He passed around photos of people he said were suspects, but no one in the group could identify any of the pictures. He also said there was a cream or white colored car that might have been seen outside the building on the morning in question and asked if anyone knew who owned it. No one did.

Polanco said that by releasing some information to the employees, the word might spread to the killer and cause him enough concern to return to the scene to determine if he had left clues or just to re-experience the adrenaline rush he had felt during the rape and killing. Polanco reiterated that the employees should keep their eyes open for anything unusual around the Pizza Hut, people acting suspiciously or talking about the crime in a suspicious manner. He also told the group that two persons might have been involved in the crime, because "Nancy was five feet four inches tall and weighed one hundred and twenty pounds, so it might have taken two people to subdue her."

Polanco did not mention whether or not Pizza Hut employees were on the list of suspects. That reasoning kept recurring, because police still believed Nancy either had known her assailant and let him into the locked restaurant or he had a key with which he let himself in. Polanco did, however, ask store employees to go down to the police department, have their fingerprints taken and give statements, purely as a routine matter.

Polanco's words only intensified the excruciatingly stressful atmosphere within the Austin area Pizza Huts. Employees were traumatized, especially those who had been close to Nancy. A few of them quit or asked for transfers within days after the murder. Many who continued to work no longer felt safe on the job, in spite of the presence of security guards. Hearing that the killer might return to the store didn't make them feel better. They wondered to themselves, and aloud, if perhaps he already had been back. Maybe they'd smiled at him, seated him, served him, not knowing who and what he really was.

As a result of Polanco's meeting with her employees, the store manager was keeping a watchful eye out. She, herself, had been badly shaken by the murder. Since she had been scheduled to work that morning, she was keenly aware that it could have been she who was in the store that morning. That thought haunted her busy days and sleepless nights. It made her feel somehow guilty, even as she realized the feeling was not warranted.

Wednesday night, four days after the meeting with Polanco, the store manager was sitting in a booth at about 9:30 doing some bookwork. Headlights swept across the dining area, indicating a car pulling into the parking lot. The lights stayed on for at least five minutes, but no one came in. The store manager watched, puzzled and a little apprehensive. The headlights went out, but another few minutes passed before a pair of young men came through the front door. One of them the store manager recognized—Chris Ochoa, who until recently had been an assistant manager at another store. She recalled seeing him at a managers' meeting. She knew the second man worked at a nearby store, but she didn't know his name. She had seen him only that afternoon, when he delivered paychecks to her store that had been inadvertently delivered to the store where he worked.

The men sat in a booth and ordered beers from the waiter. The manager sensed the taller one was staring at her as she worked, but every time she looked up, he quickly looked away. Chris Ochoa looked jittery and uncomfortable, keeping his eyes on the table. The other man's gaze constantly roamed around the restaurant. Neither spoke. When the beers arrived, they clinked their glasses and the taller man told the waiter they were having a beer "in memory of Nancy."

Chris Ochoa took only one or two sips of his beer and didn't say much, although the other man talked a bit and seemed to be checking out the room and the kitchen area. Then they left. On the way out, the taller man stopped to talk to the security guard and asked him a number of probing and detailed questions about the crime. When did they start posting a guard here? Did the police have any suspects? What kind of evidence had been gathered? Where had Nancy's body been found?

Chris Ochoa stood off to the side and said nothing except a mumbled "hello."

The guard told the manager afterward that the man told him his theory of the attack: that two men, not one, had committed the crime—something he certainly had not heard directly from Polanco, since he worked at a different store and had not been at the police officer's session with employees. She guessed that information could have spread quickly through the company grapevine.

To the manager, the guard and the waiter, this added up to the kind of suspicious behavior Sergeant Polanco had warned them about. As the men drove away, the manager asked the guard to see if he could get the car's license plate number. He tried but couldn't get it. She fretted about the incident over the next few hours, replaying it in her mind. Early the next morning, she made a phone call to the police.

For twenty-two-year-old Christopher Ochoa, this was the defining moment in his life. In the hours, days, years that followed, he must have kept going over the words and events in his life he wished he could change, but nothing could have been more starkly vivid in his mind than the visit to the Pizza Hut that night. What should have been a meaningless incident, quickly forgotten, became the major turning point in his life, an exit he should not have taken.

Later it was reported that it had been Richard Danziger's idea. In the account, they were driving home to the apartment they shared. "I've got an idea. Let's stop off at the place where Nancy worked and check out the crime scene. We could drink a beer in Nancy's memory." At least that's what was told.

According to the report, Ochoa was unsure. Richard hadn't known Nancy, but Chris knew her slightly from casual work-related contacts. Richard was the type of guy who was always walking on the edge, always threatening to step over the line. Chris, on the other hand, tried to follow the rules and stay out of trouble.

Besides being creepy, Richard's suggestion included breaking a Pizza Hut policy: Employees of Pizza Hut were not supposed to drink liquor on the premises; not in the store where they worked and certainly not in another store. Plus, Richard, at age eighteen, was too young to drink legally.

In the account, Chris protested, "Let's don't. You're going to get your ass fired and mine, too!" But Richard was driving and before Chris knew it, they were parked in front of the store. They continued arguing in the parking lot. Chris refused to get out of the car, not wanting to go inside, but Richard insisted.

Afterward, when he reported it, the version went on this way: "Fine," Chris finally said. "Let's just go inside and grab a quick one, then we're out of here."

Chris reported he sighed heavily and figured that he might as well do what Richard wanted and get it over with. He knew Richard would not give up until he got his way. They were in Richard's girlfriend's red compact crapmobile, the one that kept failing to start. Richard's girlfriend was a manager of the Pizza Hut where Richard worked, and Richard, having no car of his own, frequently drove his girlfriend's. The passenger side door was dented so badly it would not open. Chris had to climb out on the driver's side.

Chris seemed to be nervous and uneasy all through the brief time they were inside. Richard made a toast to Nancy; uncomfortable, Chris took a sip of his beer. Richard kept speculating on how the attack on Nancy had gone down. Chris just kept his eyes on the table and said, over and over, "Let's get out of here." After what seemed like hours to Chris, but probably was only a few minutes, Richard agreed to leave. On their way out, to Chris's exasperation, Richard struck up a conversation with the security guard, asking him pointed questions about the murder. Chris hung back for a few minutes; finally, just wanting to get out of there, he went to the car by himself.

Chris had little interest in hearing about crime and this one was too horrible to contemplate. He had been an honor student in high school, where he had served as assistant editor of the school's literary magazine as well as manager of the football team. He was taking a few years off, working, doing some partying and indulging his passion for rock concerts. He had moved from his hometown of El Paso to Austin, because it was easier to find work here. His brother had followed him a while later and now they shared an apartment with Richard, when he was not at his girlfriend's house, and another friend.

Chris had recently been feeling the urge to go back to school, to make something more of his life, and was planning to attend a community college the following spring.

Chris and Richard didn't spend much time together. To Chris, Richard was a co-worker who'd needed some help settling back in Austin. Chris knew Richard had just gotten out of a juvenile facility, was on probation and was trying to straighten out his life. When he'd first come back to town, he had been living at the YMCA. Chris gave him a job at the Pizza Hut and also a temporary place to stay. Because Richard was spending so much time at his girlfriend's, his roommate status at this point was practically moot. To Chris, Danziger must have seemed like a cool but occasionally annoying guy.

## Chapter 4

# Nightmare in Plain Clothes

While Jeanette grieved and waited for word about the police's search for her daughter's killer or killers, detectives unknown to her were rushing forward with their theories as to where, who and how the killer or killers might be found. Their first thoughts focused on the employees or former employees of the fast-food chain. The detectives found out that a young man named Christopher Ochoa had transferred from another Pizza Hut location, giving up his assistant manager job to become a cook at the store, which is where Sergeant Bruce Boardman and senior officer Elsa Gilchrist found him around noon Friday, a mere eighteen hours after the store manager's call to Polanco. The two detectives told Ochoa they wanted to question him about a burglary at a Pizza Hut, and they wanted him to come to the police department. They gave him the choice of driving his own car or riding with them in the patrol car.

Ochoa left his car at the restaurant and rode with the detectives.

The police were questioning Pizza Hut employees about Nancy DePriest's murder, and Chris asked Boardman if that was why they wanted to question him.

"No, it's about the burglary at the other store," Boardman told him. There had been some earlier thefts at another store to which Ochoa had been alerted. He and his brother had been questioned by police. Neither was implicated, but the record of the interviews was still in the computer, a fact Ochoa had no way of knowing.

Boardman noted that Ochoa appeared extremely nervous, from the time he and Gilchrist had introduced themselves to him.

Now, when they arrived at police headquarters, they settled in an interrogation room. When Boardman turned the topic to Nancy DePriest, Ochoa nearly broke down. The officer watched as the young man began shaking and a small rash broke out on the left side of his neck, increasing until it covered the entire left side of his face. He started to breathe heavily; his palms became sweaty. To Boardman, Chris Ochoa seemed "very shook up."

To Ochoa, Boardman must have seemed tall and hulking, compared to his own five feet three inches. Later, Ochoa said he saw Boardman as a "big old white detective." After a few moments, Boardman left him in the room, saying that other investigators wanted to speak to Ochoa. It was almost as if Boardman had been softening him up for Polanco. Chris appeared terrified from the outset.

Hector Polanco's street name was *El Cucuy* (koo-KOO-ee). In Latin lore, *El Cucuy* is a ghost-like, red-eyed creature who hides under your bed or in your closet and comes to get you if you don't watch out. While the most literal translation is the rather mild "bogeyman," when Sergeant Hector Polanco told Ochoa he was known as *El Cucuy*, what he really seemed to be saying, speaking Spanish, was *"I am your worst nightmare."*

Polanco lived up to the name, had been doing so for years, and apparently was proud of it. The Austin Police Department valued Polanco as one of their most successful investigators, one who could speak the language of the streets and put fear into the toughest suspects.

Polanco was like a heavyweight boxer; his bulk alone seemed to fill half the tiny interrogation room. When he sat down with Ochoa at the table, he loomed over the smaller man. "I want you to tell me what you know about the murder," he said in Spanish.

Looking frightened, Chris fidgeted and wiped his damp palms on his uniform pants, then replied in English, "I don't know what you're talking about."

"You've got to know something," Polanco snarled, still in Spanish. "You've got to know who did it."

Again, Chris stuck to English, refusing the falsely sympathetic "Chicano bond" Polanco was apparently trying to establish. "No! I don't know nothing!"

The question was asked in a variety of ways for the next hour. "You must know somebody. You must have heard something. Weren't you and your friend, Richard Danziger, asking questions at the same store where Nancy DePriest was killed the other night?"

After a while, Polanco went out of the room, brought back a soft drink for Chris and offered him a cigarette. Then he switched to English: "We *know* you know something—why don't you just go ahead and tell us?"

"But I don't know nothing," Chris said.

"If you know something and don't tell us, you can get charged with conspiracy," Polanco snarled. "You can be charged with capital murder. And, you can get the death penalty." A master of timing, he let that sink in.

"*But*, if you tell us what you know, you can go home," he said, more quietly.

*Capital murder? The death penalty?* Chris must have been terrified. How could he believe this was happening? He had *never* been in trouble with the law. He had been taught that police were people who help you when you're in trouble. Suddenly, that foundation of trust was crumbling beneath him.

Once more, Chris just shook his head. "I don't know nothing." He didn't say it defiantly, but fearfully shaking now.

Again, Polanco spoke forcefully in Spanish. "They call me *El*

*Cucuy*, because I send people away," he said. To Chris, the officer must have looked like a dragon with fire shooting from his eyes. It was an expression of evil intent and hatred that Chris had never experienced before.

Polanco left the room and another detective came in. Detective Edward Balagia began to play good cop, throwing Chris a lifeline. "We're not trying to hurt you, Chris. We just want you to tell us what you know, if you know anything, so you can go home."

Chris insisted he knew nothing.

"Come on, I can get my partner off you. My partner is a hothead," Balagia said confidentially.

Still, Chris kept repeating he knew nothing.

Polanco returned, the bad cop in full fury. He slammed his fist on the table. "I'm not going to play games with you. I have the District Attorney out there and he's going to charge you with capital murder and give you the death penalty."

Polanco stared at Chris, his eyes seemed to be burning with intensity. "Or," he said, "you can talk to me now, tell me who killed that girl and you can go home."

Chris didn't say a word.

"Here. Look at these." Polanco spread an array of photos in front of Chris—photos of death row from Huntsville prison, the self-proclaimed death penalty capital of the world. "If you don't talk, this is where you're going. You're going to get the needle." He tapped Chris's arm. "This is where the needle's gonna go if you don't cooperate."

Polanco pointed to another picture. "That cell is where you'll spend the rest of your life, until you are put to death. Take a good look at it, because that's gonna be your home. You're not gonna be able to hug your mom or your family anymore. You're gonna die on a gurney with a needle in your arm. Help me out here. We don't want to put you away for a crime you didn't commit."

Chris sat, silent, shaking, clutching his stomach, looking sick and shook his head.

More photos, this time from the brutal crime scene and from Nancy's autopsy, clearly showing the bullet hole in her head. Chris looked like he was going to throw up.

"Don't you feel bad for her?" Polanco asked.

The grisly, horrifying photos were meant to drive the point home for Chris. His face saddened and he looked down as police described the beautiful girl who had been so brutalized. He still said he knew nothing of what had happened to her. But he could not help knowing they were talking about murder and if they arrested and convicted him, he could die. People like him were put to death all the time, Polanco reminded him, and "Mexicans always get the death penalty."

Time seemed to lose all meaning, but hours must have gone by. It must have seemed as if Ochoa had been in the tiny, cramped, smelly room with these burly detectives for an eternity. He was weak and tired, looking around and around as if the room was spinning. More questions from Polanco, from Balagia, from both at the same time, circling and questioning and threatening Ochoa with death, dominating the small space with their bulk, their potential brute force. The whole scene was dizzying and confusing.

In that constricted, ominous atmosphere, Chris must have felt fragile, as if his mind were an eggshell, tapped over and over again with the handle of a knife until a million tiny cracks covered its surface. He must have asked himself if the cops thought they had something on him. But what could it be? Finally, looking like fear was choking him, he must have decided he'd better give them what they wanted. He started saying yes to their leading questions, their descriptions of the crime scene.

"Yeah, I heard someone talking about the murder. It may have been a black guy."

That wasn't good enough. They suggested that Richard Danziger was behind the murder and Chris was covering for him. "Who told you about the murder? How about your friend Danziger? Come on, you two were over at that store, you were asking questions. Tell us. Tell us and you can go home. If you don't, you'll get the needle."

*The needle. The needle. The needle.* They must have said that word a thousand times.

Polanco left the room again and in a moment another officer came in, a young woman with long, wavy dark hair. She seemed to have a nicer, more sympathetic demeanor, leaning towards Ochoa when she first arrived.

"Can I ask you something?" Chris groaned.

"Yes. Of course," she said.

"What about a lawyer? Can I have a lawyer?"

The question seemed to upset her. "You can't have an attorney until you are formally charged," she told him. Then she left the room, slamming the door behind her.

Chris Ochoa had never been arrested, never had any dealings with police, but he must have read enough and seen enough television to know that he had not waived his right to an attorney. Being questioned without the assistance of counsel was dangerous. However, he seemed too afraid of Polanco to say anything.

Polanco returned, hulking over Ochoa menacingly. "I'm getting tired of you," he screamed. "I'm going to put you downstairs, and you'll be fresh meat. You're new. You're young. Boy, they're going to love you."

Although Chris had never been in jail, surely he had to know Polanco was talking about jail rape and that must have terrified him. He stared at the door as if all he wanted was to go home. By then the interrogation had gone on for hours.

The room became deathly silent. Then Christopher Ochoa began giving a formal statement; one of the detectives typed on an electric

typewriter as they talked to him. The officers began typing the
statement at 4:45 P.M. and finished up at 7:15 P.M. The Miranda
Warning, meant to ensure that every suspect was given the
opportunity for an attorney, is printed in three different versions.
Throughout Ochoa's questioning, all the versions, or a combination
of them, were given several times. At the top of the standard form was
a numbered list of the Miranda rights, with the advisory that anyone
making a statement must hear them beforehand. Polanco made Ochoa
initial every item on the list, including the one that said, *"I have the right
to have a lawyer present to advise me prior to and during any questioning."* Ochoa
hesitated, appearing confused and looking more afraid than ever.
Hadn't the woman cop told Ochoa he couldn't have an attorney until
he had been charged with a crime? That is what she'd said. He hadn't
been charged, had he? No one had told him he was under arrest or
charged with anything. But he must have felt afraid to ask Polanco to
clarify for him, so he initialed all points, indicating that he had read
and understood them. *This meant he had forfeited his right to have an attorney
present during this interrogation.*

Before and during Ochoa's statement, Polanco, Boardman and
Balagia had baited Ochoa, saying Danziger was being questioned in
another interrogation room and striking fear in Ochoa about what
Ochoa's friend was saying. "Danziger's in the next room, and he's
fixing to talk. If you don't tell us what we need to know, he's going to,"
Polanco said.

Another frightening comment: "The white dude always talks and
the Mexican always gets the death penalty. So why don't you talk first?
Because if he talks first, he gets the deal—life in prison, maybe—and
you'll get the *needle*."

So Ochoa began his statement again, describing a party at the
home of Rhonda Shore, Danziger's girlfriend, the night before the
murder—a party that had lasted until the predawn hours of that
bloody Monday, October 24. He told them it had been Richard's

girlfriend, Richard, Chris and a woman, a friend of Rhonda's they'd invited to be Chris's date. They'd drunk a lot of beer and whiskey as they played a drinking game. When the party broke up, Chris felt too drunk to drive home, so Richard's girlfriend called one of Chris's roommates to come get him. When the roommate got there, he didn't think Chris was too drunk to drive, so the roommate advised Chris to drive himself and the roommate would follow to make sure he got home all right. Richard didn't come with them, so Chris assumed Richard spent the night at his girlfriend's, as he often did. Chris said he thought it was between four and five o'clock in the morning when he got to bed. He woke up around eight thirty or nine, but didn't have to be at work until later, so he watched TV. Later that morning, a news bulletin blared out the bare details of a brutal crime at the store.

Later, some reported that Polanco had micromanaged Ochoa's statement that implicated Richard Danziger in Nancy's murder.

According to the statement, after that early Monday party, the next time Chris saw Richard was late Tuesday, October 25, the day after the murder. He said Richard came back to their apartment and the conversation naturally turned to Nancy. All the Pizza Hut employees were shocked by her murder. Richard asked Chris if he knew whether the police had any evidence or leads in the case. Chris said he didn't know of anything new.

When this information got into the statement, it read: "Richard then paused for a moment and then stated to me, 'Well I did it!' I was shocked and I stated, 'What do you mean?' Richard then went on to tell me that he was the one who committed the robbery, rape and murder of Nancy DePriest at the Pizza Hut.

"Richard had parked his girlfriend's car, the red one, at an apartment complex parking lot across the street from the restaurant. He knocked at the west door, posing as a produce delivery man, and Nancy let him in. After getting money from the safe, Richard took a closer look at Nancy."

An exhausted Ochoa continued. "Richard stated that his intention was to rob the place, until he got inside and saw how pretty Nancy DePriest was," the statement read. It continued with, "Richard stated he never did notice her good looks until after he had robbed the place. Richard then told me that he 'had a little fun' with Nancy DePriest. I assumed that the way Richard meant this was that he had sex with her. Richard also stated that he tied Nancy up so he could make sure that she couldn't get away or try to struggle. Richard then stated to me that 'after I finished with her, I put a bullet through her.'

"Afterward, Richard drove straight over to his girlfriend's apartment. Then he stated to me that if the cops ever questioned him about the murder, he would have a perfect alibi by stating that he had been with Rhonda."

Polanco must have wanted the statement to contain a plausible explanation as to why Richard confessed to Ochoa. "I then asked Richard, 'Why are you telling me all of this?' I then stated, 'Aren't you afraid I'm going to go and tell the cops?'

"Richard then stated, 'Go ahead. Tell the cops. They won't believe you. They'll think you're the one who did it.' Richard gave me a hard stare and kind of smirked at me. Then he told me he had to tell someone so he could get it off his chest and ease his conscience."

All the points the detectives wanted to make clear had to be covered. They kept on stirring fear and bearing down on the frightened Ochoa. Richard allegedly took a .22 caliber pistol from his girlfriend. In the store drinking incident, Richard, not the security guard, was indicated to have the information about the attack. "Richard asked the security guard, 'Do you think it could have been a .22?' The security guard told Richard that he didn't know anything and that no news about the murder had been released to him."

The police pressed on, now concentrating on showing Richard's involvement. Chris's statement appeared to indicate that he was a willing but easily intimidated informant: "When the police officers questioned me about the Pizza Hut murder, I told the officers what

Richard had told me. The reason I hadn't come to the police with information sooner is that I was scared of what might happen to me if Richard found out that I had talked to the police."

The timing of a phone call from Rhonda's supervisor, Alex Martin, to her apartment that morning, when he was trying to find out why the store was not open, was covered as well: "Richard stated that the telephone rang (after he arrived at Rhonda's apartment after the murder) and he answered it. Richard stated the person calling was Alex Martin . . . Richard then stated to me that this would be a great alibi, because, since he answered the phone, everyone would think he had been there all the time with Rhonda. Richard was extremely confident he would get away with the murder."

Ochoa concluded the telling statement: "With what I know about Richard and what he has told me, there is no doubt in my mind that he is the person responsible for the murder of Nancy DePriest."

Then he added what appeared to be an afterthought: "There's something else that I want to mention. When I first heard about the murder of Nancy DePriest at the Pizza Hut, the first thing that popped in my head was that the suspect was probably a current or ex-Pizza Hut employee. The reason I think this is that a Pizza Hut employee knows all of the normal working procedures and could take advantage of when the restaurant is most vulnerable to being robbed. This is especially true of the morning shift, because there is usually only one employee working in the restaurant, preparing the place for the lunch hour rush. Someone who has experience in opening up by themselves knows exactly what the set up is and Richard has a lot of experience in opening up a restaurant by himself."

At last, the interrogators seemed to have concluded they had covered all the areas that anyone might later question, and Christopher Ochoa signed the three-page document with the declaration, "I have voluntarily given this statement to Detective Edward Balagia while at the Austin Police Department." The statement also bore the signatures of two witnesses.

But there were frightening lapses not yet voiced, which might have led outsiders to question what was the truth. Suppose the Tuesday conversation in which Richard had supposedly confessed to Chris had never taken place. Suppose Richard had not even been at their apartment that day. Was Ochoa being led through a carefully orchestrated script? Could, woven into the fabrication, have been such details as the .22 caliber weapon, Nancy's hands being tied together, what allegedly had been said to the security guard at the Pizza Hut the night he and Danziger drank a beer to Nancy? Had Chris really known any of these details until he heard them? Clearly, Polanco and the others felt the resulting story accounted for evidence and facts they knew about the crime. But did the evidence justify their crusade against this man or had they rushed to judgment?

After the interrogation was over, Polanco and Boardman drove Ochoa to Brackenridge Hospital for blood and hair samples to be taken for forensics examination. He had given a sperm sample during the long afternoon of interrogation.

Chapter 5

# To Tell
# the Truth

Throughout the long, arduous questioning and resulting statement, it was reported that Polanco had told Ochoa: "Just tell us what you know and you can go home."

Ochoa had been interrogated for more than seven and a half hours. At some point they had given him food. Now, for his own safety, they said, they were going to put him up at a motel. He was given strict orders to stay in his room, order food from room service, but he was NOT to contact anybody or tell anyone where he was. Otherwise, Polanco threatened, there was a real danger that Richard might come after him.

That must have sounded plausible to Chris, and he agreed. He was told the police would pick him up Monday morning for further questioning. On the way to the hotel, they stopped at his apartment to pick up clothes for him and while they were there, they conducted a search, for which both he and Richard had signed their consent.

For Chris, the weekend must have been almost as horrible as Friday had been. He was left alone at the hotel, isolated, simmering in a dark caldron of despair and fear. How could he know what he had gotten himself into? What was going to happen to him now? He was unable to sit still, unable to sleep, unable to watch television. Image after image had been evoked by the police of the death row cell, Nancy's autopsy photos, the bullet wound, a puncture to her head. The bullet exiting through her eye was exceptionally horrifying. Finally a frantic Chris called his apartment and talked to one of his roommates.

"I think I'm going to need a lawyer," he told the man and explained what had happened. "Call my mom."

By calling his roommate after the police had warned him not to contact anyone, Chris enmeshed himself deeper. Polanco picked him up Monday morning and took him into the same small, smelly interrogation room where Ochoa had spent Friday afternoon and evening. "Now we know you're guilty. We know you called your roommate."

A stunned look on his face, Chris shrank into his chair. How could the police know he had called his home? Had they tapped his home line? Didn't they have to get permission from a judge or something? Or were they watching him all weekend? Why? To make sure he didn't run away?

"And we know you asked for a lawyer," Polanco said menacingly.

"Why can't I ask for an attorney?" Chris asked, bewildered. "I thought I had a right to an attorney."

"Only guilty people call for attorneys," Balagia answered.

Under United States law the detectives had to allow Ochoa to call an attorney. But he felt powerless. These men obviously could do whatever they wanted. And what they seemed to want now was Chris Ochoa on death row.

Polanco charged that Ochoa had lied during his statement Friday, deliberately withholding facts about his role in the murder, Chris only dropped his head, his shoulders slumped. Defeat was on his face.

They gave him a polygraph test and told him he had failed. That is, they said, he was shown to be lying on such key questions as "Did you have anything to do with this crime?"—to which Chris had answered no. They said he had failed the question that asked if his first statement was accurate. They told him the polygraph showed it wasn't an accurate statement. They told him the District Attorney wasn't buying his statement. "You're lying," they told him. "We want the truth and we'll stay here all day until we get it."

After the polygraph, Polanco and Balagia brought Chris back to the interrogation room. Worn and traumatized from the long hours of questioning on Friday and his solitary, fear-filled weekend, Chris cowered in a chair. The detectives, though, seemed fresh. Now, they accused Chris of not having simply listened to Danziger's confession. He must have been there with Richard; he must have had a hand in the crime. Chris seemed crippled by fear, a fear that threatened to engulf him in a smothering black shroud.

Repeating their threats to charge him with conspiracy, with capital murder, with the death penalty, the detectives told Chris he must have been in on the robbery with Richard. They asserted Richard had first suggested it to Ochoa while they were at Rhonda's on Sunday night. Chris would pretend to be drunk, so he would need his roommate to follow him home, which would give him an alibi; he was at home at 5:30 A.M. and clearly not with his accomplice, Danziger. Then, the detectives told Chris their theory that he set his alarm clock for six thirty and met Richard at a fast food eatery at seven o'clock to work out the details. When they finished the plan, they drove to the Pizza Hut in separate cars—Chris in his and Richard in his girlfriend's.

From a parking lot at a nearby apartment complex, Polanco said, Chris and Richard observed a woman arriving for work in a silver car. Chris recognized her as Nancy DePriest. A man had followed her into the parking lot on a motorcycle and after flirting with her for a couple of minutes, he took off on his bike.

Nancy was now alone in the store. Polanco told Chris his theory that Chris had stood outside the restaurant as a lookout while Richard went in posing as a produce delivery man and that Chris knew

Richard had a gun to use as a threat, because Richard had shown it to him. But Chris was surprised when he heard a gunshot, so he ran to his car and drove away "like a bat out of hell." The lookout story still had Richard telling Chris about the rape and murder the following day.

Polanco, Balagia and Chris went over the story all morning, in the same way they had with the statement on Friday. Polanco asked leading questions. They were filled with crime details and Chris then answered them. In some places, Chris was now able to add details himself. There were photos of Nancy and continuous theories from the questioners. Chris heard about all the available evidence which pointed to him. Hidden elements of the crime scene came out. Later it was said only someone who had been there would know details only the killer could be aware of.

At around noon, the detectives turned on a tape recorder to capture this latest version on a cassette, to be transcribed later. The taping, of course, called for Chris to actually make the statements himself. The tape was turned off when Chris began stuttering from fear.

This confession was typed from the tape, with Chris sounding disjointed and confused. His stammer was more pronounced and it was obvious it was taking him some time to think of his answers.

In it, Chris said Richard asked him, "Hey man. You want to get some extra bucks?"

"I said, 'What are you talking about, man?' He said, 'Well, would you like to (inaudible).' I said, '(inaudible)' and he said, 'Well, I've been watching this place (inaudible).' So anyways—ah—he said, 'You want to come in with me and stuff and help me rob the place?' I said, 'Naw, man.'"

Again, Polanco and Balagia led Chris through the events following his purported Tuesday conversation with Richard, up until they picked him up on Friday. When they got to the Wednesday visit to the store, to "toast Nancy's memory," Ochoa told them that Richard asked the security guard a lot of questions and posed rhetorical questions to Chris about where Nancy had been found, where she had been shot, what the place looked like when the police got there.

After going through the entire story, the interrogators started over again, asking Ochoa about the details of Sunday night, October 23. This time, Ochoa told them Richard said, "I'm running a little low on cash. I need to get some money somewhere—if I can get hold of a gun and stuff."

"Did he say where he would get hold of a gun?" Balagia asked.

No, Chris told them. He said he, himself, never saw the gun. Then he amended his answer: "Never saw the gun. I never saw the gun. Oh, I saw it. Right. Before he walked in the Pizza Hut, he showed it to me."

Asked to describe the gun, Chris said it was a small black gun. He couldn't tell them much about it as he didn't know anything about guns.

When Polanco specifically asked Chris what the handle looked like, he said it could have been brown. "Did it look like a revolver?" Polanco asked. "Did it have a cylinder in it?

Chris said it did. It looked similar to Polanco's gun.

Balagia pointed out that Polanco wore a blue steel revolver with a brown grip and asked if that was the kind of gun Chris had seen. To which Chris answered, "Yeah. Something like that."

Polanco leaned forward. "Do you know what an automatic looks like? The ones you pull back?"

"Yeah."

Polanco described an automatic in detail and asked, "Was it like that?"

"No," Chris said. "Not like that."

Asked to resume his account of Sunday night, Chris told them, "Richard said, 'Come on. Let's do it.'

"I said, 'No, I don't want to do it.'

"Then he said, 'All you have to do is watch. Watch out for anybody.' He said he would do it all (inaudible). 'Just wait for me in my car and stuff and you in your car. We will go our separate ways and stuff and they won't suspect a thing.'

"Then I said, 'No man. It sounds too fishy. I've never done this before.' Then after a while, I said, 'Fine. I'll go watch. If they call me, I don't know nothing.'"

Balagia asked how Chris was supposed to warn Richard if someone pulled into the Pizza Hut parking lot. Here the tape ended and had to be turned over. When the recorder was ready, the detective went through the preliminaries again: those present, Ochoa, Balagia and Polanco; he read Chris the Miranda warning again. Then he said, for the benefit of the recorder, "As soon as the tape ended we turned it right around, without any hesitation. Is that correct?"

Chris said that was correct and resumed his answer. "I was supposed to go to the back, to the big old brown fence they have there. I was supposed to bang on it hard and stuff. Real hard. That would warn him to get out the front door or whatever. He said something like that and—ah—anyways, that's his plan."

At that point, Balagia backtracked to the time Chris left Richard's girlfriend's house earlier in the morning of October 24, asking him again what time he got home. This time, Chris said he probably got home about 5:15 or 5:30, rather than four o'clock, as he had stated earlier. And, he said, he set his alarm for 6:30. He and Richard had met at the fast-food place where Richard gave him the plan. Chris said he arrived at the meeting spot at around 7:00 or 7:15 and Richard was already there, driving his girlfriend's car. He was wearing khaki pants that could have been his work uniform, a white, long sleeved, button-front shirt and white sneakers.

Then, he said, they left at 7:00 or 7:15 (although he had just said they arrived there at about that time). Polanco showed Chris a diagram he'd drawn, indicating the locations of the Pizza Hut, the gas station and the two apartment complexes, and asked Chris to point out the spots where they had parked their cars.

"All right. Here. Somewhere around there. I don't remember quite where." He pointed to an approximate location. He also gave an approximate location where he said Richard had parked. By that time, he said, it was probably about 7:20.

They got out of their cars and Richard showed Chris where he should stand lookout. While they were there, he said, they saw "a car drive up and stuff, and a motorcycle and stuff like that." He identified the car as silver or gray and said Nancy DePriest got out of it.

"Did you know Nancy?" Balagia asked.

"Well, yeah. You know that's when I really freaked out because you know there was no way of stopping." He told them he knew Nancy, because she used to buy meats and "stuff" from the store where he was assistant manager, because she would "run out of stuff" at her store. He showed Balagia, on the diagram, where the motorcycle parked, across the lot from where Nancy had parked the car on the east side.

"Who got off the motorcycle?" asked Polanco.

"Some big guy and stuff, you know." He said he didn't recognize the man. "Then he went in and he was flirting with her for a couple of minutes and he took off and stuff."

"How did he take off?" Balagia asked. "What did he take off in?"

"I think on his motorcycle," Chris put a finger on the diagram, "off this way, because I wasn't really paying attention. I didn't really want to know." He couldn't remember what time he saw the motorcycle drive away, but his best recollection was that it must have been 7:30 or 7:35.

He never saw Richard inside the store, he said, but he waited about twenty minutes and then heard one gunshot. That scared him and he ran to his car and took off "like a bat out of hell."

The next time he saw Richard was Tuesday afternoon about four o'clock. He repeated what he'd told the detectives earlier, that Richard had confessed to killing Nancy, after he'd "had a little fun with her."

"Did he say what caliber of gun he used?" Balagia asked.

Chris shook his head. "No. Not at that time." Immediately, he corrected himself. "Yeah, he did. He did, at the end of the conversation. He said he used a .22 or something like that."

"Did he tell you any specifics of how he had sex with her?" Polanco asked.

"Ah—he was going to start but I didn't want to hear nothing, because I was pretty pissed. I had just freaked out. He said he had a little fun with her and I naturally said, 'Well, sex and stuff?' And he said, 'Well I tied her up and stuff.'"

"Did he say how he tied her up?"

"No. I think he mentioned a rope or something, but I don't know if that's what he used or not."

"What did he say he did after he killed her?"

"Well, he got in the red car and took off. Then he got to his girlfriend's place and stuff and as soon as he got there, the phone was ringing and it was his supervisor."

The *lookout* confession was completed at one o'clock in the afternoon and consisted of more than twenty-five transcribed pages. At two points on the tape—first when it started and again when it was turned over to the second side—Chris was read his Miranda rights. At the end of the tape, he confirmed the statement, "There were no threats or promises made against you in the middle of this conversation." Polanco asked him to look at the clock, state the time the tape ended and asked him whether he had any questions.

"Uh…no. The only question I have is what is going to happen to me," the transcript read.

Chris had been told he would get only a few years in prison for being the lookout. Polanco promised, "You'll get some time, but not much." To Chris, this sounded a lot better than the *needle in his arm.*

Even after the latest confession, however, Polanco and Balagia continued to badger Chris. They told him they were convinced they had not yet heard the full story. They continued to lead Chris on, their questions dragging him deeper and deeper into the murder. *He'd actually gone into the restaurant, hadn't he? Hadn't he, maybe, actually taken the money from the safe? Had Nancy recognized him? She knew Chris from managers' meetings. Right? Is that why they had to kill her?*

Horrified, Chris stuttered. "Nnnn—no. No! I didn't do any of that," he insisted.

His protests were met with the now familiar threats. They would not let him go. He was completely within their power. He had no rights. There was nothing he could say or do. He would get the *needle* if he didn't tell them the truth.

He tried to tell them what they wanted to hear, but fear was in charge of him now. His stammering became almost uncontrollable. They kept turning off the tape recorder and yelling at him because he hadn't gotten it right. Their threats of the death penalty were more frequent. All Chris could hear was *the needle. The needle. The needle.*

Balagia finally exploded. "Man, I'm tired of you," he yelled. Then he lifted his chair and hurled it at Chris, sitting a couple of feet away. The chair bounced off the wall, but Balagia caught it by a leg when it was within centimeters of hitting Chris in the head. It was a practiced move, one he had done many times before.

Nevertheless, Chris looked petrified. The officers were intimidating. He must have felt they were going to beat the crap out of him. Their menacing in-your-face manner never let up.

"Come on. Just help us," Balagia said. "You were there. You took part in it. Just tell us." They turned the tape recorder off, apparently giving up on the idea of getting a coherent statement from their terrified suspect, who was now a babbling basket case. Whatever had been taped that afternoon, after one o'clock, was never made available to outside authorities and was, perhaps, not even preserved. Balagia began typing instead, initiating the new statement at 5:00 P.M.

Terrified, horrified, completely traumatized, Chris gave up. There was no way out. He was exhausted. He was beaten. He was a confessed accomplice to rape and murder. They would never let him go home. But by now, he was probably clinging to that forlorn hope.

By five, Polanco and Balagia had a new, more cohesive statement ready for Chris to sign. In the new statement, the sentences were smooth and apparently well thought out. There was no evidence of stammering or hesitancy in his words. Gone were the frequent pauses and corrections that had been prevalent in the transcribed tape.

Although this was actually his third statement, including the almost incoherent taped one, this version began, "This is the second statement I am going to give Detective Balagia. On 11/11/88, at 4:45 P.M. I gave Detective Balagia my original statement. I am giving this second statement because of the fact that I left out a lot of details in my first statement, and I didn't give a complete and truthful statement to Detective Balagia on 11/11/88."

In this latest version, Chris said Richard had chosen that particular Pizza Hut, because "it was at a location that offered numerous and easy getaway routes. Richard went on to state that he knew all the procedures at the Pizza Huts and the surroundings would be familiar to him. When I asked him how he would get into the store, he said he had an easy way to get in and that I would have to trust him.

"Then Richard asked me to join him in the robbery. I was reluctant, but Richard was persistent and said we could split the money and each of us could receive at least $200. We decided we would meet in separate vehicles (easier for the getaway and nobody could place us together) and we would meet at the fast-food restaurant at seven in the morning."

At the planning meeting, Chris said Richard pulled up his shirt and revealed a blue steel semi-automatic pistol that he had stuck in the front of his waistband. Then, he said, after they parked their cars in the apartment complex, they waited a while to watch the restaurant to make sure nobody was there.

Here again, his story changed from his previous ones: "As we watched, I observed a silver car pull up and park in the north side parking lot at the pizza hut. A man on a motorcycle followed it into the lot. I recognized Nancy DePriest as she got out of the car. Nancy went into the restaurant and the man got into her car and drove away, leaving his motorcycle parked on the north side of the Pizza Hut. As we watched, he drove back in the car, parked the car and drove off on his motorcycle. All of this took place in about twenty minutes."

The new statement continued to add new details. In it, Chris said he and Richard approached the Pizza Hut together, that Richard had a key with which he unlocked the door and went in, Chris following. Nancy was in the kitchen cutting dough. She looked up at them, stunned.

"Richard ordered her to give him all the money. Then Nancy recognized me and asked, 'What's wrong, Chris? What's going on?'

"'Give us the money,' Richard ordered. When he had the money, Richard said, 'Let's have some fun.' Nancy was real scared and she said, 'You have the money, now leave me alone.' Richard slapped her and yelled at her to shut up."

The police had disclosed details of the sexual assault to Chris, using leading questions. At this point, exhausted and afraid, he began saying yes to everything.

"Didn't Nancy say at one point, 'No. Stop it'?" Polanco said.

"Yeah. That's what she said," Chris, grim-faced, answered.

Polanco continued. "Then Nancy started screaming and yelling, 'Stop, it hurts.'"

"Yeah."

The long interrogation continued in the same vein, portraying acts that were so sadistic, so heinous, they seemed to exceed any information that was needed to account for known facts or evidence. According to the statement, Chris and Richard both came to orgasm twice while assaulting Nancy vaginally, orally and even anally—after Danziger had shot her in the head. The anal assaults apparently were introduced to account for physical evidence found by Dr. Roberto Bayardo, chief medical examiner for Travis County, who said he had found abrasions and bruises of the rectum and anus. Dr. Bayardo later testified that the bruises and abrasions had been the result of "some instrument having been introduced repeatedly into her rectum."

By this time, Chris appeared exhausted and terrorized—his voice barely a whisper.

He described the anal attack in grim, pornographic detail, in words that sounded as if Richard, especially, had loved every minute of the horror he was inflicting on Nancy and all the while she was crying and begging them to stop.

Five hours had passed since the detectives began typing the statement, more than twelve hours after interrogation had begun that day. Chris knew the general details of the statement. But neither before nor after signing did he read it.

After Ochoa signed the confession, the detectives arrested him for capital murder and sexual assault and brought him before a magistrate for arraignment. The female magistrate asked if he had an attorney. When Ochoa answered that he didn't have an attorney, the woman tried to find out why the accused was brought before her without benefit of legal counsel. Apparently unable to get a satisfactory answer, she demanded that Ochoa and the lawyer from the District Attorney's office confer with her in her chambers, where she gave everyone present a good dressing down, loudly and vehemently. "I want this man to have an attorney," she demanded. "Immediately."

A public defender was called to represent Chris. He appeared to be young and inexperienced in defending capital crimes. Chris told him everything that had happened in regard to the murder of Nancy DePriest and said that he was innocent of the murder and rape. The attorney seemed to accept what he said, but went to talk to the police. When he came back, he told Chris the police had told him about Chris's confession. "You confessed to murder," the man said. "You have to plead guilty."

"No, I'm not guilty," Chris protested.

"You must be guilty. The police have a signed confession. You have to plead guilty."

Ochoa was adamant. He would not plead guilty to this horrible crime. The public defender threw up his hands in defeat and a new, more experienced lawyer was appointed to represent Chris. After meeting with Ochoa and hearing his story, the new attorney said, "The police have a detailed confession. The only thing to do is plead guilty."

"No," said Chris. "Isn't it your job to prove me innocent?"

The man seemed completely unconvinced of Chris's position. "I'll tell you what my job is. My job is to try and save your life. For me to do that, you have to plead guilty."

Chris kept protesting his innocence and the attorney kept trying to persuade him to plead guilty. Days passed and Chris was adamant, daily insisting he was not guilty. Every day he received a phone call from his mother in El Paso, who told him the police were calling her and telling her she should persuade her son to plead guilty. Finally, she got sick and had to go to the emergency room.

That same day, Chris Ochoa notified his attorney he would plead guilty to the assault and murder of Nancy DePriest.

## Chapter 6

# One Little Truth

About six hours after Chris's interrogation began, several officers, including homicide detective Boardman and officer Gilchrist, along with an Assistant District Attorney, were dispatched to find Richard Danziger. Investigators had been told he could probably be found at the home of Rhonda Shore. When the detectives appeared at the door, he was sitting nonchalantly on a couch in the living room.

"We would like you to come down to the station to talk about the DePriest murder," Boardman told him.

Looking unruffled, Danziger grinned. "I've been waiting for you. In fact, I've been wondering why it has taken you so long to get to me."

Boardman realized Danziger probably knew police had been talking to numerous Pizza Hut employees, so it wasn't as offbeat a statement as one might imagine. But he was surprised when Danziger pointed a finger at Rhonda and said, "I was with her that morning. She's my alibi."

*Why would he need an alibi?* Boardman must have wondered. The policeman hadn't accused Danziger of anything.

Boardman assigned two other officers to drive Danziger to the police department, while he and Gilchrist stayed behind to conduct a search of Rhonda Shore's apartment, to which she had consented, and to confiscate any of Danziger's belongings that might be considered evidence. Gilchrist gathered up Danziger's few belongings, consisting of several pairs of jeans, some sweatpants, personal papers and the gray and black duffel bag he used as an overnight bag.

They also asked Rhonda to go to the station for questioning, and she said she would, but she had to arrange for her mother and stepfather to care for her children.

Two uniformed officers drove Danziger in a marked patrol car to the police department, where he was led inside through a special, locked entrance, rather than through the main entrance. He was taken to an interview room furnished with only a table and three chairs, where he was met by Sergeant Polanco, who read him his Miranda warning from a small blue card: "You have the right to remain silent. Anything you say can and will be used against you in a court of law. You have the right to speak to an attorney and to have an attorney present during any questioning. If you cannot afford a lawyer, one will be provided for you at government expense."

When Danziger answered that he understood those rights and waived them, he was asked to sign the card. He did so, although he must have wondered why they were acting this way since, by law, police must read the Miranda warning to anyone who is under arrest, and Danziger had been told he was not under arrest. However, in certain cases, the warning is read prior to investigative interviews, such as when interrogating a suspect.

Obviously Danziger did not consider himself a suspect, and he did not request an attorney.

For the next four hours, with grueling questioning, many times the same questions repeated over and over again by Polanco, Boardman and Detective Edward Balagia, Danziger told the same story. He had spent Sunday night, October 23, with Rhonda in her home. They had partied until five in the morning, then went to bed. The next thing he knew, the bedside phone was ringing. Through sleep-fogged eyes, he could see the bedside clock: 8:35.

According to Danziger, he picked up the phone and said, "Thank you for calling Pizza Hut. This is Richard."

"What are you doing there? Why aren't you at work?" The voice was that of the lead manager, Alex Martin. Only then did Danziger realize he had overslept. He should have been opening the store.

"Dude. There was a party here last night and it got late. I spent the night in Rhonda's guest room. Must have slept through the alarm. Or maybe I forgot to set it."

The manager was furious and told them both to get to the store. Frantically, Rhonda scrambled to get her young sons up, dressed and fed while getting into her uniform. Richard observed the single mother circus from a distance as he ironed a work shirt in the kitchen, washed, dressed and put his few overnight things in his duffel bag.

Then, Danziger told police, Rhonda's car wouldn't start. She had been having trouble with the motor lately. He pushed it out into the alley. Rhonda began running around to find someone who could help her give the car a jump-start. The kids had to be taken to school and day care. It took more than an hour for them to make it to work. The manager was smoldering. Richard was late and Rhonda was in disgrace. Two other servers were there, madly trying to catch up with all the prep duties, because the restaurant was due to open in an hour.

The first he'd heard about the murder, Danziger told the detectives, was when customers started arriving for lunch. Everyone who came in was talking about the awful events at the store less than four miles away. There had been a break-in. The whole store was blocked off, with police cars and television trucks everywhere. A young woman had been inside, and she'd been hurt, raped—maybe even killed. She was an employee, and they heard she'd been alone in the restaurant. Their customers asked the employees if they knew the victim.

Alex Martin called his supervisor and learned Nancy DePriest had been raped, shot and left for dead; that she was on life support at Brackenridge Hospital. The crew worked in stunned silence. The answer to their customers' question was, yes, they knew Nancy DePriest.

Polanco and Boardman kept after Danziger, sometimes two against one, other times one on one. No matter how hard they pressed him, though, Danziger never changed his story by one word. They couldn't even shake him on the time. Danziger insisted he definitely was at Rhonda's at 8:30 and from then on he was visible to his girlfriend, her kids and the employees at work.

What Danziger didn't know then was that he and Chris Ochoa were the prime suspects in the murder, that Chris was also being questioned in another interrogation room, as was Rhonda Shore, in a third room. Not only did the police feel his actions on Wednesday night when he drank a toast "to Nancy's memory" were suggestive of guilt, but also he seemed to know too much.

When Polanco asked Danziger what he knew about the murder of Nancy DePriest, Richard said forthrightly, "I don't know much." Then he went on, "Just that Nancy was shot in the back of the head with a .22 caliber handgun and the restaurant was flooded by stuffing a blue work apron into the sink."

Boardman actually kicked Polanco under the table to underscore the significance of Danziger's statement. Nobody was supposed to know those details. The police had tried to keep all that secret—the caliber of the weapon, where Nancy had been shot, the flooding, the blue apron used to plug the sink.

"Where did you get that information?" Boardman pressed.

"From the security guard," Danziger replied.

"I talked to the security guard," Boardman said firmly. "He didn't know all that himself."

"Then I guess I must have heard it from Alex," Danziger replied.

Boardman left the room, called Alex Martin and returned minutes later. The manager had said he didn't know any details of the crime. "You couldn't possibly have known those things unless you were there during the crime," Boardman snarled.

Danziger had no other explanation. He'd heard it all somewhere, but couldn't say where. The detectives took him through it all again. Where Danziger had gotten the information, why he had been late to work, what he and Rhonda had done after the phone call from the manager, but he never changed his statement and they elicited no new information.

By that time it was past ten o'clock and the police had nothing to show for those four intense hours with Danziger. The only thing left was to collect all the physical evidence they could and they asked him if he would provide them with samples of his hair and bodily fluids—blood, saliva and semen. These would be submitted to the Department of Public Safety laboratory for analysis and comparison with materials gathered at the restaurant. Danziger agreed, telling them, "You won't find anything from me at the crime scene."

He signed their request and also a consent to search the apartment he shared with Chris Ochoa and two other roommates. Boardman took Danziger to Brackenridge Hospital, where Nancy DePriest had died only two and a half weeks earlier. He remained in the room while a male nurse took samples of Danziger's pubic hair, head hair, saliva and blood. The hospital provided a receptacle for semen; back at the police department, Danziger was asked to masturbate in one of the interrogation rooms to provide the semen for testing.

Despite the late hour, the detectives were not through with Richard Danziger. He and Ochoa were the first promising suspects they had, and they were determined to break them. Polanco and Boardman had failed to put a dent in Danziger's story, so Detective Edward Balagia took a turn at the suspect. However, he could only repeat the questions Polanco and Boardman had been asking for the last several hours.

"What can you tell me about the murder at the Pizza Hut?" Balagia asked.

"I have an alibi," Danziger told him, still sounding as positive as he had been when he was picked up, hours earlier. He went through his story again, emphasizing that he'd been miles from the scene when the murder was committed. Once more he stated unequivocally, "You don't have any evidence to link me to the murder."

"Your reactions are pretty unusual for someone accused of such a crime as capital murder," Balagia told Danziger accusingly.

"You're not going to pin a capital murder on me!" Danziger vowed.

When Balagia asked what he knew about the crime scene, he repeated everything he'd told the other detectives. Also, he said, he knew the police had no likely suspects and no strong leads in the investigation.

"Where did you get this information?" Balagia wanted to know.

Again, said Danziger, from the security guard, from the manager of the store where he worked and from other employees. This was a brutal murder and people were talking. There was no way those kinds of things could be kept secret.

"What were you thinking, asking the security guard those kinds of questions?" Balagia asked. "What were you trying to find out?"

Danziger answered that he was simply curious about the case and was trying to be helpful in solving it.

*Yeah. Right.* Balagia didn't buy that story for a moment. Everything about Danziger seemed strange. To him, here sat a young man suspected of murder and he was behaving as if he didn't have a care in the world. He was throwing around terms like "alibi," "crime scene" and "evidence linking me to the crime" as though this were a TV drama about someone else, not a real life crime that had cost a young woman her life, had cost a little girl a mother and could cost Danziger his freedom—or his life. He kept insisting that investigators were wasting their time by talking to him, that they could never pin anything on him.

"Why are you so sure we can't pin this on you?" Balagia asked.

Danziger shook his head impatiently. He seemed to be implying, *Why don't you get it? I've told you and told you, and you still don't get it. What is it you don't understand?*

He simply sighed and said, slowly and deliberately, "You. Have. No. Evidence. Against. Me."

To Balagia, this was not the behavior of an innocent man. Instead, it was the coolness of a sociopath, someone who was capable of just about anything, without any sense of remorse.

By one o'clock in the morning, the detectives figured they'd gotten all they could from Danziger, at least for now. Except for one thing. Polanco asked Danziger for his shoes—white high top sneakers that apparently were the teenager's only footwear. Maybe they could get something from the shoes to tie him to the crime. Danziger handed them over as readily as he had given them his bodily fluids. Finally, he was released and went barefoot into the night, unaware that only a few hours earlier, Christopher Ochoa had told a different story.

A short while later, a call came into the police department through the emergency line from Richard Danziger, asking to be connected to Sergeant Polanco. After several minutes, Polanco came on the line and Danziger told him he was going to his mother's house in Beeville, Texas, a few hundred miles southeast of Austin. He was keeping his word to the police that he would call if he left town.

Two days later, police dispatched officers to arrest Danziger in Beeville and bring him back to Austin.

Chapter 7

# Adrift in the Void

Day after day, night after night, totally unaware of the passage of time, Jeanette sat in her rocking chair and thought of suicide. She didn't want to live without Nancy. Most nights as she rocked, she held her loaded .22 pistol in her hands. She existed on soda and cigarettes, chain smoking four packages a day. She lost thirty pounds. Her unemployment checks stopped coming, so she had no money and no energy to look for another job. Her friend and neighbor Doris Barnes regularly brought food and encouraged Jeanette to eat. Sometimes she ate. A lot of times she didn't.

Her sister JoAnn realized what bad shape Jeanette was in and came to see her every day. Together, they walked the country trails and Jeanette picked up aluminum cans, which she sold. The cans brought in enough to keep her supplied with cigarettes.

Other times, the sisters sat out in the yard and talked, while her dog played at their feet. "I want to die," Jeanette told JoAnn. "I want to be with Nancy."

"No, you don't," JoAnn scolded. "You know you don't want to put Mother through what you're going through. Do you know what that would do to her? Have you thought about what it will do to me?"

Jeanette knew her sister was right. She couldn't inflict on her family the utter despair she was feeling. Those daily visits with JoAnn kept Jeanette going.

Finally, as time passed, Jeanette emerged from her grieving enough to understand that she had to go back to work. She was in a convenience store filling out an application when the owner of the store where she had last worked saw her. He offered his condolences about Nancy, then wanted to know what Jeanette was doing. She told him she was looking for a job; that she hadn't worked since Nancy's death.

"You can come back to work for me," the man offered.

So she accepted a job at one of his stores. Somehow she made it to work each day.

In mid-November, Austin police got in touch with her and said they had arrested two men, Richard Danziger and Christopher Ochoa, for raping and killing her daughter. Jeanette asked if she could have pictures of the men, so she could see what heartless beasts looked like. They agreed, and the photos arrived on her birthday, November 23. She had expected the killers to look like monsters, so she was surprised to see two ordinary looking young men.

The police told Jeanette that Chris Ochoa had confessed to participating in the robbery and the assault and killing of Nancy, but had named Richard Danziger as the one who fired the shot that ended her daughter's life. Danziger, on the other hand, was claiming both of them were innocent. There would be a trial at some point; the police would notify her of its time and place.

In March of 1989, Jeanette was notified that Chris Ochoa had made yet another confession, his third, in which he confessed that he was the one who had shot Nancy, not Richard Danziger. He said he was making this statement, because the one he had given in November was not exactly the way everything happened. He said that, basically, it was truthful in the sequence of events that led up to the murder, but it was not truthful as to how he detailed exactly who did what and exactly what happened on the morning of Jeanette's daughter's death.

"I am the person who killed Nancy DePriest," this new statement read. "I took the pistol from Richard Danziger and shot Nancy DePriest in the back of the left side of her head. I shot her one time. I shot her because Nancy DePriest recognized me and I didn't want to go to prison for robbing the Pizza Hut and raping Nancy DePriest."

He made her kneel on her knees; she was begging and pleading with him not to kill her. She kept repeating, "Please don't. Please don't." He pulled the trigger and Nancy slumped forward. He let her go and her body fell, face first on the floor.

"I then asked myself, 'What have I done?' And Richard Danziger took the gun out of my hand and that is the last time that I touched or saw the weapon."

Ochoa also changed the details of how the rape occurred, emphasizing that he had been the leader in the attack and Richard had gone along with everything he suggested.

Jeanette, still numb with grief, wondered if it really mattered which of these beasts had fired the bullet that killed her daughter. Nancy was still dead, and both men were guilty and deserved to spend the rest of their lives in prison.

Later that spring, the other women who worked with Jeanette at her new job began trying to coax her into getting out, socializing, anything except going home every night to her rocking chair, her cigarettes and her boundless grief for her daughter. She refused to be coaxed, totally uninterested in anything outside her sorrow. Knowing that Jeanette was divorced, several of the women kept trying to set her up with dates, but she refused. She didn't think she would ever have enough energy, enough love, to maintain another relationship—ever.

The clerk who worked the morning shift, coming on as Jeanette was getting off in the mornings, told her about a man who came in every morning after Jeanette left. He was really attractive, the woman told Jeanette. Trim and buff, with a twenty-eight-inch waist and a strong, muscled chest. And he really knew how to wear his tight jeans. When he came in, the other women couldn't keep their eyes off him.

One morning, at shift change, the clerk said, "There he is! There he is."

"Who?" Jeanette asked, getting her keys out of her purse, ready to go home and fall into bed.

"The man in the jeans, getting out of the brown truck. That's Mr. Tight Jeans. That's the kind of guy you should date."

"I don't need to date any kind of guy," Jeanette informed her. "I don't need a date. I don't want a date. I don't want to go out. Not even with you girls."

Mr. Tight Jeans came in and Jeanette watched him pick up a few items. When the man came to the counter to pay, he mentioned that he hadn't seen her in the store before. She told him she was usually gone by that time.

"I guess I'll just have to come by earlier," he said, grinning.

Sure enough, the next morning he came in before her shift ended and took a soda from the cooler. After he paid for it, he hung around the store while he drank it.

"Do you need something else?" Jeanette asked.

"Nope."

So they made small talk. He told her his name was Jim Popp. He worked the night shift and commuted to Dallas for his job. She learned that those muscles the other clerks had been admiring came from moving diesel engines around.

Every morning Jim came in, and finally, he asked her to go out to dinner. She told him she just wasn't up to dating at that point. But he kept coming in.

More time passed. It was October again, a year since Nancy's death. At the first of the month, the morning clerk told Jeanette she was quitting. So they planned a going away party. A few days before the party, the clerk reminded her it was for couples and Jeanette should bring a date. She protested that she didn't know anyone.

"How about Tight Jeans? Has he asked you out?"

"Yes," she admitted. "But I'm not ready for that."

"Jeanette, when are you going to be ready? Do you think Nancy really wants you to do this? To shut yourself off from the world?"

Jeanette thought of her daughter, so full of life. Who had fun wherever she went. Who loved people and invited them generously into her life. While Jeanette was considering this, Jim came into the store.

"Ask him," the clerk urged. "If you don't ask him, I'll ask him for you."

So Jeanette took a deep breath and asked timidly, "Jim, are you busy Saturday night?"

"Nope."

"Would you mind accompanying me to a party for a woman I know?"

"Glad to oblige," he grinned.

Saturday, Jeanette worked the day shift and Jim picked her up from work at five o'clock, so they could eat before they went to the party. They went to what she considered the best pizza place in the world. Immediately, Jeanette felt she had known Jim forever. They talked constantly, falling over each other's words. They never made it to the party, staying at the restaurant until seven, then driving around for awhile. Finally, Jim parked by Cedar Creek Lake. It was a beautiful, warm, star-studded night. Jeanette felt relaxed for the first time since Nancy's death. She could have sat on those banks forever, soaking in the peace, not only of the lake, but also of Jim Popp. Eventually, he told her his house was on the lake.

Suspicious, she asked him if he was enticing her into his boudoir. He denied it, but mentioned they would be more comfortable at the house, so she agreed. By then it was eleven o'clock. At his house, they watched a baseball game on TV and talked some more.

That was the beginning of what she knew would be the best relationship she'd ever had. She moved in with him the next day.

It wasn't long before Jim Popp asked Jeanette to marry him, and Jeanette was amazed to find she wanted to do it. She knew, without a doubt, that he was the one with whom she was supposed to spend the rest of her life. But despite her newfound security, she was still traumatized by Nancy's death. Jeanette was anxious about the murder trial of Richard Danziger that had been set for March of the following year. She didn't want to bring her fears and anxieties into her new marriage, so she and Jim decided to wait until after the trial to marry.

Chapter 8

# The Portals
# of Hell

For the next few months, Jeanette found that life with Jim Popp provided her with the kind of strength she'd never found in her previous relationships. With him, she began to rise from her pit of despair and enjoy brief periods of peace and even some rare moments of joy. Even so, Nancy was never far from Jeanette's mind, though now she was able to think about her daughter without completely losing her composure.

As the actual trial date neared, though, Jeanette was plunged once more into the depths of anguish she'd experienced during those awful days after Nancy's death. She was determined to attend the trial, but when March 3 came, Jim couldn't go to Austin with her, because of work commitments. Unwilling for Jeanette to face the trauma of the trial alone, Edith Sparks insisted on accompanying her daughter to Austin.

The Austin District Attorney's office had insisted on paying all their expenses, including the hotel and their meals. Jeanette was told a member of the District Attorney's staff would pick Edith and her up every morning and return them to the hotel in the evening. The DA's staff tried to keep the reporters away from Jeanette who, with the sad anticipation of the trial now so near, was again thrown into an abyss of grief for her daughter. Flashbulbs seemed to be popping off constantly. Cameras were always in their faces.

Assistant District Attorney Clair Dawson-Brown, who would be prosecuting in court along with ADA LaRu Woody, described the judicial process to Jeanette, explaining that her office had chosen to charge Danziger with aggravated sexual assault rather than murder. She explained that the rape was considered a capital crime, committed in the course of a robbery, and the District Attorney's office thought they could get a stiffer penalty than they could if the charge was murder.

This made no sense to Jeanette, but she accepted their judgment. She would later learn that murder in the course of a robbery or sexual assault is also a capital crime, although conviction for a capital crime does not always mean the death penalty is involved. Possibly, considering the lack of physical evidence or even circumstantial evidence tying Richard Danziger to the crime and the fact that the case rested solely on the confession of Christopher Ochoa, the District Attorney's office thought it had a better chance of proving rape and robbery than it did murder and robbery.

Travis County District Attorney Ronald (Ronnie) Earle had been first elected in 1976, the year the Supreme Court reestablished capital punishment. Texas quickly set records for executions, exceeding the number of the next top five death penalty states combined. (By 1990, death sentences in Texas reached almost one hundred. By 2001, it passed two hundred, by 2003 it hit three hundred executions and by 2007, it had passed the four hundred mark.) This was in spite of Texas law that says to win a death sentence, prosecutors must first convince jurors "beyond a reasonable doubt" that a defendant is guilty of capital murder, which is an ordinary murder compounded by at least one of several aggravating factors, ranging from murdering someone you know is a police officer or a fireman who is acting in the line of duty, to killing a child under six years old or intentionally committing murder in the course of committing another crime, such as kidnapping, robbery, aggravated sexual assault or several other criminal actions. Second, the jury must find—again, beyond a reasonable doubt—that "there is a probability that the defendant will commit criminal acts of violence that will constitute a continuing threat to society."

Earle vigorously backed the Court's decision at first, as did most other law-and-order District Attorneys in the state. As late as 1982, Earle said capital punishment was "society's right to self-defense," emphasizing that there are times when society should use the death penalty to send a message that it will protect people in vulnerable situations. Early in his career, however, one of his mentors reminded him that when he asked for the death penalty, "The burden is on you to show that no lesser punishment would do that job."

That warning stayed with him through the years and after prosecuting violent crime for fourteen years, Earle's beliefs about capital punishment had changed somewhat. He reserved his recommendation of the death penalty for those brutal murderers he believed would kill again, even in prison.

Christopher Ochoa had no previous record and Richard Danziger's juvenile record did not contain violence; therefore, it must have seemed unlikely that either one of them would commit murder in the future.

Jeanette had decided not to attend the trial until it was time for Chris Ochoa to testify. She learned about the first few days of testimony from ADA Clair Dawson-Brown and ADA LaRu Woody, as well as from news reports. From the first moment of the trial, Dawson-Brown and Woody built their case against the defendants, brick by brick, layers upon layers of minute detail and called as witnesses every person they determined might be even remotely

involved in the investigation, police and civilians, no matter how small
their parts were. Dawson-Brown began with Nancy DePriest's
husband, Todd, then moved on to Pizza Hut employees and police
officers who were the first responders on the day Nancy died.

Todd DePriest described for the court how he had followed his
wife to work on October 24, arriving at the Pizza Hut at 7:01 A.M.
He watched her enter the building by the east-facing door, then he
drove their fifteen-month-old daughter to the sitter's and returned to
the restaurant to get his motorcycle, arriving there about 7:45. Nancy
came to the door so he could give her the car keys. He kissed her
goodbye and left for work at Bergstrom Air Force Base. This was the
sum and substance of DePriest's knowledge of the events of that
fateful morning.

To pinpoint the time of Nancy's death as accurately as possible,
Dawson-Brown called a witness who was a supervisor of the Pizza Hut
warehouse, where all the stores got their supplies. The warehouse
supervisor said he got a phone call from a woman at the restaurant
sometime between 8:00 and 8:30 A.M. requesting supplies as soon as
possible. The witness said he had worked with Nancy for a while and
recognized her voice. He dispatched a van to the store and around 9:30
the van's driver called to say he couldn't make the delivery, because no
one was there to receive it.

The next witness was the deliveryman, who testified that he had
already scheduled a stop and couldn't go directly from the warehouse,
so it was between 9:15 and 9:30 when he arrived at the store where
Nancy worked. He knocked on the back door, but got no response.
After a minute or two, he heard the telephone inside start ringing, but
no one answered. A small gray car, whose make and model he didn't
recall, was in the parking lot, along with a brown car. The cars led him
to believe someone was inside, so he continued to knock and call out
for about five minutes, but no one came to the door. He called his
boss, who called the store and received no answer, so the driver left.

Later, the deliveryman returned to the restaurant and saw police officers there. When asked by Dawson-Brown if he knew Richard Danziger, he said he did not.

Lester Davis, the supervisor of seven Pizza Hut restaurants, including the one where Nancy worked, testified that he called Nancy DePriest for his daily, routine check with his managers between 8:30 and 8:55 and received no answer. After finishing his check of the stores, he drove to the store he received no answer from in his car. He got there about 9:30 and entered the store through the west door, which was unlocked. The lights were on inside and the dough machine was running. He walked through the store, calling Nancy's name, but got no answer. Then, in the hallway, he stepped in water ankle deep and thought at first there was a plumbing problem. Immediately, he knew he was wrong. On the floor between the men's and ladies' restrooms lay Nancy DePriest, naked, her hands tied behind her back, brutally restrained. Knowing he shouldn't touch anything, including the phone, he ran across the street to the gas station and called 911. It was 9:33.

The first police officers arrived at 9:37 and Davis unlocked the east door to let them in, rather than bringing them in through the back door, where he had entered. When asked who had keys to the store, the supervisor explained the way keys were distributed and why, emphasizing that each store could be opened only by its specific key or a master key, of which there were only a few and those in the hands of upper level employees.

Davis also testified that each restaurant had its own safe, with the combination known only to each store's managers, assistant managers and shift leaders.

The store manager, Nancy's supervisor, testified next. She told where the money was kept, that someone with the combination must have opened the safe and that only about one hundred and fifty dollars had been taken.

The next three witnesses were the first officers at the scene. One officer, who said he diagrammed the scene, found a key ring and a .22 caliber shell casing, which was strangely flattened and deformed. He also discovered the cause of the flooding in the hallway: a blue apron had been stuffed into the mouth of the sink drain in the men's restroom, causing the basin to overflow. Another officer, Mike Alexander, said Sergeant Hector Polanco later told him Nancy DePriest had been shot with a .22 caliber gun.

Four EMS personnel responded to the call and all four gave essentially the same testimony: They had immediately put Nancy on advanced life support; it was all too apparent that she had been shot with a small caliber gun.

Going over each detail, Dawson-Brown called everyone who had been at the murder scene, including two sex crimes investigators, robbery detail personnel and forensics investigators. All of them essentially gave the same facts. Those who testified they were aware that Nancy had been shot in the head, that the hall was flooded and that a blue apron had been stuffed in the sink, all denied discussing those facts with anyone. They said they didn't tell any outsiders, they did not talk to the press; they only spoke to the police officers.

An employee of the Emergency Department at Brackenridge Hospital testified that Nancy DePriest was brought in at 10:05 A.M., given a number and, because she hadn't yet been identified, was referred to as "Mrs. B." He described examining Nancy for rape: injecting saline solution into her vagina and aspirating the liquid onto a slide to examine it for sperm. Then he did pubic combing, took oral and vaginal swabs and drew blood. He noted that she appeared to have ligature marks on her wrists.

He testified that Nancy was moved to the Intensive Care Unit at Brackenridge, where X-rays and a CT scan of her head were done. The physician on duty when she was admitted to the floor testified that she was breathing with the help of a ventilator. She had no response to pain, no gag reflex and no corneal reflex. At 10:45 P.M. she was pronounced brain dead and was prepared for organ transplants in accordance with her wishes, as relayed to the hospital by her husband.

William Beechinor, an investigator on the robbery detail, testified that he was dispatched to Brackenridge Hospital, where he examined Nancy's body for fingerprints, but found none. Afterward, he said, he talked briefly with Todd DePriest.

Patrolman John Hardage testified that he searched Christopher Ochoa's car, which had been impounded. He found several items, including a pawn ticket, clothing and tennis shoes, which he delivered to the Department of Public Safety Crime Laboratory Service.

An APD fingerprint expert, Charles Dermody, described how he worked the scene, processing the fence behind the building, along with other objects outside. He processed the three entrances, the coolers, the safe area, the two telephones and the areas that were not wet in and around the bathrooms. Dermody retrieved prints from glass on an interior door, the entries to both bathrooms, toilet paper holders and the phones. He was able to identify some of the prints as belonging to the supervisor, Nancy DePriest and another employee. Some areas, where Dermody would have expected to find prints, were clean. In fact, they appeared to have been carefully wiped.

Later, after Richard Danziger and Christopher were arrested, Dermody compared their fingerprints with those he had lifted from the murder scene. They did not match. *He concluded his testimony by admitting that he did not find any fingerprints linking Richard Danziger to the crime.*

A hush fell over the courtroom as Robert Bayardo, chief medical examiner and forensic pathologist for Travis County, entered the witness box. Dr. Bayardo testified that he had done 8,809 autopsies. He stated that he had performed the autopsy on Nancy DePriest at 8:50 A.M. on Tuesday, October 25, and concluded that she had died of a gunshot wound to the head. He said the wound was consistent with a gunman standing behind the woman as she was kneeling.

According to Bayardo, the gun was held farther from her head than twelve inches. It was not a "close range or contact" type of wound.

Dr. Bayardo said Nancy's rectum and anus were bruised, abraded and dilated. He concluded that some instrument had been introduced repeatedly into her rectum. He repeated some of the tests that had been performed in the Emergency Department, collecting oral and rectal swabs, combing head and pubic hair and clippings of her nails, which he turned over to the Austin Police Department.

The testimonies of Sergeant Hector Polanco and Detective Bruce Boardman were essentially the same testimony, almost word for word, even though it had been more than a year since the murder. Nancy DePriest had already been taken to Brackenridge Hospital when the two men arrived at approximately 10:07. A number of other officers were already present. They told of finding the spent, flattened shell casing and Nancy's purse, clothing and car keys. They described the scene and all that had been done to collect evidence, including the discovery of hairs and blood. Sergeant Polanco said he interviewed Nancy's husband Todd DePriest, who submitted to tests for hair and semen comparisons.

Boardman said several suspects were brought in over the next two and a half weeks and were interviewed by Polanco, Detective Edward Balagia and himself. In his testimony, Boardman stressed that it was department policy not to give details of a crime to a suspect, to keep the suspect in the dark and in that way, prevent someone from confessing to a crime he did not commit. He said the police *were not interested in listening to any false confessions.*

Polanco told of his plan, which he devised several days before he heard of Richard Danziger or Chris Ochoa, because he "had an inkling" it would lure the suspect to return to the scene of the crime. On the stand, Polanco admitted that, in putting his plan in motion, he could have told Pizza Hut employees there might have been two persons involved in the crime. He surmised this, because Nancy was five feet four inches tall and it "might have taken two people to subdue her."

Five days after that meeting, the manager who had been Nancy DePriest's supervisor called Boardman to tell him she and some other employees had seen something they thought was suspicious. She said that on November 9, their paychecks were not delivered and she sent an employee to pick them up. She called the central office to tell them what had happened and they said Danziger was on his way over to her store to bring the checks. He got there around 3:00 P.M. He seemed nervous and in a hurry, and she barely glimpsed him as he left.

She told of Ochoa and Danziger's trip to the Pizza Hut that night, of recognizing Danziger as the employee who had delivered paychecks that afternoon and of the two men drinking a toast to Nancy.

When her recently-hired security guard reported to her that the men were asking questions about the crime, she became concerned, and it bothered her to the point where she couldn't sleep that night. The next morning, she called Polanco.

That call led Polanco to Richard Danziger and Chris Ochoa. Both detectives related how they took both men into custody and interrogated them and, finally, how Chris Ochoa confessed he and Danziger had raped and killed Nancy DePriest and had taken money from the safe.

Polanco said no tape or video was made of the interview. Both methods of recording the interrogation were made available to the detectives.

Detective Edward Balagia testified he took Chris Ochoa to Brackenridge Hospital for the collection of blood, hair, saliva and semen samples, to which Chris had consented. Balagia told the jury he had taken two statements from Chris Ochoa. The first was a taped oral statement and the second was a written statement, with Polanco present, which Balagia typed.

Every detective, every investigator, every patrolman, all emergency services personnel—in fact, everyone who was present at the crime scene the day Nancy DePriest was killed and every person who searched for evidence, including the search of Christopher Ochoa's car, everyone—was asked by the prosecutor if they had discussed the case with the press or with either of the accused killers. Some of the witnesses denied even knowing the details themselves, and all those who were privy to the details stated unequivocally that they had not told Danziger, Ochoa or anyone else any of the details of the crime scene.

To some observers, it seemed almost as if there was doubt about the veracity of Chris Ochoa's confession, and the prosecution went out of its way to impress on the jurors that Ochoa could not have known the details to which he confessed if he had not been present.

Forensics technicians gave testimony next.

Joe Ronald Urbanovsky, a chemist for the Texas Department of Public Safety laboratory in Austin, described testing the samples of hair, blood, nails, saliva and semen that were sent to him in the DePriest case. He said the DPS lab was not capable of DNA testing at that time, but they had sent the samples to a private lab.

Urbanovsky explained that he tried not to use all of Nancy DePriest's blood that was available to him, but froze some for future testing, if necessary. He said she was blood group A, a secretor. From the oral swabs taken from Nancy, he found no semen protein, although he found A and H antigens. On the vaginal swabs, he found antigens A and H and PGM 1+. He compared these findings with samples taken from Todd DePriest, Chris Ochoa and Richard Danziger. Vaginal swabs from Nancy were positive for P-30, indicating the presence of semen, but he found only a 1+ PGM subtype. Todd DePriest could not be eliminated as the semen donor, since he was a PGM 1+1 subtype. Danziger, a PGM 1+2+ subtype, and Chris Ochoa, a 1-1+ subtype, could not be eliminated either, based on the tests. Since Nancy was a I+I+, she could account for the PGM subtype. Although the three men could not be eliminated, neither could it be proven that any of them could have been the semen donor.

Urbanovsky testified that no blood or seminal stains were found on the blue apron that had stopped up the sink at the restaurant, but several hairs were found. Hairs also were found on a piece of black cloth present at the scene. Human blood was found on Nancy's bra, but it couldn't be typed. No trace evidence was taken from her fingernails, no blood, no tissue, no hairs.

The prosecution next introduced the rectal swabs taken from Nancy at the hospital. The chemist said they were positive in the presumptive test for blood, but no spermatozoa were detected.

Dawson-Brown asked, "If seminal fluid had been introduced in the rectal cavity two days prior to the time a rectal swabbing was done, would you expect to find spermatozoa still in the swab?"

The chemist answered that it would be highly unlikely. The sperm and P-30 deteriorate over hours, due to bacteria.

He said he examined the tennis shoes belonging to Danziger and the floor mat from Ochoa's car and found no significant stains.

In conclusion, Urbanovsky said, *No evidence affirmatively linked Danziger to the assault on Nancy DePriest, but he could have been the donor of semen found in her vagina, along with 45 percent of the male population in the United States.*

After the chemist finished explaining how he performed the blood tests and why the results were inconclusive, Dawson-Brown drew the court's attention to hair, fiber and DNA testing. Juan Rojas, an analyst with the DPS Criminalistics Section, explained that although hair analysis is not an exact science—in fact, he said it is more of an *art* than a science—analysts could use it to exclude people from a group of suspects. Tests on samples that didn't contain roots, where DNA is found, were determined to be "consistent with" or "not consistent with" a specific suspect or "person of interest." Rojas said he compared the head and pubic hairs that had been obtained from Todd DePriest, Nancy DePriest, Christopher Ochoa and Richard Danziger with hairs found at the crime scene. He determined that hairs taken from Nancy's panties were probably her own. One hair, a broken strand without a root, was inconsistent for pubic hair from Todd, Nancy and Ochoa, Rojas said, but it "could have come from Richard Danziger."

More questions not answered included the fact that none of the hairs found on Danziger's clothing was consistent with Nancy's hair sample.

Moses Schoenfield, the laboratory director of the Analytical Genetic Testing Center, testified that his laboratory had just begun testing for DNA. He said he could find no information on the semen donor. Nancy, Danziger and Ochoa were all the same type in two major analytical respects. There was no indication of a significant amount of semen from Todd DePriest. And he stated unequivocally that *there was no physical evidence to implicate Richard Danziger.*

After Schoenfield finished his tests, he forwarded the samples to Ed Blake, another analyst, for further testing. Blake said that after his tests, he could eliminate both DePriest and Danziger as the semen donors, but he could not eliminate Ochoa. He emphasized, however, that if someone's semen is deposited second, it might mask other semen already present, particularly if it is in a much greater quantity—at least ten times the amount of the first semen.

In closing, Blake also stated that *he found nothing to implicate Richard Danziger in the rape of Nancy DePriest.*

The last forensics expert LaRu Woody called was Calvin Story, the firearms examiner from the crime laboratory at the Austin Police Department. After Story's credentials were established for the record, Woody asked, "What type of analysis do you make as a ballistics expert? What type of things do you look for?"

Story laid out his area of expertise cogently and succinctly. "The primary test in the ballistics section is to examine evidence bullets, test-fire suspect weapons, compare those tests with the evidence bullets to determine if the evidence bullets were fired from that particular weapon."

"Then," asked Woody, "is it fair to say that what result you get depends on what evidence you have to work with?"

Story nodded. "That is correct."

"For example, you can't determine if a bullet was fired from a specific weapon unless you have a weapon. Is that correct?" the ADA asked.

"Yes. That's correct."

"If you had some information, could you determine what caliber of bullet was used in this particular crime?"

"Yes."

"What kind of evidence would you require to make that determination?"

Story shifted in his chair so he was speaking to the jury as well as to Woody. "I would need either a fired cartridge case or a fired bullet."

"What would you look at, on the bullet, to make a determination of what kind of weapon fired that bullet?"

"You take many different characteristics into account, one being the diameter of the projectile; the most important being the weight of the projectile. Using these two basic bits of information, you can normally determine the caliber of weapon it was fired from."

Woody nodded. "All right. Now let me ask you, what would you look at on a casing to determine its caliber?"

Story said that, normally, the fired cartridge case will have the caliber stamped on its head. He could more easily make a determination as to what weapon a bullet and casing were fired from if he had both the bullet and the casing.

Woody showed Story a small plastic evidence bag, which she described as a State's exhibit. "Can you identify this for the jury?"

"Yes. This is a .22 caliber fired bullet." Story confirmed that it was the same bullet Sergeant Hector Polanco of the Austin Police Department had given him to examine and that it had been in his, Story's, custody since that time, until he turned it over to an investigator from the District Attorney's office a few weeks prior to the trial.

Continuing the same line of questioning, Woody had the ballistics expert identify another exhibit for the State, a fired .22 caliber cartridge case, a case Detective Bruce Boardman had turned over to Story the same day Polanco had given him the bullet. Story said it was his opinion that the bullet was fired from a .22 caliber weapon having six lands and grooves, inclined to the right. These characteristics of six lands and grooves, the right hand twist and the width of the lands and grooves had at one time or another been used by every firearms manufacturer in the United States. Based strictly on the bullet, Story said, he was unable to narrow it down to the manufacturer to any degree.

Taking the bullet and the casing together, however, Story said he was able to draw some specific conclusions. Adding to the bullet characteristics, including the shape of the casing, the firing pin impression and the location of the firing pin and extractor and ejector marks, Story concluded that the two pieces of evidence were fired in a Browning .22 long pistol.

The expert admitted that while he thought the Browning pistol was the most likely weapon to have fired the bullet, other manufacturers including High Standard and Ruger made weapons with similar characteristics.

Having established what Story thought was the caliber and manufacturer of the weapon that fired the fatal bullet into Nancy DePriest's head, Woody directed Story to the type of gun it might have been.

"When only one fired cartridge is found at a crime scene, this normally indicates the weapon used was a semi-automatic," Story said, "because a semi-automatic will automatically eject the fired cartridge case after the cartridge has been fired.

"A revolver, on the other hand, would have to be manually unloaded. The revolver normally holds six rounds. It would be unusual for a person to open a revolver and manually eject a single fired cartridge case. It is more common to see all six, or more than one, ejected. It is more common for a person to fire all six bullets and then eject the cases." For that reason, Story told them, if a single cartridge case was found, the weapon that fired the bullet was a semi-automatic.

Woody summarized the firearms expert's testimony for the jury. "So it is your opinion that this bullet and the cartridge case were fired from a .22 caliber semi-automatic handgun?"

"Yes," Story said in a grim voice.

Judge Perkins declared a short recess before moving to the next witness and Jeanette and her mother went outside to a small patio to talk. A man approached them tentatively and introduced himself as an emergency medical technician.

"I was the first EMT to treat your daughter," he said. "I don't know if this will help you or not but I thought I should tell you."

"What?" Jeanette asked.

He shook his head somberly. "She wasn't alive. She had been gone a long time—in her mind. So she probably didn't suffer. . ." he choked and tears started trickling down his cheeks.

Jeanette patted his arm. "Thank you for telling me. It does make things easier for me."

Chapter 9

# The "Alibi" Girlfriend

After the technical testimony had been completed, the prosecution was scheduled to continue constructing their circumstantial case against Richard Danziger by introducing his "alibi girlfriend," Rhonda Shore. Jeanette wanted to hear what this woman had to say.

So, early in the morning of the fifth day of the trial, a car from the District Attorney's office picked Jeanette and her mother up to take them to the courthouse. That day, Richard Danziger's alibi girlfriend would take the stand. A Victim's Service advocate met Jeanette and her mother at the courthouse and told them her job was to be of any assistance she could to Jeanette. Death threats had been made against Ochoa and Danziger, so everyone was thoroughly searched as they entered the courthouse. Purses were rummaged through, bodies were scanned.

Jeanette and her mother were escorted to seats in the second row in the courtroom behind the prosecution table, catty-cornered to the defense table where Richard Danziger would sit in a few minutes. When he was brought into the courtroom, it was the first time Jeanette had seen him, although she recognized him from the picture the Austin police had sent her more than a year earlier. He was tall, slender and had a cocky manner. He had on gray pants and a blue shirt, through which she could see the bulk of a bulletproof vest. He was met at the defense table by his court-appointed attorney, Berke Bettis.

His eyes zeroed in on her immediately; she found his stare challenging and somehow threatening. Jeanette's mother asked her why the defendant was staring at her and Jeanette said she had no idea. She didn't know, but she met his long stare with one of her own.

Even when the presiding judge, District Judge Robert (Bob) Perkins entered the room, Danziger never shed his rebellious stance. Jeanette didn't see any member of Danziger's family. If they were there, they did not approach the defendant's table or hug him when he entered.

When Dawson-Brown called Danziger's girlfriend Rhonda Shore to the stand, court observers took note that this could be crucial testimony in the case against Richard Danziger. The witness told Dawson-Brown she took over the management of the Pizza Hut when she was promoted to general manager, which is where she met Richard Danziger and Christopher Ochoa, who both worked there at the time. She had known Ochoa previously, however, and a short while later he moved to another store. She said it was against Pizza Hut policy for employees to become romantically involved, so, although Richard was spending three to four nights a week at her house prior to October 23, they were trying to keep their relationship as invisible as possible—at least she was. She said Danziger didn't own a car, but she sometimes let him borrow hers.

On Saturday, October 22, she said she worked part of her shift, then took off so she could go to San Antonio with a female friend. She left her two sons in the care of her mother, since she planned to spend the night. Her friend drove and Rhonda left her red car parked at her duplex. The two women got back to Austin late the following day. Her mother brought the children home, and after Rhonda fed and bathed them, she got them ready for bed. Then she started ironing the clothes they would need for the following week.

According to her, Richard and Chris came over and she continued ironing while the men sat in the living room and talked. Chris had brought beer and they all had some, except Richard, who never drank much. Later, just before midnight, another female friend came over and stayed a couple of hours, then went home. Rhonda said her memory of the events after that were hazy. She vaguely remembered that Chris wanted to go home about two o'clock in the morning, and Richard went outside with him, ostensibly to drive them in Chris's car. A few moments later, they came back in and said they had broken the key. She didn't remember seeing the key, however. They ended up calling their roommate to come and get Chris.

Rhonda had no recollection of how long Richard's roommate stayed at her house. She did remember the roommate saying he needed to go home and reported that soon afterward he left. She didn't know if Chris left with the roommate. She did remember that Richard stayed with her. She was under the assumption that the roommate and Chris went home in the roommate's car, although she didn't remember seeing Chris's car at her house the next morning. She didn't recall what time she and Richard finally got to bed, but knew it was really late.

The next thing Rhonda recalled was the phone ringing and Richard answering it. She struggled to wake up and saw that the sun was shining. She told the court Richard had never answered the phone at her house before, because she had warned him not to do so. She was afraid he would answer and it would be her mother calling, and "Mom would have a fit."

When the girlfriend opened her eyes, Richard was sitting on the side of the bed saying, "Pizza Hut. This is Richard. May I help you?" With a shock, she realized it was Monday morning and, as opening cook, Richard should have been at work at eight o'clock. Her shift started at eleven. When she heard Richard answer the phone, she waited to find out who was calling. Richard looked over at her and said, "It's Alex Martin."

Martin, the general manager of another Pizza Hut, also supervised Rhonda at the store where she worked. Trying to mislead the manager about the nature of her relationship with Richard, she pretended to be in another room and took her time answering the phone. When she finally got on the phone, the manager was furious, because Richard was late opening the store. He was also angry, because he knew Richard had spent the night with her. And as store manager, she bore the ultimate responsibility for both situations.

As soon as she got her supervisor off the phone, she woke her sons and they hurriedly prepared for school and work. Rhonda didn't put on any makeup, just shoved it into a bag to take with her and apply when she got time. As quickly as possible, she helped the children get ready. She felt weary that she had the responsibility for three people and Richard only had to get dressed and watch them scurry around.

She told Dawson-Brown she thought only fifteen minutes had passed when they got out to the car. Her frustration increased when they got in the car. She got in first and unlocked the doors for the others. She remembered she had to pull the driver's seat up, which seemed strange, since she hadn't driven her car since Saturday evening and the seat had not been pushed back at that time.

"Did Richard Danziger have a key to your car?"

"Not that I know of."

"Where did you keep your car keys and house keys when you were home?" the ADA asked. "Say you walked in from work or something to your home, where did you put your car keys?"

"In my kitchen, by one of the cabinets. I had two hooks there and I would always hang them up there, because my little ones would quite often get the keys and you could spend forever looking for keys in toy boxes. So I hung my keys up every single time."

"To the best of your recollection, is that where your keys were that morning?"

"Yes."

"You specifically remember having moved your car seat up that morning?" Dawson-Brown persisted.

"Yes."

Dawson-Brown asked Rhonda what she did when she couldn't get the car to start that morning.

Shore said she panicked, all too aware her store wasn't open and her supervisor was angry. She ran in the house to call him and tell him the car wouldn't start, but they would get there as quickly as possible. That news only made Martin more upset.

"Your job is on the line," he yelled over the phone. "And so is Danziger's."

Even more frantic at that point, Rhonda ran up and down the street, knocking on the neighbors' doors to see if someone would help her jump-start her car. The neighbors closest to her either didn't have a car available or no one was home. She couldn't find anyone to help her. Richard suggested giving the car a push to see if it would start, so they pushed it into the alley. It didn't start, but she saw a man she had seen before, a man who kept the trash picked up and the alley clean, and he agreed to look at the engine and see if he could tell what was wrong. He couldn't. Finally, Richard's girlfriend flagged down a woman in a big car. She couldn't remember what kind of car it was or what the woman looked like, but the woman agreed to help start the car.

She said Richard did not volunteer to look under the hood and didn't seem at all upset that they were late for work and he would probably lose his job.

When they finally got the car started, they drove to the elementary school one of her sons attended, only a block and a half from home. She dropped the boy off at the door and rushed to the sitters' house, where she would leave her younger son. She couldn't remember the name of the street or the names of the women who ran the day care. She did remember that they were foreign-born. At the sitters', she got out and walked her son to the door, to make sure he got inside safely. After that, she headed toward work, taking William Cannon to I-35 to 183 to North Lamar, normally a half-hour drive, providing it was after nine o'clock in the morning, when most of the morning commuters had arrived at their destinations.

Richard didn't say much on the drive, but Rhonda unloaded on him about all the dire things that lay ahead of them, because the manager was so upset. When they arrived at work, three people were there, including the manager, and all of them were busily getting the store ready for opening at eleven o'clock.

"Had they gotten some of the preparations done already by the time you arrived there?" asked Dawson-Brown.

"Oh yes. They had been doing a real good job of getting the store ready to open. They were well into it."

Rhonda didn't tarry to talk to anyone, but went into the restroom and put her makeup on. When she went back out into the prep area, she tried to stay clear of the manager, because she knew he was angry. As soon as he could get free, however, he called her aside and warned her about what could happen, because of the fiasco that day. He said she could be terminated, but it wasn't his decision. He said the two new area supervisors were going to have a talk with her.

"Now," Dawson-Brown said, "thinking back over all the occurrences of that morning, do you have any idea of when that phone call from the manager came in?"

Without any hesitation whatsoever, Richard's girlfriend answered, "It was probably about 9:15."

"How have you come up with that?"

"Because we didn't get up there till after ten o'clock. And with getting the kids to school and to the sitters' and the drive, it would have taken me an hour, an hour and ten minutes from the time I woke up to the time I walked in."

Seeming satisfied, the prosecutor moved on to the events of later that morning—news of the attack on another Pizza Hut employee.

They opened the store on time, and several customers had come in when one of them stopped Rhonda and asked her what was going on over at the other Pizza Hut. She didn't know, but went to find Alex Martin. He started making phone calls and a little later, he said something had happened over there.

In an effort to show Richard Danziger's sudden interest in the other store, Dawson-Brown asked Rhonda about the reported mix-up in employee checks. Somehow, the checks for the other store were sent to their location that day. Rhonda was making arrangements to have the checks sent to the appropriate store, but while she was doing it, Richard took off with the checks and delivered them to the right store. He had not discussed it with her, and she wasn't aware of his actions until he had left, when another employee told her. He had never done that before; it was certainly not in his job description, and she had made arrangements for someone from the other store to come over and pick up the checks.

Again, Dawson-Brown moved to another topic, Richard Danziger's actions after the murder of Nancy DePriest. "During the period of time from October 24 to November 11, did Richard Danziger ever make a comment to you about his whereabouts on the morning of October 24?"

"It seems like it was a couple of days later, or the next day or something. He said, 'I was with you. Right?' And I just laughed and said, 'Yeah, you were with me.' You know, not giving it a second thought."

"Could Richard Danziger have left your duplex on the morning of October 24 without your knowing it?" Dawson-Brown asked.

"Absolutely."

"Are you a light sleeper?"

"No. I'm a pretty good sleeper, and when I drink, I'm a way heavy sleeper."

"Have you had problems with alarms not waking you up?"

"Yes, I have. I had gone through three alarm clocks during that period."

"Had you been unable to hear the alarm clock on occasions before?"

"Oh, many times before."

"Do you know if Richard Danziger was aware of your heavy sleeping?"

"I'm sure he was."

Regarding the Friday the police came to her house and picked up Richard Danziger, Rhonda said she was asked to accompany them to the police department, but had to make arrangements for her mother to take care of her children. She thought it was eight thirty or nine in the evening before she got there. The first thing they did was ask for the floor mat from her car, which she gave them. They questioned her until about one o'clock in the morning. When they released her, she went to her parents' house, where she spent the rest of the night. The next time she spoke to Richard was the following Sunday, when he called her from his parents' home in Beeville. He told her about his session with the police, how they had taken his shoes and he had taken a cab to his mother's home in his bare feet. He also told her he had given samples for testing, but he assured her the police wouldn't find anything. He said, "I gave them what they wanted. They won't find anything."

She said she talked to Richard twice that night, because he asked her to call his roommate and see if she could find out what had happened with Chris Ochoa. He also wanted her to assure his roommate that he had submitted to all the tests and that the police wouldn't find anything. He asked her to move to the same town as his mother, but she put him off.

"At that time, had you been told not to speak with Richard Danziger?"

"Yes. The police told me not to speak with him."

"But you did anyway?"

"I did anyway. I didn't feel he had anything to do with the murder and he wasn't really taking it to heart either. It all happened too fast and I just couldn't believe it. I couldn't absorb it."

At that point, Dawson-Brown asked the witness if she saw Richard Danziger in the courtroom and Shore pointed out the defendant.

For the prosecution, the central thrust of Rhonda Shore's testimony seemingly had been to establish a timeline for the events of the Sunday night and early morning hours of the Monday Nancy DePriest was killed.

Then it was time for cross-examination by Richard Danziger's court-appointed attorney, Berke Bettis.

## Chapter 10

# Cross Attack

Even though it was late in the afternoon, Bettis showed no sign of wanting to call it a day. Instead, he seemed to be eager to attack Rhonda Shore's testimony. "I believe that prior to your testimony today, you had given two written statements to the Austin Police Department. Is that correct?"

"That is correct."

"And, also, you have testified before the Travis County grand jury, which testimony has been reduced to writing. Is that correct?"

"That is correct."

Bettis turned to the judge. "Your honor, at this time, I ask to have an opportunity to review the prior statements of the witness before commencing cross-examination." Dawson-Brown immediately asked for a sidebar. After some wrangling, she agreed to turn over the grand jury testimony, along with some notes Shore had made to refresh her memory before testifying before the grand jury.

Bettis reminded the court that the grand jury testimony had lasted six hours and asked for time to study it. The court first offered twenty minutes, then after listening to Bettis' protest, the judge gave him thirty minutes. After notifying the jury of the brief recess and that they would be late returning home that night, court was recessed. It was 5:10 P.M., and the jury was called back at 5:45.

Again, Berke Bettis addressed Shore. "At the time you became manager of the Pizza Hut, had the locks to all the local Pizza Huts been recently changed?"

"Yes."

"So if I have it straight, the locks had been changed for a couple of weeks before you transferred?"

"I'm not sure when the locks were changed but they were changed before I got to the new store and then they were changed shortly after I got there."

Bettis appeared surprised. "They were changed twice?"

"Yes. At my store. I was issued a key when I got up there, and then shortly after that, I was issued another key."

"Okay. Now, did that key to your store open any of the other stores?"

"Not that I know of. It was my understanding that the supervisors had a master key that would open all the stores and that individual keys were assigned to each store, and they would only open that store."

"Okay," Bettis smiled in understanding. "Did you ever see Richard in possession of any key other than the one for the store you worked at?"

"No."

Bettis steered Shore to the Sunday night before the murder and she told essentially the same story she had told on direct examination. When he asked what time the roommate came over to get Chris, she said she didn't know. It was late, probably 2:30 or 3:00.

"Do you recall telling the Travis County grand jury, in response to when the roommate came over, that 'It was late. I don't know. I guess it was probably 3:30 or four o'clock in the morning'?"

The girlfriend shrugged. "I probably said that to them, yes. I know it was late and I didn't make any note of the time. It was late."

Prodded by Bettis, she said her last recollection of that night was sitting on the couch and no one was there except Richard. She didn't even remember going to bed and she didn't remember Richard going to bed. She said the next thing she remembered was the phone ringing. It rang only once.

"All right," Bettis said. "Isn't it true that the first thing you noticed after you heard the phone ringing was Richard moving in bed beside you?"

"Yes."

Bettis became insistent. "At the time the phone rang, Richard was in bed."

"I believe so. Yes. The phone was on the side he was on."

"Okay." Bettis nodded and looked at a thin sheaf of papers in his hand. "I'm looking at your notes, and I'm going to read you something that is here that I have never seen before and ask if you can explain it to me. It says, 'Talked in sleep. He said my name three times. One time he said, "Got to get the dough out of the proffer."'"

She nodded. "Yes."

"Who is that referring to?"

"Richard."

"After the phone rang and you talked to the manager, what did you do about getting ready to go to work?"

"Well, I washed my face. I grabbed my uniform and put it on, got clothes for the kids."

"And dressed the kids? Helped them dress?"

"I got their clothes out. They dressed themselves."

"Okay. Who got the kids up?"

"I guess I did."

"Do you remember?"

"I don't remember getting them up, no."

"Okay. Did you get them breakfast or anything?"

"I wouldn't have sent my son to school without anything. I would have found him something."

Bettis looked at the grand jury transcript again and said, "When you got to the car, you mentioned today that you had to move the seat."

"Yes."

"I looked through your two previous statements, the grand jury testimony and your notes, and I don't see anywhere where you had previously referred to that."

"I had not."

"When did you remember that detail?" Bettis demanded.

"Last Thanksgiving. Do you want to know why?"

"Absolutely." He smiled benignly.

"Okay. I was at my sister's house and we were finished with the Thanksgiving meal. We were sitting around talking about when we were kids, teenagers, and we used to 'borrow' the car and how we had to put everything back. And that we always had to put the seat way back, put the radio dial on the right station."

"On that Monday morning, was the car in the same place you had left it before you left to go to San Antonio?"

"Yes."

"When it wouldn't start, did you check it to see if there were any obvious causes?"

"Yes. I checked the lights. The radio. Nothing had been left on."

"After the car wouldn't start, you called the manager, then went to get a neighbor and finally located someone to help you jump-start it. Is that right?"

"Yes."

"Whose jumper cables did you use?"

"Mine."

"Did you have those in the car?"

"No."

"Where were they?"

"They were out in the store room in the backyard of the duplex."

"Who went to get those?"

"I did."

"Let's go back to the phone call from the manager again. Tonight, what time do you think that phone call took place?"

"The phone call that woke us up in the morning?"

"Yes."

"9:15."

Bettis shook his head. "You previously told us you gave some testimony before the grand jury. Do you recall the prosecutor asking, 'Why is it that you think the phone rang at 8:35 in the morning?' And you responded, 'I thought it rang at 8:15. I don't know. Fifteen minutes after the hour stuck in my mind for some reason. I don't know.' Do you recall making that statement?"

"Yes."

"Do you then recall that the prosecutor continued, 'Do you think it was maybe 9:15?' and you responded that it might have been 9:15?

"And you testified, 'Mother called me that morning and talked to me and she thought it was around nine o'clock, and then at that time when I talked to her, I already knew my battery was dead. So I really can't pinpoint [the time].'

"Do you remember that statement?"

"Yes."

"Do you now recall whether your mother called you?"

"No. She told me she called. I was telling the grand jury what she told me."

"But you don't have any independent recollection."

Abruptly changing the subject, Bettis asked, "During all the time you knew and associated with Richard Danziger, did you ever see him in possession of any type of a gun?"

"No."

"Did you have any type of gun?"

"No."

On that note, Bettis passed the witness back to the prosecution and redirect examination with Claire Dawson-Brown, who followed a new line of inquiry, asking the witness about an incident that Sunday night, when she took possession of Richard Danziger's wallet and he took it away from her.

Bettis interrupted, asking that the jury be excused so he could make an objection outside of their presence. The judge agreed, and Bettis asked to question the witness on *voir dire.*

"The prosecutor was about to ask you about an incident on the evening of October 23, involving yourself and Richard Danziger. Would you tell the court whether this incident involves certain events relating to your conjecture about the nature of certain contents of Mr. Danziger's wallet?"

"Do I think—I don't understand the question."

"Did you and Mr. Danziger have a scuffle that involved possession of his wallet?"

"Yes."

"Did you ever look inside that wallet?"

"After the contents were removed."

"On that occasion, did you look inside it?"

"Yes."

"Did you see the contents removed?"

"I didn't see them as they were removed."

Bettis glared at her. "Have you previously, in your statements to the police and before the grand jury, speculated that the contents of that wallet might include some type of drug?"

"Yes."

"Do you have any personal knowledge that there was any such drug?"

"No."

Bettis turned toward the judge again. "Your honor, at this time, I'm going to object to this line of questioning by the prosecution, for the reason that it is an attempt to put before the jury an impermissible suggestion of an extraneous offense or improper conduct on the part of the defendant, which is not within the purview of proper impeachment, not proper impeachment in this case, but moreover, is mere speculation on the part of this witness. Therefore, even if it were the proper time for such impeachment, its limited probative value would be grossly outweighed by its prejudicial effect. It represents mere speculation by the witness, and I ask that my objection be sustained and the prosecutor be instructed not to follow this line of questioning."

Judge Perkins hesitated, then spoke to Dawson-Brown. "All right. Since the jury is out, you may go ahead and establish what it is you're proffering here."

"Judge," she sounded exasperated. "What the State is proffering is the incident of the tussle over the wallet."

The judge nodded. "I think you can go into that question and answer."

Turning to the witness, Dawson-Brown asked, "Did you swap pants with Richard Danziger that night?"

"Yes."

"And was his wallet in your pants when you did that swapping?"

"Yes."

"Did you pull his wallet out and start looking into it?"

"Yes."

"Did he take some action to keep you from looking in his wallet?"

"Yes. He chased me down and tackled me. He grabbed the wallet from me. Then he took something out and then returned it to me for inspection."

"Do you have any idea what he took out?"

"Only speculation."

"Do you know what it was?"

"No."

Dawson-Brown took a deep breath and tried another tack. "But from the acts that Richard Danziger did that night, he did not want you to see an item which he removed from his wallet."

"Yes."

To Perkins, Dawson-Brown said, "Your Honor, I ask that you instruct her not to speculate. But certainly the events involving the wallet and the actions of Richard Danziger indicate there was something in that wallet he did not want her to see, and he removed it. This is certainly relevant to this inquiry."

The judge put up his hand definitively. "I'll sustain the objection by the defense. First of all, there's no knowledge of what the item was. Secondly, there's no showing of relevance."

Looking exasperated, Dawson-Brown tried again: "Judge, there's going to be an issue of a key; did Richard Danziger have a key that allowed him access to that Pizza Hut? And I ask that the witness be instructed not to speculate as to what was in there, just testify as to the observation of Richard Danziger's actions approximately nine hours before this Pizza Hut was entered, in which we will introduce testimony to show that Richard Danziger did have a key. I think his actions are relevant; in tackling this woman, removing some items that would fit that wallet and then hiding it from her. And I ask her to be instructed not to speculate."

At that point, Judge Perkins' voice had a razor edge. "The only thing about it is that could have been anything in that wallet. There could have been a love note to some other girl. There could have been anything. And so I'll sustain the objection. You can bring in the jury, please."

When the jury was brought in, the prosecutor renewed her redirect examination of the witness, focusing again on the time element of that fateful October morning when Nancy DePriest died. Again, the girlfriend admitted confusion about the time her phone had rung that morning, whether it was 8:15 or 9:15.

"You and I have talked about this quite a bit, haven't we?" asked the prosecutor.

"Yes," the witness admitted.

"Have you thought about how much time it would have taken you, from the moment you woke up to the moment you got to work?"

"Yes, I have."

"Have you added all those times together?"

"Yes."

"How much time do you think it was from the moment that phone rang and woke you up to the moment you got to the Pizza Hut that morning?"

"To drive and do everything, had to have been an hour and ten minutes. Right around there."

"And knowing that and knowing how much work had been done by the time you got to work, what is your best recollection, thoughts, on what time that phone rang that morning?"

"9:15."

At that point, Dawson-Brown passed the witness and, with no more questions from the defense attorney, Rhonda Shore left the stand.

Chapter 11

# The State's
# Star Witness

It had taken more than a week of testimony to show without a doubt that Nancy DePriest had been brutally attacked and raped. And in those days, the State had given concrete evidence that Nancy DePriest had been murdered, shot in the back of the head with a .22 caliber weapon. However, in spite of all the testimony by police officers, members of the medical community who had ministered to the dying woman, every criminal forensics examiner who had participated in the investigation, friends, family members and colleagues, there was no physical evidence to tie any known individual to her murder.

On January 30, the State finally was ready to present its star witness, Christopher Ochoa. Realizing how hearing Ochoa's testimony might be devastating for Jeanette, Dawson-Brown suggested that Jeanette might not want to be present that morning. However, Jeanette insisted.

"It isn't a matter of whether I want to hear it or not. I have to know exactly what happened. I'm going to hear every word. Do you actually think he could say anything that would hurt me any worse than what he did?" She was wrong. It would hurt more than she could have imagined in her most frightening nightmare.

From the moment Chris Ochoa entered the courtroom, Jeanette couldn't help staring at him. He was smaller than she expected, with a quiet, polite manner that surprised her. The contrast between Ochoa and Richard Danziger couldn't have been more pronounced. Even after a week of the trial, Danziger appeared sure of himself, although when he glanced at her, Jeanette sensed anger as well as curiosity.

The jurors looked at Ochoa curiously, then quickly looked from him to Jeanette to see her reaction. All she could think of was that this man, who looked so small and so scared, had confessed that he shot Nancy. Jeanette closed her eyes and tried to wipe away that vision— her daughter bound, gagged and so afraid, with this little man shooting her.

Before Christopher Ochoa testified, the prosecution brought another matter before the bench, outside the presence of the jury. Claire Dawson-Brown informed Judge Perkins that her question had to do with the plea agreement Christopher Ochoa had signed. Apparently, there were two versions of the plea agreement.

"The original, signed agreement has some matters mentioned on it which I don't believe should come up before the jury," she told the judge. "They have to do with the taking of the polygraph and passing of the polygraph by Chris Ochoa and the agreement with Ochoa that he will testify at all times and cooperate at all times, including any pre-trials and probation revocation hearings.

"Because I understand that this may not be admitted in front of the jury, I would like to offer, outside the presence of the jury, the original signed plea agreement between the District Attorney's office, Chris Ochoa and his attorney, Nate Stark, and substitute in the presence of the jury a copy of the plea agreement in which those sections which could be found objectionable have been whited out and taken out. I made every attempt. I've shown it to defense counsel to make it look like nothing has been taken out, so the jury doesn't in any way attempt to speculate what could have been there. I'd like to show the court right now. I've already shown the defense counsel."

Bettis said he had no objection to the entering of the corrected plea agreement for the purpose of introduction in the presence of the jury. He requested a copy of the full, original agreement be included in the record for the purpose of any appellate review.

Dawson-Brown agreed. "I want to introduce a full copy of the original after I show it to Chris Ochoa and ask him to testify that it is the original, then have him look at the edited version and state that he understands."

The judge looked up penetratingly. "I don't even know if you need to do that. There's not any objection."

"The problem is, Mr. Ochoa is extremely worried about, in front of the jury, admitting that this is the true agreement, since he's been urged only to tell the truth here."

The bailiff swore Chris Ochoa in. Then Claire Dawson-Brown began her examination. "Mr. Ochoa, have you, with the assistance of your counsel, Nate Stark, entered into a plea agreement with the Travis County District Attorney's office?"

"Yes, ma'am."

The ADA tendered the plea agreements to be marked for identification as State's exhibits. Then she showed the first one to the witness. "Mr. Ochoa, is this the original plea agreement signed by Carla Garcia of the District Attorney's office, by yourself and your attorney, Nate Stark?"

"Yes, ma'am."

"You have an original copy of this, is that correct?"

"Yes, ma'am."

"In that agreement, you have agreed that you will give a complete and truthful confession in this case, is that correct?"

"Yes, ma'am."

"And this is involving the death of Nancy DePriest. Is that correct?"

"Yes, ma'am."

"And that you must pass a polygraph examination arranged by the Travis County District Attorney's office that may include your statement to be truthful and that you are telling the truth about who was with you. Is that correct?"

"Yes, ma'am."

"You also agree that you must testify truthfully before any judicial body regarding any matter relative to this investigation and prosecution and any other person's involvement in this investigation, including any pre-trials and probation revocation hearings. Is that correct?"

"Yes, ma'am."

"And you have pled guilty to murder by using a deadly weapon, is that correct?"

"Yes, ma'am."

"That we will recommend that you, Chris Ochoa, receive a life sentence."

"Yes, ma'am."

"That if Richard Danziger is sentenced to T.D.C., we will notify T.D.C. that you, Chris Ochoa, cooperated with the State in this investigation and prosecution of Richard Danziger?"

"Yes, ma'am."

"Let me show you the State's next exhibit No. 221. Is this a copy of your original plea agreement with portions taken out of it about the polygraph and about probation revocation hearings?"

"Yes, ma'am."

"And you understand that before the jury, we will be introducing this State's exhibit No. 222 as to the plea agreement. Is that correct?"

"Yes, ma'am."

"You understand that the law in the state of Texas does not allow you to let the jury know that any polygraphs have been given. Is that correct?"

"Yes, ma'am."

"And you understand you're not supposed to mention that before the jury and that's the reason you're going to have to testify that State's Exhibit No. 222 is the true and correct plea agreement?"

"Yes, ma'am."

At the end of the brief session, Ochoa was taken out of the courtroom, the original plea agreement was introduced for the record and the amended agreement would be admitted in the presence of the jury.

When the jury returned, Ochoa took the stand again and started answering Dawson-Brown's questions, tears already streaking his face. His voice was practically inaudible and Dawson-Brown asked that the microphone be turned up so Ochoa could be heard. As he stumbled over his answers, Jeanette thought he must be feeling extreme remorse for what he had done to her daughter.

Asked his age and place of residence, Chris said he was twenty-three years old and currently incarcerated in the Travis County Jail, where he had been ever since his arrest. Then the prosecution addressed the issue of the plea agreement, so the jury could hear its details.

"Mr. Ochoa, is part of your plea agreement that you agree that you will give a complete and truthful confession?"

"Yes, ma'am."

"Did you agree that you would testify truthfully before a grand jury, judge, jury and/or any other body regarding any matter relative to this investigation and prosecution, that being the murder of Nancy DePriest and any other person's involvement in this investigation, including any pre-trials?"

"Yes, ma'am," Ochoa's voice was barely above a whisper.

"Did you further agree that you would plead guilty by indictment or information to murder by using a deadly weapon?"

"Yes, ma'am."

"And you have already pled guilty."

"Yes, ma'am." Jeanette had to lean forward to even hear his repeated soft replies.

"Did the State agree that they would withhold prosecution of you for any other offense arising out of this murder offense?"

"Yes, ma'am."

"And is it your understanding that the State will recommend that you receive a life sentence in this case?"

"Yes, ma'am."

After establishing other facts, such as the date of the plea agreement and the name of his attorney, Nate Stark, Dawson-Brown was ready for Chris to begin his terrible story. They began with his move to Austin and his acquaintance with Richard Danziger, beginning in the fall two years before the murder, with Danziger's leaving Austin that year and returning to the city early in the fall of 1988, when they became roommates at an apartment in north Austin. Chris said he didn't socialize much with Danziger, simply provided him a place to stay.

When Dawson-Brown asked him what he and Richard Danziger did on the night of October 23, he said Richard needed a ride or something to his girlfriend's place.

"And, you know, I really didn't want to go, you know. I didn't want to give him a ride, but he said, 'Come on, let's go buy some beer. Go have some beers.' And I changed my mind, so I said, 'All right. I'll take you.'"

"Who was there when you arrived at her house?"

"Rhonda and her two little boys."

"What was she doing when you arrived? Do you know?"

"She was ironing."

"Where was she ironing?"

"In the kitchen."

"What did you and Richard Danziger do right after you arrived?"

"We were drinking beer, started drinking beer and started playing some cards."

"Did Richard's girlfriend stay in the kitchen ironing?"

"Yeah. Yes, ma'am."

"Did Richard Danziger bring up a subject with you during that time while Rhonda was in the kitchen?"

"Yes, ma'am."

"What was that?"

"He stated, you know, he needed some money and that he had a way of getting some money, and I was kind of puzzled about that."

"Did he explain what he meant to you?"

"Yeah. He said, you know, he knew a place where he can get some money, and I asked him, you know, we're talking about. . .yeah, you know, that Pizza Hut."

"Did you ask him what he meant?"

"He said he was going to rob the other Pizza Hut."

"Did he tell you how he was going to do it?"

"First, I didn't want to know, but he kept on, you know, telling me, 'Come on.' He told me he needed some help. He wanted me to help him. And I plainly stated I didn't want nothing to do with that. But I was kind of drunk by then. I guess I was, yeah, I was kind of drunk by then, drinking pretty much. And he kept on, 'Come on, help me out,' you know. And I said no. Finally, I said, 'All right, what you got in mind?' And he said Pizza Hut and I asked which Pizza Hut. He said the one near the freeway. I asked him why and he said, 'That's an easy getaway, the freeway. It's easy.' He said he'd been thinking about it, he'd been watching it, that he wanted to do that one, because he'd been staking it out, watching it."

"Did he tell you how he planned to do the robbery?"

"I asked him, but he said not to worry about it."

"Did he mention any plans he had for any sort of weapon?"

"He said he knew where to get a gun."

"Did you ask him where?"

"Not really. I didn't want to know about it, you know. I was . . ."

"Do you know what time it was when you decided to go home?"

"About five in the morning."

"Had any arrangements been made by you and Richard Danziger to meet anywhere?"

"Yes. There was an arrangement made to meet at a fast food place about, I guess about seven. I'm not too sure."

"What was the purpose of the meeting there?"

"To go over final minute details."

"To do what?"

"To rob, you know, the store. Pizza Hut."

"Did you drive your car home?"

"Yes, ma'am. Another roommate followed me home that night, and I got home, set my alarm clock for 6:30. Didn't really get that much sleep that night."

"Did you wake up?"

"Yes, ma'am."

"What did you do?"

"Put on some jeans, red shirt, some sneakers. Started my car and I took off toward the meeting spot. Richard was not there when I got there, but he drove up. He was in Rhonda's car."

"What did you all do there?"

"He came up and said he would get coffee and something. Then we started going over last minute details. He told me I was going to be lookout. I said, 'All right, I guess.' He flashed me a gun."

"Where was the gun?"

"Inside his pants."

"Did he tell you where he got that gun?"

"No, he didn't. No, ma'am."

"Do you know whose gun it is?"

"No, ma'am."

"Do you know where that gun is now?"

"No, ma'am."

"You followed him to the Pizza Hut or he followed you up?"

"He followed me up."

"Where did you park?"

"Some apartments right across the street from the Pizza Hut, right behind the parking lot, right behind the apartments."

"Do you know what time it was?"

"Oh, I don't know; 7:30. I'm not too sure."

"What did you and Richard do once you got to the apartment complex and parked?"

"Got out of the car and we went and stood across the street from the Pizza Hut. Just looked. We were watching it for a while. After a while, a silver car drove up and a motorcycle. A girl got out of the car and I recognized her. It was Nancy DePriest."

"How did you know her?"

"I had bumped into her a few times, business, you know, managers' meetings."

"Did you know who was on the motorcycle?"

"No, I didn't."

"What did they do?"

"Talked for a while, and then she went inside and he took off in the silver car. And Richard told me we would have to wait for a while. At that time, I realized, I guess, he was going to have me go in there with him."

"Did anybody come back to the Pizza Hut?"

"Yes. That guy did. He parked the car, got on his motorcycle and he left."

"What did you do after he left on the motorcycle?"

"We started walking towards the Pizza Hut. Richard had the gun. And he pulled a key out of his pocket."

"Was it on a key chain or what?"

"No. It was just a key, a plain key. He opened the door with it. The door not facing toward the freeway, but the other one. The east side, I guess. We walked in and Nancy was cutting dough. She said, 'What's up?' Then she looked up and said, 'Chris, what's up?'"

"She recognized you," Dawson-Brown asked.

"Yeah."

"She said your name."

"Yes, ma'am."

"What was said to her?"

"Richard told her to shut up and give him the money. He wanted the money. All the money."

"Where was the gun?"

"He had it in his hand."

"Did he show it to her?"

"Yeah. You know, she got kind of scared, real scared, and she went down to the safe. We took her to the safe, in the back."

"What did you see or hear next?"

"Oh, he got the money. It was in a big, old, white coin bag. There was a vinyl bank bag you put bills in. That was what it was in. He came back, came back towards . . ."

"What happened next?"

"'Well, we're going to have a little fun now.'"

"Who said that?"

"Richard. Richard did. He took off, you know . . ."

"What did he do?"

"He pushed her down on her knees and he took out his penis and he started having oral sex."

At that point, Jeanette closed her eyes, trying to shut out the awful image that had suddenly assaulted her. She put her hands over her ears, but she couldn't shut out the soft tones, the awful words magnified by the witness's microphone. Jeanette's mother had become ill and her husband had to come to Austin to take her home, thus Jeanette was left without family to comfort her as she listened to Christopher tell his story of rape and murder.

"What do you mean by that?"

"Put his penis in her mouth."

"What were you doing?"

"I was watching."

"Where was the gun?"

"He had it on her head. And after, you know, he didn't ejaculate, pulled out, he picked her up. He told me to come on and he brought her out into the hall and took off her blouse and bra. And he had me go get an apron."

"Where did you get the apron from?"

"From back there somewhere. I don't remember where they're at, you know. I just saw a pile of them and got a blue apron and a sweater and we put them down."

"You said he had taken off her shirt and bra."

"Yes."

"Did you do anything with those?"

"He threw the bra at me and told me to tie her hands behind her back. After that, he pushed her down on her back."

"Where?"

"On the aprons."

"Where was the gun?"

"He had it, you know, pointed. . . he had it pointed at her."

"What was Nancy doing at this time?"

"She was crying, 'Stop. Stop.' Richard told her to shut up. He hit her. She's crying."

By this time, Jeanette was crying, too, her whole body shuddering, her eyes clenched shut. She didn't want to hear this, but somehow she felt compelled to listen. As if she would be letting her daughter down if she refused to listen to the last moments of Nancy's life.

"So she was lying there?"

"She was down there. And then he had taken off her pants at the same time he took her blouse and all her clothes. He laid her down on her back and then he proceeded to take off, pulled down his pants. He started having intercourse with her."

"What did he do with the gun while this was happening?"

"He had it. He had it pointed at her."

"Did he give you the gun?"

"Not at this point, no. He got me to sit down on her shoulders, you know, on my knees on her shoulders so she wouldn't move, and she was kicking. And he told her not to move no more or else, you know, he would blow her away."

"And he had intercourse with her at this time."

"Yes, ma'am. After a while he pulled out and ejaculated all over her."

"What part of her body?"

"Right here, the stomach area, I guess. The stomach area. And he turned around, he looked at me and he says, 'It's your turn now.'"

"What did you do?"

"He said, 'You're going to do it.' So I said, 'All right.' Then I proceeded to take, you know, pull out my penis, and he told me, 'You're going—you're going to have fun with her, too.'"

"Did you put your penis in her vagina?"

"I put my penis in her vagina. I ejaculated inside of her and pulled out. And after that—"

"Was Nancy saying anything to you?"

"Said, 'Don't. Stop. Stop.' Kind of felt bad at the time. Anyway, then Richard told me he wanted to tie up her legs and gag her."

"What did you gag her with?"

"A scarf."

"What did you tie her legs with?"

"Her blouse."

"What happened next?"

"He told me he wanted me—he said, 'Help me drag her to the booth over there up front where the video games are.' So I proceeded—so I helped him."

"How did you carry her up there?"

"He put his hand under her shoulders and I got her ankles. We took her up there to the booth."

"What did you do with Nancy DePriest when you took her up to that booth?"

"Richard pushed her down on the booth."

"You were helping him, weren't you?"

"Yes. Put her down on the booth and he—"

"On her back or on her stomach?"

"No. On her back. And then he took off—he asked me to take off the blouse (from around her legs). He just yanked it off. And he proceeded to have, he proceeded to have intercourse again with her."

"Where was the gun?" Dawson-Brown asked.

"He handed me the gun at that point, told me to—"

"Did he place his penis in her vagina at that time?"

"Yes, ma'am, placed his penis in there and had intercourse." Chris kept his head down, refusing to look at the defendant, at anyone. Danziger just glared at him, fury and puzzlement warring in his eyes.

Chris lifted his eyes to Dawson-Brown when she asked the next question. "Do you know if he ejaculated?"

"Yeah. Yeah. When he pulled out and he turned around and said, 'Your turn again.' And Nancy was, through the gag, you could tell she was asking for help. And then I proceeded to have intercourse with her and I ejaculated inside her vagina and pulled out. And then, at that time, I had already handed the gun back to Richard."

"What happened next?"

"After that he turned her around, on her stomach, on her shoulders, I guess, on the booth."

"You said, 'I guess.' Did he or didn't he?" Dawson-Brown demanded.

"Yeah. And he proceeded, he took, you know, proceeded to have intercourse again with her. Anally. And he ejaculated all over her back. And told me it was my turn. So I had intercourse with her and I ejaculated and then pulled out. And at that point, you know, we were discussing that we were going to have to kill her because she recognized me, she knew who I was."

"Were you discussing this in front of Nancy?"

"Yes."

"What was she doing?"

"She was scared. She was crying. She was asking for help. Anyways, we discussed, you know, he said, 'All right. We're going to have to kill her' and yanked her down."

"You agreed, didn't you?" asked Dawson-Brown.

"Yes. He yanked her down from the booth and then, you know, he took her over to the hallway where the bathrooms are."

"You were helping, weren't you?"

"Yes. I was."

"What happened in that hallway?"

"Put her down on her knees."

"Who had the gun?"

"He had the gun at the time, but he said, 'You kill her.' He handed it over to me and then I put it to the back of her head and pulled the trigger."

"How were you holding her?"

"Holding her with my right hand, shoulders. Pulled the trigger with the left hand. And she just fell face-first to the floor."

"What did you and Richard Danziger do next?" Dawson-Brown wanted to know.

"Took her to the women's bathroom. I held the door open. He just picked her up from her shoulders and dragged her into the bathroom."

"What happened when you got Nancy DePriest into the bathroom?"

"He took off the gag from her mouth, yanked it off, then he proceeded to have intercourse with her, first the vagina, then he went up to her mouth."

"Was Nancy DePriest bleeding?"

"Yes."

"Was she moving?"

"No. At the time, I thought she was already dead."

"What did you do?"

"I was standing there, shocked."

"What did you do, Chris?" Dawson-Brown asked again.

"He had intercourse with her orally and he ejaculated all over her neck, then he said, 'It's your turn.' Then I proceeded to have intercourse with her, her vagina, then at that time I didn't ejaculate inside her. All over her stomach. After that he told me to go get some aprons, and. . ."

"Where did you get the aprons from?"

"From back there in the back where I got them to put on the floor."

"Did he give you any other instructions?"

"Told me to get the clothes and told me to wipe down anywhere we might have put our fingerprints."

"Whose idea was that to wipe down?"

"That was his idea. I went back there to get the aprons and clothes. I was wiping down as I went."

"Where did you wipe?"

"Around the safe area, around the safe. Not the top, just around the safe, the bottom where the hole is. And doors, the door we came in through, the counter where the booth was, the ledge. Went in . . ."

"Went in where?"

"Then I went into the bathroom."

"What was going on in the bathroom?"

"Richard had her turned around. He had the water running. And then he told me he needed some help."

"What did you do?"

"He needed some help washing her down. He put her up in the vanity up there. She was like on her side. She was in a fetal position. And he started washing her off."

"How did you wash her off?"

"Water was running. We were splashing water on her."

"Where did you wash her? Where did you and Richard Danziger wash her?"

"I washed her on her top side and he washed her on the bottom half."

"Did you wash her good?"

"Yeah, I guess. I wasn't paying too much attention. Then we stopped. Then he said, 'Let her go.' Her head just, I just saw it drop. Her head just hit the ground."

"She fell off?"

Ochoa only nodded, refusing to raise his eyes.

## Chapter 12

# A Horrible Story

Jeanette trembled and tears ran down her face as Chris Ochoa testified. When he described the horrible, degrading, agonizing things he said he had done to Nancy, Jeanette felt physically sick. Suddenly, her stomach roiled and she tasted something dark and viscous in the back of her throat. She kept swallowing, but the geyser in her throat kept threatening to gush into her mouth. Out of her mouth.

Jeanette had been warned by the District Attorneys not to voice any emotion, any reaction to Ochoa's words, because an outburst from her could trigger a mistrial. So Jeanette sat there and listened to the awful things being spoken on the stand. In Jeanette's mind, seeing her daughter in the final, excruciating moments of her life made her anger and anguish grow. Finally, when Ochoa described how he and Danziger had raped Nancy again, even though they thought she was dead, how Danziger had engaged in oral sex with the lifeless girl and then bathed her afterward, Jeanette couldn't stand it any longer. She bolted from the courtroom. In the ladies' room, crying and gasping, she vomited until nothing was left in her stomach. Even then, her body was assaulted by spasm after spasm, in painful, nauseating waves, trying to rid itself of the awful memory she had just heard. To Jeanette, it seemed as if the savage acts had happened to her. For a long, long time, she held on to the sink to keep her trembling legs from buckling.

While Jeanette was out of the courtroom, Dawson-Brown led Chris Ochoa through the final few minutes of his testimony for the prosecution. He recited what he and Richard Danziger had done to cover up their crime. He said that while they were in the bathroom washing Nancy, he heard the telephone ring several times. According to his words in the courtroom, the two men paid no attention to the phone, and Chris watched Richard stuff aprons into and around the vanity and in the drain. Chris said they left the water running and Richard wiped the bathroom down. Then, he opened the bathroom door and Richard dragged Nancy outside and left her in the hallway.

Dawson-Brown showed him two of the State's exhibits, both of them photos of Nancy DePriest. "Is this how you left her?"

"Yes, ma'am."

"After you left Nancy DePriest lying in that hall bleeding, what did you do?"

"I went and got the bag and he told me to go get the money, the money bag, and give it to her—to him. He went back inside the bathroom for something. I don't know. He left, and then he came back out and started going out. We started going out the west side door. I was just following his lead, following. He was leading. Push it open, but then he changed his mind. Then he turned back around, went out the east side door with the key. Used the key. He opened it back out."

"How did he try to go out the west side door? Used his hand?"

"His elbow on that thing. He used his elbow. And he turned back around and went, opened the east side door. I was following him. He had the money bag. I ran out. As soon as he opened the door, I ran. I ran as fast as I could to the car and I got in my car. I didn't look back at him. I took off and…"

"Did you have blood on you when you left that restaurant?" asked Dawson-Brown.

"Yes, ma'am."

"Did Richard Danziger have blood on him when he left that restaurant?"

"Yeah, I guess. Yeah."

"Where did you go?"

"Well, as I was cutting the corner, my radar thing fell off. I had it on the sun visor and it slipped off the visor. I reached down to put it back up. I took off and went home, went to the apartment, took off my clothes, put them in a bag and put them in a dumpster, and I just stayed there to watch the news."

Ochoa said that the next morning he got up, went to work and discovered he wasn't needed there. Then he came back home and watched the news on TV. He went to a concert that night. He watched the news the next morning. And then, in the afternoon, Richard Danziger came home.

Dawson-Brown asked what he and Danziger had discussed that afternoon.

"If I wanted. . .if I wanted half of the money. I told him, 'No. I don't want nothing. I don't want nothing about it. I'm already deep in it as it is.'"

"Did you talk about what had happened?"

"Yeah. He asked me if there was, you know, any clues, any evidence."

"What else did you discuss that day?"

"At that time when he told me, you know, about the money, I said, 'I don't want no part of it.' I told him I was thinking about turning myself in."

"What did he say?"

"He said, 'I wouldn't do that.' And he said, 'Besides, you know, they're just going to think you're the one that did it anyway. They ain't going to believe you.' I didn't say much at the time. I got kind of scared."

"Why were you scared?"

"He gave me a stare, same stare I've been getting waiting for this trial when I bump into him. Before he left he just gave me a stare that, you know, like a threatening stare."

"He didn't threaten you verbally, did he?"

"Not verbally, no. But you get that feeling. And I got shaken up a bit."

As Dawson-Brown asked the witness to describe the mundane events of the following day and a half, a picture emerged of a callous personality who felt no emotion about his brutal attack on an innocent woman.

A savage story told, but was it true?

An audible sigh of relief came from spectators who had, like Jeanette, been locked in a whiplash of emotion in the courtroom when Dawson-Brown's questions took the witness and the observers in a different direction.

The prosecutor asked Ochoa about the events of Wednesday, November 9, 1988, the night Ochoa and Richard Danziger made their ill-conceived visit to the place where Nancy DePriest had died. Ochoa told her he and Richard had been together for a while that night at the home of Richard's girlfriend, and Richard had asked him if he wanted to go see where Nancy had died.

"I said I didn't really want to go down, you know. I wanted to go to some kind of guitar contest. I said, 'Just take me home.' We got in the car and drove down the freeway. I thought he was going to forget about going to the Pizza Hut, but he didn't. He pulled up there and we discussed it a little bit. I didn't want to go in."

"Why did Richard want to go there? Did he tell you?"

"I don't know. I really don't know. Just wanted to go there. We went in, sat down, ordered a beer."

"Did you all talk about what had happened there on October 24?"

"A little bit, yeah."

"What did Richard say?"

"I don't recall, you know, but it was something about that. I didn't really touch my beer. I didn't even finish my beer." His lack of emotion was mystifying. Was there something missing in his answers?

"Why not?"

"I just, I didn't want any part to do with anything. I already felt bad enough as it was and being in there just played on my mind. We went out. I paid for the beers. The security guard was waiting outside. And Richard started talking to him. I went to the car."

"Could you hear what Richard was saying to the security guard?"

"Yeah. He was asking him if they had any evidence, any leads yet. The cop, the security guard, said the police officers wouldn't release any information at that time."

"Did the security guard ask your name?"

"I can't recall if he asked us our names or not. Richard asked him about the gun, what kind of gun was it. The security guard said he didn't know, you know. Richard asked if it could have been a .22."

"Do you remember if the security guard asked Richard where he was on the morning of October 24, 1988?"

"I don't remember exactly. He could have asked him that when I was back in the car, waiting in the car, you know. I didn't really pay too much attention to what they were saying. I just wanted to get home."

Again, Dawson-Brown changed the subject of her questions. "Had you ever found out from Richard Danziger where that gun was?"

"No, ma'am."

"Do you know today?"

"No, ma'am."

"Weren't you curious?"

"No." The witness's tone was distant but firm. "I had never been in that kind of a situation before. I didn't want nothing else to do with it. I figured the less I knew the less—the less—I guess, I guess the more I knew, the more involved that I'd be. You know what I'm saying."

"You were pretty involved?"

"Yes. I was pretty involved. But you know what I'm saying. I had never been in trouble in my life before. And you go and do something like this, it plays on your mind, plus I was feeling pretty bad at the time."

"Now," said Dawson-Brown, giving him the measured gaze of someone trying to maintain patience. "The police interviewed you on November the eleventh. Is that right?"

"Yes, ma'am." Ochoa's eyes seemed to film over.

Her voice tightened like a grasp. "Isn't it true that you told them you didn't have anything to do with this, but that Richard Danziger had confessed to you that he had done it?"

"Yes, ma'am."

"That was a lie, wasn't it?"

"Yes, ma'am."

"Now, you told this jury just a few minutes ago that you thought about going in and telling the police. And here you had the opportunity to tell them and you didn't do it. Why not?"

"Yes. I got brought into the station and Sergeant Hector Polanco was questioning me."

"You could have confessed then, couldn't you?"

The witness shook his head ever so slightly. "I could have, but the way he interrogated me scared the heck—scared the living daylights out of me."

"Did you think you were going to prison?"

"I thought I was going to get the death penalty. He kept on threatening me with that. 'You're going to get the needle. You're going to get the needle for this. We got you.' You know."

"But you weren't willing to confess, were you?" Dawson-Brown persisted.

He looked pale, listless. "I was scared. I was scared that if I confessed, you know, I'm going to get the needle anyway."

"So you told them Richard Danziger did this and confessed to you."

"Yes, ma'am."

"They talked to you again on Monday, November the fourteenth, didn't they?"

"Yes, ma'am."

You told them you were with Richard Danziger, but you didn't go in the Pizza Hut. Isn't that right?"

"Yes, ma'am."

"And you lied to them about the type of gun that was used, didn't you?"

"Yeah. I wasn't too sure. I didn't know. I don't know anything about guns."

"You know the difference between a revolver and an automatic, don't you?"

"At that time, not really. But anyways, Polanco—"

"You lied to them, didn't you?"

"I lied to them. Polanco was, you know, I just wanted to say anything 'cause he was intimidating me."

"You lied about how Richard and you got in that store, didn't you?"

"Yes, ma'am."

"You said what?"

"I said something about produce."

"Why did you lie about that?"

"I don't know. At the time I was just, I was trying to—I guess I was trying to see if I could get away with lies. They knew, you know. They knew," he said in almost a whisper.

"You're a very good liar?"

Chris shook his head. "Not really, 'cause, you know, if I would have (been a good liar), I would have walked out of there."

"They interviewed you later that day and took a second written statement."

"Yes, ma'am."

"This is November the fourteenth, Monday."

"Yes, ma'am."

"You admitted to being in there, didn't you?" She faced him accusingly.

"Yes, ma'am."

"But you lied about shooting Nancy DePriest, didn't you?"

"Yes, ma'am."

"And you lied about some other things in that statement, didn't you?"

"Yes, ma'am."

"You told them Richard Danziger was the one who shot her, didn't you?"

"Yes, ma'am."

"You lied about the gag, didn't you?"

"Yes, ma'am." His voice was a monotone as if repeating scripted words over and over again.

"Why did you lie about the gag?"

"I don't know. My mind just—I guess I didn't want to look bad gagging a person. To me, you do something like, it's demeaning."

Her words had a razor edge. "What you did to Nancy DePriest was demeaning with or without a gag."

"Yes, it was. I understand that."

"You lied about some other things, too, on that written statement on the fourteenth. You lied about how many times you sexually assaulted her, didn't you?"

"Yes, ma'am."

"And you lied about how Richard Danziger ejaculated, didn't you?"

"Yes, ma'am. Said I felt guilty."

"You *were* guilty."

"Well, do you know what I'm saying? I felt remorse."

Dawson-Brown moved the witness forward to the following year, 1989. "You made a final written statement to the police on March 7, 1989. Is that correct?"

"Yes, I did."

"Was your lawyer there with you?"

"Yes, ma'am."

"Did you tell the truth in that statement?"

"Yes, ma'am. Before I told the statement, my lawyer talked to me. All that time I spent in jail sitting in my cell. That's when it really got to me. Said I took another person's life."

"You admitted—"

"I had to admit it."

"You admitted to shooting Nancy DePriest."

"Yes."

"And you admitted to how it all happened."

"Yes."

"Are you telling this jury the truth now?"

"Yes, ma'am."

Dawson-Brown paused a minute, her eyes locked with those of Christopher Ochoa. "Have you told some people you didn't do this?"

"Yes, ma'am."

"Who did you tell?"

"My family and my roommate."

"Was that after you told the police that you did it?"

"Yes, ma'am."

"Why did you lie to your family?"

"I didn't want them to think I could have done such a thing like that. Plus I was scared that if I did admit to them, they would just shun me aside, which is understandable."

Dawson-Brown turned to the jury box. Her voice was taut. "Look those jurors in the eye. Look each of them in the eye. You are under oath. Are you telling the truth?"

The knot Ochoa must have felt in his stomach was invisible. "Yes," he replied.

With those words, a hush fell over the assemblage for a moment. No one moved. No one spoke. Finally, Dawson-Brown broke the silence.

"Pass the witness."

## Chapter 13

# Time is Whenever You Want It to Be

Then, it was the defense's turn to question Chris Ochoa about this horrendous rape/murder. The defense attorney stood up and addressed the witness.

"I'm Berke Bettis. I'm one of Richard Danziger's lawyers. I'm going to go over the testimony that you've given here in court today and the statements that you gave to the police in the past, as well as some statements you made to members of your family. You understand what we're going to be doing here?" Bettis looked grim, intense as if he had been sleepless the night before.

"Yes, sir," Ochoa replied flatly.

For what felt like an interminable period of time, Bettis asked the witness about what seemed like every minute detail of Ochoa's life, up to and including his confessions to the police that he had killed Nancy DePriest. Bettis went through the confessions separately, almost question by question, asking Chris what he recalled telling the detectives.

Ochoa's eyes and tone appeared glazed as he answered mechanically, almost in rote.

Yes, he remembered telling the police he knew nothing about the murder, but Richard had confessed to him that he had killed Nancy DePriest, after he had a little fun with her.

Yes, he remembered telling the lookout story. About waiting outside while Richard went in. And then hearing pops like gunshots and fleeing the scene.

Yes, he remembered changing his story even more, admitting he went in with Richard. Yes, he remembered telling the police about all the vile, degrading things the two of them had done to Nancy before Richard shot her in the back of the head.

And yes, he remembered giving his final confession, when he detailed for the police all that he, Chris, had done and that he, Chris, had been the one who shot Nancy DePriest.

Then Bettis asked, "In the second statement, did Sergeant Polanco ask you, 'Excuse me, did you ever see the gun?'"

"Yes, he did."

"And you responded to him, 'No, I never saw the gun.'"

"Yes."

"And he asked you again, 'At any time?' And you responded, 'Never saw the gun. I never saw the gun. Oh, I saw it right before he walked in the Pizza Hut, he showed it to me.'"

"Yes, I do recall."

"Sergeant Polanco at that time asked you, 'What did it look like?'"

"Yes."

"You said, 'It was a small gun like this, a small black gun. I don't know too much about guns.'"

"Yes, I did."

"Sergeant Polanco said, 'What about the handle?' You said the handle could have been brown."

"Yes."

"Sergeant Polanco said, 'Did it look like a revolver?' And he reached in his shoulder holster and pulled out his revolver and showed it to you, did he not?"

"Yes." Ochoa's replies remained curt, barely audible as if something was missing.

"You said, 'One of those,' referring to his revolver."

"Yes, sir."

"And he said, still holding his revolver, 'Did it have a cylinder in it?'"

"Yes," Ochoa murmured.

"And you said, 'Yeah, like that.'"

"I did."

"Continuing on, Detective Balagia said, 'By saying this, you're pointing to Sergeant Polanco's. It's a blue steel revolver with a brown grip.'"

"Yes."

"You said, 'Yes, something like that.' Polanco said 'Small like this,' again showing you his gun."

"Yes." Ochoa nodded.

"Sergeant Polanco said, 'Do you know what an automatic looks like, the one you pull back?'"

"Yes."

"You said, 'Yeah.'"

"'Was it one like that?' he asked you. Did you say, 'No, not like that'?"

Ochoa nodded. "Yes."

Now Bettis turned from the matter of Ochoa's incorrect description of the gun used in the murder. He carefully questioned the witness about every aspect of Ochoa's interrogation, the first and second confessions. Finally, he said, "The first time you went down to the police station was on November 11."

"Yes."

"And you've told the jury that Sergeant Polanco scared the living daylights out of you."

"Yes, I did."

"And he kept telling you that you're going to get the needle."

"Yes."

"And after that, on November 11, he took you back to your apartment to get some clothes?"

"Yes, he did."

"Then they took you to the hotel down on Town Lake."

"Yes."

"And they left you there till Monday?"

"Yes, sir."

"And on Monday, you came back to the police station and you gave an oral statement that was tape-recorded."

"Yes, I did."

"Then, later that day, did you talk to the police some more?"

"Yes. Talked to Balagia."

"And after you talked to Balagia, was that when you decided to give your next statement that day?"

"Yes."

"And they were still talking about giving you the needle."

"After that, no. That's when I started coming out with more details, the truth of the matter, getting closer to the truth. Still didn't want to admit to myself, I guess, you know, something like that, somebody has a conscience, you know, you don't want to admit it, unless you're proud of the thing and you're going to come right out and say it. But that's why I gave three statements. And the last one, I had time to think about it. I was by myself. I felt bad. That's the only way. Can't ever bring her back, but I can at least try that much." Ochoa's face and voice were tired, flat and lifeless.

After a few more questions, Bettis elicited information from Ochoa that after he confessed the second time, no one in the police department ever again spoke to him about his getting the needle. And, upon Ochoa's third confession, made in March of 1989, he assumed full responsibility for the shooting, although he still insisted Richard had given him the gun. At that time, the plea bargain was made.

Ochoa would testify at Danziger's trial that he had pulled the trigger and he would be given life in prison.

At this point, it may have seemed to the jury and court observers that the prosecution had offered their most dramatic telling pieces of evidence: First, a beautiful young wife and mother had been callously raped and murdered, and second, Christopher Ochoa had confessed, in court, before witnesses, that he had participated in the rape and he had pulled the trigger, firing the bullet that ended Nancy DePriest's life.

The State was not through, however. Once again, Dawson-Brown called witnesses to testify about the time line of the morning of Nancy's death. Although he did not testify as to the time he and Richard Danziger had gone to the Pizza Hut that morning, Ochoa said in his confession to police that they had arrived there around 7:20 or 7:30 and waited around a while. While they were waiting, they saw Nancy DePriest arrive in her car, her husband Todd DePriest arrive on his motorcycle and the departure of Todd DePriest in the car with his child. Then Ochoa told of DePriest's return, leaving the car keys with his wife and leaving on his motorcycle. No one mentioned that Todd DePriest had testified that he and Nancy had first arrived at the Pizza Hut at around seven o'clock. When he returned from the babysitter's, it was around 7:45.

After standing in the bathroom a while, Jeanette was able to gather herself together somehow. When she returned to the courtroom, Christopher Ochoa was no longer on the stand. There was no doubt in her mind that Ochoa had been telling the truth about what happened to Nancy. He seemed to know every minute, each excruciating detail. Nevertheless, his lack of emotion was strange, almost scripted. But why would someone who was innocent say he had committed such a savage act? Surely this couldn't happen. No, he had confessed the truth.

Dawson-Brown called the supply manager, who testified that a woman sounding like Nancy had ordered supplies between 8:00 and 8:30. Lester Davis, who had discovered Nancy's body, had testified he started calling his stores between 8:00 and 8:30 and had received no answers at two of the stores—the one where Nancy DePriest worked and the one where Richard Danziger worked. First, he set in motion a chain of events to find Danziger, then he finished calling his other stores. When he still received no answer at Nancy's store, between 8:35 and 8:55, he decided to go there to see what was wrong.

Danziger had said, in his statement to police, that he had been awakened at Rhonda's at 8:35 by his lead manager. Rhonda had given various statements, had testified before a grand jury and then at this trial and she had given various times for the phone call, ranging from 8:15 to 8:35 to 9:15. She said she just wasn't sure, but thought it must have been 9:15, based on the amount of time it took them to get to work following the phone call.

Now, Dawson-Brown called Alex Martin, the lead manager who made that call to Rhonda's home. Martin said he had been awakened by his supervisor, Lester Davis, telling him Rhonda Shore's store was not responding to phone calls. Martin called the store in question himself and received no answer. Knowing that Richard Danziger was supposed to open that morning, he called Danziger's home and spoke to one of his roommates, who said he didn't know where Richard was. Finally, he called Rhonda, to tell her that her store was not open and instruct her to either go open the store herself or find someone to do it. Pronto.

The telephone at her house was answered by Richard Danziger. The manager asked Danziger why Danziger was there, and he told the manager about the party the night before and that he had spent the night in the guest room and either forgot to set the alarm clock, set it incorrectly or just didn't hear it.

Martin said he asked to talk to Rhonda and after a minute or two, she came to the phone. After he had told her to get over to her

Nancy DePriest was a beautiful, young twenty-year-old mother with her whole life ahead of her before she was the victim of a senseless murder.

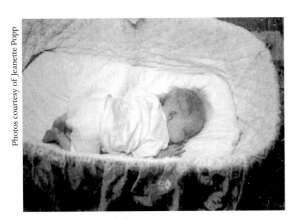

Nancy DePriest as a baby.

Nancy DePriest, shortly before she was murdered.

Nancy and Jeanette pose for a family portrait.

February 17th, 1998

Governor George Bush
State Capitol
P.O. Box 12428
Austin, Texas 78.701

RE: Murder Confession

Dear Governor Bush Sir,

My name is Achim Josef Marino, #573519 and I am currently confined in the McConnell Unit of the T.D.C.J.-I.D., serving three life sentences plus three ten-year sentences for crimes committed at Austin, Texas in both 1988 and 1990. While in Austin in 1988, I also robbed, raped and shot a 20 year old women at the Pizza Hut at Reinli Lane. This was in late October of 1988, after purchasing the murder weapon via the Austin American Statesman classified section. The womens name was Nancy Lena Depriest, and I have not been convicted for this crime. Approximately a month after this crime, I was arrested in El Paso, Texas, where the murder weapon was confiscated by the El Paso police department, however, the federal government ultimately convicted me for it. At the time of my arrest, I had the keys as well as two currency bags from the Pizza Hut with the name of Pizza Hut bank on the bag, in my possession and which remained in my personal property in the county jail

for approximately 14 months. My friend, Janet Vaughn of P.O. Box 4973, El Paso, Tx., 79914, picked up my personal property after I was transferred to T.D.C.J.-I.D., for parole violation. She later took these items to my parents home where they remain to this day. Included with this confession to you is a B.A.T.F. report in conection with the confiscated murder weapon, and the purchase of it in Austin, Texas, shortly before the murder. In 1990, after I was re-paroled by T.D.C.J.-I.D., I was once again arrested in Austin, Texas for robbery on approximately 5/30/90. While in the county jail, I was told by my cell mate, Raughleigh Lawson, that two men named Danzinger and Ochoa had been convicted for that crime. I tell Raughleigh at that time that they had gotten the wrong people, that I knew the guy who had done it. He then told me that Danzinger and Ochoa had plead guilty to the murder. Governor Bush Sir, I do not know these men nor why they plead guilty to a crime they never committed. I can only assume that they must have been facing a capital murder trial with a poor chance of aquittal, but I tell you this sir, I did this awfull crime and I was alone. Early last year, I wrote the Editor of the Austin American-Statesman, Chief Elizabeth Watson of the A.P.D., and Ms. Susan Maldonado of the Austin office of the

A.C.L.U., confessing to this crime because I believed that I was about to be killed here at the prison, and therefore I wanted to clear my conscience somewhat in regards to the lives of Dansinger, Ochoa and their loved ones. However, the confessions I'd made to these people, was ultimately ignored. Now, I make this confession for a different reason. My life is no longer in danger, but my conscience still sickens me. I can not help Nancy Lena Dupriest or her family, but at least I can attempt to make ammends to Dansinger and Ochoa and their loved ones by doing my Christian duty and come clean about this terrible crime, a crime which has been enlarged and magnified by the arrest and conviction of two innocent men. Additionally, I have had a spiritual awakening and conversion, resulting in me becoming a Christian. This is a direct result of joining the Alcoholics Anonymous/ Narcotics Anonymous Twelve Step Program, some 21 months ago and whose 12 steps and guiding principles caused me to have a spiritual awakening which ultimately lead me to the answer, Jesus Christ, His Father our Creator, the Holy Spirit, and ofcourse, this confession. The Christian life-style and value system demands that I do this, even at the loss of my life, which

I am fully pre-pared to lose and ex-pect to loose. I am deeply sickened, disgusted and mortified for the crime I have committed, as well as my entire past life. I grieve for Nancy Lena Dupriest, her loved ones, as well as those of Dansinger and Ochoa, and also my family. Prior to my Christian conversion and healing, I was insane. Never the less, there can be no excuses for my crime, because I knew exactly what I was doing. I am pre-pared to pay the price for my actions. Governor Bush Sir, a copy of this letter/confession to you will also be sent to Ronny Earle of the Travis county District Attorney's Office. I wish to respectfully remind you, that in the event that you all decide to once again ignore this confession that you all are legally and morally obligated to con-tact Dansinger and Ochoa's attorneys and families concerning this confes-sion. Thank You. God bless you and your family,

Yours in Jesus
Christ,
Achim J. Marino
#573514
McConnell Unit
3001 S. Emilly Dr.
Beeville, Texas 78102

Marino's letter gives a detailed account of events that took place on the day of Nancy's death.

Richard Danziger, shortly before his arrest and conviction for his alleged role in the rape and murder of Nancy DePriest.

Achim Josef Marino, the man who said he was Nancy's real killer.

Chris Ochoa, posing with former Illinois governor, George Ryan.

Chris Ochoa and Jeanette Popp, standing outside the Pizza Hut in Austin, Texas, where the body of Nancy DePriest was discovered by a co-worker.

Jeanette, outside of the Austin courthouse, protesting the death penalty.

Chris Ochoa, speaking at a symposium for the Innocence Project, at the University of Wisconsin.

Jeanette Popp with her husband, Jim.

Jeanette Popp, speaking out against the death penalty, at a public engagement for the Texas Moratorium Network.

On February 6, 2002, Chris Ochoa and Richard Danziger were officially exonerated of the murder of Nancy DePriest. Shown here are Chris and Jeanette celebrating the men's freedom shortly after the judge's decision that they were innocent.

Nancy's gravesite in tiny Newcastle, Texas, just a few miles outside of Graham.

Clockwise from top left: Chris Ochoa tears up his prisoner number at a speaking engagement for the Innocence Project. Chris enjoys his first meal after his exoneration of the murder of Nancy DePriest. Chris with Innocence Project founder Barry Scheck.

store, he started to get ready himself, because he lived closer to the store and could get there sooner. Before he could leave the house, however, Rhonda called to say she couldn't get her car started. Martin told her he didn't care how she got there but she should get there as fast as she could. When he arrived at the store, Martin said, one employee was waiting and another arrived soon after. Half an hour later, he said, Danziger and Rhonda arrived.

Pressed by Dawson-Brown, Martin testified it must have been 9:00 A.M. when he was awakened by his supervisor. With that, Dawson-Brown passed the witness for cross-examination.

Berke Bettis began his cross-examination by reading the witness's two statements he said he gave the Austin Police Department. When Bettis finished reading, he asked Martin, "With regard to the first statement you gave to Sergeant Bruce Boardman of the Austin Police Department, do I understand from this statement that you do not, did not at that time, recall how you learned the store was not open?"

The witness said that was right. He couldn't remember if his supervisor had called or if he had called the store himself.

"Let me ask you if you had made certain statements to Sergeant Boardman in this statement: 'On 10-24-88, I discovered that the store had not been opened. I knew that, according to the schedule, Richard Danziger was supposed to open the store. This was before 8:30 A.M.'"

"Yes, sir. I made that statement."

"Did you mention calling Richard's roommate?"

"Yes, sir."

"And then you said you called Rhonda Shore's house. 'The reason I remember about what time this was is because I was going to have to write it up for living with another employee. It was close to 8:30 A.M. when I called.'"

"Yes, sir. I made that statement."

"Then, after detailing what Richard said when he answered the phone, did you say in your statement, 'I asked Richard what he was doing answering the phone at that house at 8:30 in the morning'?"

"I said that."

"Did you further state that 'I arrived at the store around 9:00 A.M. I was the first to arrive'?"

"Yes, sir."

"Also, in that statement, did you make the following remarks to Sergeant Boardman? 'With regard to what I had been told or heard about this case, I know the following: One, she was shot in the head. Two, she was sexually assaulted. Three, her hands were tied behind her back. Four, it happened in the foyer where the restrooms are. Five, the bullet did not come out. Six, she must have been surprised while rolling dough. Seven, they got the money. Eight, I may have discussed or theorized what I thought to be the caliber of the gun, based upon my knowledge of guns. The theory was that the gun was going to have to be a .32 caliber or smaller. With regard to the exact caliber of weapon used, I have no personal knowledge nor have I been told. I am sure that Richard and I discussed the case while working. I had been told by my supervisor that the floor had been flooded.' Did you make all those statements, sir?"

He agreed he had.

"Pass the witness," said Bettis.

On redirect examination, Dawson-Brown asked Martin, "Did you come on your own, along with your wife, on November 21, for a second statement to the police?"

"Yes, ma'am."

"Getting back to the November 14 statement, did you say, 'I arrived at the store around 9:00 A.M. I was the first to arrive. Then two other employees arrived between 9:15 A.M. and 9:30 A.M. It was 10:00 A.M. or after that Richard and Rhonda arrived. They walked in together'? Were those your best estimates at the time?"

"Yes, ma'am."

"Now," said Dawson-Brown, "in your second statement, November 21, did you state, 'The more I thought about it, I'm not certain of the exact time I received a phone call from my supervisor, nor of the exact time that I called my store manager and spoke to her and Richard Danziger'?"

"Yes, ma'am."

When Dawson-Brown had finished with the witness for the second time, Bettis approached for re-cross.

"What did you specifically say to Richard Danziger when he answered the phone at Rhonda's house?"

"Specifically, I can't say."

"Well," drawled Bettis, "if the first statement you gave to the police contained the statement, 'I asked Richard what he was doing answering the phone at that house at 8:30 in the morning,' can you think of any reason why you would have inserted the phrase 'at 8:30 in the morning' if you had not said that?"

"No, sir. I cannot say anything to it."

"But at the time you made this statement, that was in fact your best recollection of precisely what you said."

"Yes, sir."

Bettis passed the witness and Dawson-Brown had no redirect, so the witness was allowed to step down.

The prosecution was not through with the topic of the time line of that fateful Monday morning. Assistant District Attorney LaRu Woody called, as the State's next witness, Maria Carrizales, who identified herself as an investigator for the District Attorney's office. The investigator testified that she had driven the route from Rhonda Shore's apartment to the restaurant where Nancy DePriest was killed. That restaurant was located twelve miles from the apartment where Danziger spent the night with Rhonda on October 23, 1988. The witness named the car she was driving and that she drove within the speed limit of fifty to fifty-five miles per hour on one trip and then she was asked to drive the same route as if she were in a hurry.

Carrizales said she got on the interstate and drove southbound before turning west on William Cannon Boulevard to a little past Congress Avenue, then took a residential street that ran behind a group of duplexes to the one where Rhonda Shore lived. The twelve mile drive, made between 8:00 A.M. and 10:00 A.M., took her sixteen minutes. When she said she drove as if she were in a hurry, she said she made the trip in eleven minutes.

LaRu Woody did not ask her about traffic conditions. Those in the courtroom who were familiar with Austin traffic were more than likely aware that I-35 southbound between 7:00 and 8:00 A.M. is a thirty-mile long bottleneck, with cars bumper to bumper, sitting idly for long periods of time. Many commuters complained that they could read a Texas newspaper during their morning commute. If she had started driving at eight o'clock, the time elapsed would have been far different than if she had started at nine or nine thirty. Rarely is there an opportunity for a driver to approach anything remotely resembling the speed limit during those hours. By nine o'clock, however, the traffic is generally cleared out and drivers proceed at a more rapid pace.

Next, Woody asked Carrizales to describe taking a different route, this time from Rhonda Shore's duplex to a location identified as the babysitter's, then on to an elementary school and subsequently to the Pizza Hut where she and Richard worked. The investigator said she was asked to make that drive under two conditions: at the normal speed limits and again as if she were in a hurry.

Carrizales described a circuitous route from the driveway she had previously mentioned, along some residential streets, back to William Cannon Boulevard to South Congress, heading east, to another smaller street where the elementary school was located. Eventually she arrived back at I-35, which she took northbound all the way to State Highway 183, which brought her to the store where Richard and Rhonda worked.

Woody asked, "Driving the legally posted speed limit, how long did it take you to make that drive?"

"Twenty-nine minutes," Carrizales answered.

"And then you were asked to make the same drive as if in a hurry?"

"Yes. That time, it took me twenty-four minutes."

"On making the drive from William Cannon to the day care center and to the elementary school, did you stop at each of these locations?"

"Yes."

"Did you bring your car to a full stop at the day care center and at the school?"

"Yes."

The defense attorney only asked the witness a few questions and Woody dismissed her.

After one final witness, a guard in the jail, who testified to an altercation between Chris Ochoa and Richard Danziger in which Danziger accused Ochoa of "squealing" on him, the State rested its case.

# Chapter 14

# No Way Out

Then it was time for the defense to put on its case. Berke Bettis called as his first witness Danziger's roommate who had taken the early morning phone call on Monday, October 24, 1988, from Alex Martin. Martin had been looking for Danziger and the roommate told him Richard wasn't at home.

The roommate said he was awakened by the phone call and looked at the clock as he picked up the receiver. It was 8:30. He said he received a second phone call from the manager, about other things related to work, and that call came at 8:45.

On cross-examination, Dawson-Brown elicited an admission that the man might be unsure about the time of the first phone call.

When Bettis called Richard Danziger to the stand to testify in his own behalf, Jeanette shook her head in disbelief. Throughout the trial, to her he had appeared brash, unremorseful, even disinterested at times. His gaze kept roving over the courtroom. At first, she thought he might have been looking for a friend or family member, but eventually she decided he just couldn't sit still. She wasn't too sure how closely he was following the testimony.

He gave inappropriate responses sometimes, late responses sometimes and other times his responses did not relate to the questions at all.

Bettis's preliminary questions elicited the information from Richard that, at the time of the murder of Nancy DePriest, the eighteen-year-old man was on felony probation for forging his mother's signature on a check. One of the conditions of his probation was that he would get a job and support himself. He hadn't been able to get a job in Beeville, where his mother lived, so he moved to Austin to look for work, with the permission of his probation officer. He got a job at the same Pizza Hut where Chris Ochoa worked and for short intervals at other restaurants. Ochoa said he would let Richard live with him and his roommates for a while, until he got on his feet. He didn't socialize with Ochoa, however. He said the only thing Ochoa did was go to concerts. He himself had to work all the time, Richard said.

Bettis led Danziger through the events of the evening of Sunday, October 23, 1988, which varied little from the account given by Rhonda Shore. He denied any conversation with Chris Ochoa about robbing a Pizza Hut. He told of answering the phone the next morning when the lead manager called. After the phone call, he said he ironed his work shirt. Rhonda got her kids ready to go to school. Then, when they got in the car, it wouldn't start.

"What did you do when the car wouldn't start?" Bettis asked.

"I didn't do anything. She got out of the car. She tried to start it the normal way she tried to start it. And then we tried to push-start it, but it wouldn't start. So we—there was a couple of people down the road in a car and we got a jump-start from them, eventually." He said that when they got the car started, they dropped the kids off and went to work.

"When you got to work, do you have any idea about what time it was?" asked Bettis.

"Around ten, a little bit after, a little bit before."

"Whatever time it was, you put it down on your time card?"

"I'm pretty sure."

"Whatever the time card says is going to be fairly accurate."

"Pretty much."

When Bettis asked Danziger why he went to the Pizza Hut where Nancy worked, he said, "I did it, because it was in memory of—in thought of—Nancy. I did it, because it was in thought of Nancy. I didn't even know the girl."

"Had you ever met Nancy DePriest?"

"No. That's a public fact. You can go through all my records or whatever. I never even met the girl."

"Well, then . . ."

"Or lady."

"Why would you want to drink a beer in memory of her, or in thought of her?"

"Because it could have been me. Because I went to my store to open up. I was late."

"You say you worked the same shift as Nancy?"

"Yeah."

"Why did you leave without finishing your beer?"

"I did finish my beer. Somebody buys me a beer, I finish it."

"Did Chris finish his?"

"I don't think so. He was getting too nervous. He just started freaking out, pretty much."

"Did he tell you why he was nervous?"

"No, he didn't."

"On the way out of the Pizza Hut, you had some conversation with the security guard."

"Yes, I did."

"Whose idea was that?"

"Mine."

"Why?"

"Because I wanted to know what was going on."

"What business was it of yours?"

"It wasn't none of my business, really. I was just being nosy."

"Did you learn anything of any consequence from the security guard?"

"Yeah. The back sink was clogged up and that is about all I pretty much know."

Moving ahead, Bettis asked, "When the police officers came over to your girlfriend's duplex and first had their conversation with you, what did you tell them?"

"I don't remember."

"Did you tell them that she was your alibi?"

"Yeah. I remember that day specifically, because I was late and I was, that was the day Nancy got killed."

"Okay. But then on the later date, when you were talking to the police you told them that Rhonda Shore was your alibi?"

"On that day? I don't know what you're trying to say."

"Okay." Bettis drew a deep breath. "I'm not clear, apparently."

Listening to the answers Danziger gave to the questions posed by his attorney, Jeanette felt he would have been better served had he stayed off the stand.

At that point, Judge Perkins asked the attorneys to approach the bench. After a brief conversation, he told the jurors that, since one of them had to be in Houston the following day, there would be no court, but that they would start again at 8:30 A.M. Thursday morning and Richard Danziger would continue his testimony at that time. He expressed the opinion that he hoped by Thursday afternoon he would be able to give the jury his charge and closing arguments by the State and the defense could begin.

When Danziger took the stand on Thursday morning, Bettis returned to the morning of October 24, 1988, when the defendant said he was awakened by a phone call from his lead manager. "What's your best idea of what time he called?"

"About 8:35."

"How are you so sure?"

"Because I was late for work and I picked up the telephone and I looked at the clock. He asked me, 'What are you doing there?'"

"Was there a clock for you to look at?"

"Yeah, a digital clock."

Bettis told Danziger he would like to move ahead in time to the date when officers from the Austin Police Department and members of the Travis County District Attorney's office came to Rhonda's house while Richard was there. "You remember about what time of day that was?"

"About six o'clock. I'm pretty sure, because she was getting ready to go out with her parents to eat."

"Were you surprised to see the police officers there?"

"Yes."

"How many of them were there?"

"About six of them, I imagine."

"What did they tell you when the came into the apartment?"

"One ran to the kitchen and the other one ran to the back bedroom with Rhonda, and I was sitting in the living room."

"Who spoke to you, if anybody did?"

"I think it was Boardman or Balagia."

"What did they say?"

"'I'm from the police department.' And they wanted my name."

"Did you tell them?"

"Yes."

"What did they say then?"

"'Would you mind answering some questions down at the police station?' I go, 'No.'"

"Did you tell them your girlfriend was your alibi?"

"Yeah. Later on, before we left I did, 'cause I figured that would just delete me. I didn't feel like they would waste their time on me, because I wasn't there."

"Did you go down to the police station with them voluntarily?"

"Yes, I did."

"After you got down there, how long did you stay at the police station?"

"I think about nine hours."

"During that period of time, how many different police officers came in and out of the room and talked to you?"

"I don't know. A lot of them."

"Not just Boardman and Balagia and Polanco?"

"No. A whole bunch of different people."

Bettis's next question seemed to be completely off any subject pertinent to Danziger's testimony. "How did you get from your second job to your job at the Pizza Hut?"

"I walked, unless I had my girlfriend's car."

"In terms of walking between the jobs, how far was that?"

"Twenty, thirty minutes."

"How many pairs of shoes did you own at that time?"

"At that time, just one."

"Was that the same pair the State has put in evidence before the jury?"

"Yes."

"What time did you finally leave the police station?"

"I think it was around three o'clock in the morning."

"At that time, were you barefooted?"

"I had my socks on."

"When you were at the police station, did you ever refuse to answer any questions they asked you?"

"No, I didn't."

Danziger answered all of Bettis's subsequent questions in the affirmative: Yes, he had voluntarily given the police samples of his blood, his urine, his head hair, his body hair, his pubic hair and his semen.

"At any time, did anybody ask you to make a written statement?"

"No, not until after I got arrested; they asked me if I wanted to make a written statement. I said, 'Yeah, I'm going to say the same thing I did four days ago.' But they didn't take one."

"Richard, after you left the police station that morning, did you go back to Beeville?"

"Yes, I did, after I called to say I was leaving town."

"Called who?"

"Polanco. I called 911. They connected me with Polanco."

"You told him you were going to leave Austin and where you were going to be?"

"Yes. 'Cause they asked me if I was going to leave town to call them, so I called them."

"After you got to Beeville, did anybody get in touch with the police department?"

"Yes, my mother did."

"She tell them where you were?"

"Yeah, she did."

"Where you could be reached?"

"Yes."

"Richard, you heard the police officers describe you as being calm, cool and collected. You heard one of them say he didn't think you could be intimidated. Why were you so calm when you were talking to the police officers who were accusing you of a horrible crime?"

"Because I didn't have nothing to hide, that's why. I thought they were questioning everybody. So I thought I was just one of them. I wasn't pissed off or nervous or anything."

"Richard, are you a person who shows emotion easily?"

"No."

"How do you feel about the death of Nancy DePriest?"

"I express my condolences to the family. I feel it wasn't necessary."

Veering off on another path, Bettis asked, "Have you ever owned a gun, Richard?"

"No, I haven't," Danziger answered. "I'm underage to buy a gun."

Bettis gave his client a level look. "You're underage to buy a beer, too. You did that."

"Yes," Danziger admitted.

"When was the last time you held or fired a gun?" Bettis asked.

"When I was probably about fifteen, in Jacksonville, Florida."

"What kind of gun was it?"

"They were rifles and it was at a shooting range."

With hardly a pause for breath, Bettis changed his line of questioning again. "Richard, how did you feel when you were sitting over here, listening to Chris Ochoa sit up in that witness stand and accuse you of this crime?"

"I was pretty pissed off," Danziger said forcefully.

"Why?"

"Because if you sit here for fifteen months, for something you didn't do, you'd get pretty pissed off, too. I couldn't do nothing! I couldn't jump or do nothing. I couldn't do anything."

"Well, this is your chance, now, to do something. This is your opportunity to tell your side of the story."

"That's what I'm doing."

"Richard, did you sexually assault Nancy DePriest?"

"No. I didn't." Danziger's voice was firm.

Jeanette thought he sounded like he might be a little angry at that very moment. Was he acting like he was confronting in this trial a bitter trick of fate or was he a liar able to convince himself he wasn't at fault for this horrible crime when he was?

"Were you present when Chris Ochoa sexually assaulted Nancy DePriest?"

"No, I wasn't."

"Were you present when Chris Ochoa murdered Nancy DePriest?"

"No. I wasn't. I was sleeping."

On that note, Bettis passed the witness to the State.

Dawson-Brown immediately attacked the subject that had occupied hours of testimony already, the morning Richard Danziger answered the phone at Rhonda's house, the morning Nancy DePriest was killed. She began by introducing into evidence Danziger's time cards from October 1988 and then questioned him about each one. It quickly became apparent that he rarely worked more than six hours a day and frequently worked only four hour shifts. Other days, he worked even fewer hours.

When they had gone through the stack of time cards, hour by hour, day by day, Dawson-Brown asked, "Now, during this time, were you pulling down a second job?"

"I worked there for two weeks. Then I took a three-day break."

"You did?"

"If I remember correctly," Danziger said. His features wore an expression of weary disdain.

"You sure?"

"I'm not positive."

"Let's talk about your second job," Dawson-Brown suggested. She produced a couple of photocopies that he identified as his time sheets from that restaurant.

Bettis interrupted, saying he hadn't had a chance to look at the sheets. He took a moment to study the photocopies, then turned to the bench. "Your Honor, the second time card that appears on this photocopy is perfectly legible and I have no objection to its introduction. But the first time sheet shown here is illegible for me or any other person to accurately interpret."

Judge Perkins glared at him. "Well, I guess the jury will be the judge of that. I'll overrule the objection. That will be admitted."

Dawson-Brown questioned Danziger about each sheet, starting with the one she had introduced, saying it was dated September 30, 1988. "Does that look like 9-30? September 30?" she asked.

"I don't know," Danziger insisted.

Giving up on the question for the moment, the prosecutor asked the witness about the other cards. The next date was Saturday, October 1, then Friday, October 7 and then Saturday, October 8. "And you never went back after October 8?"

"No. I quit."

"So, in actuality, you worked only four days at that job?"

"I think it was two weeks, if I remember correctly. I thought it was two weeks."

Dawson-Brown put a hand on each hip. "If the record shows here that you worked on September 30, October 1, October 7 and October 8, would you dispute that?"

"Not if it says that," Danziger said diffidently.

"You're not willing to read these?"

In an exasperated tone, Danziger said, "I can barely read them."

Dawson-Brown bristled. "You want me to bring somebody down here from the second restaurant?"

"Go for it." His tone sounded defiant to Jeanette. "I can't read it. My attorney can't read it."

A surprised murmur rippled over the courtroom and the jurors looked astonished. Judge Perkins glared at the assemblage, quickly silencing the room. Jeanette just shook her head. It was inconceivable to her that a person fighting for his freedom would so blatantly antagonize the very people who held his future in their hands.

Dawson-Brown waited in the ensuing silence for a moment, then began asking Danziger about his financial situation at the time of the murder. Half an hour later, the jury had been made aware that the defendant had needed money. He was working fewer than forty hours a week, he didn't own a car and he slept on a bedroll in the apartment he shared with Chris Ochoa and two other roommates. Additionally, he was on probation for forging three checks on his mother's account. The total amount of the checks was fifty-five dollars. As a condition of his probation, he was required to make restitution at twenty-five dollars a month, he had to pay a probation fee of forty dollars a month to the Bee County Probation Department and he had to pay a fine of twenty-five dollars a month. All these fines and fees had been assessed on September 8, the first payments due the first of the next month, and he admitted he hadn't made a payment by October 24.

Finally, Dawson-Brown asked, "So you really weren't on that good a financial basis, were you?"

"I thought I was," he insisted. "I don't think I was hurting."

"Isn't being twenty-four days behind on your obligation to a court for a felony forgery hurting?"

He shrugged. "Well, they always give you leeway."

"Oh they do?" Dawson-Brown sounded amazed. "Does everyone give you leeway, Richard?"

"No."

From there, Dawson-Brown backtracked and after a few frustrating minutes, she had explored Danziger's work history as far back as December 1987, when he would have been seventeen years old. "Prior to December of 1987, where did you work?"

"December of '87? Nowhere. Or San Marcos."

"Did you live in San Marcos?"

"Yes."

Berke Bettis rose to his feet. "Bench conference, Your Honor?" He and Dawson-Brown talked for a few minutes away from the microphone, after which Judge Perkins asked the defense counsel, in full court, "Do you have an objection?"

"I have an objection," Bettis said, nodding his head.

Perkins excused the jurors, sending them to wait in the jury room. When the last one had filed through the door, he turned to Dawson-Brown. "My understanding of the line of questioning by the State is to ask the defendant about his background, more specifically, to ask him about a mental health commitment. Is that it?"

Dawson-Brown answered that she wasn't talking about a mental health commitment. "I just want to go into this witness's background. I think the jury is allowed to know his background, where he's from, what he'd been doing, to assess his credibility as they would any other witness.

"The State intends to ask this witness if he was living in San Marcos and where in San Marcos. And, I believe, if he answers truthfully, he will admit that from March 17, 1986, through December of 1987, he was in a San Marcos treatment center operated by Brown Schools, a prominent name in mental health facilities, facilities for the treatment of drug abuse as well as correction centers.

"He was not there on a state commitment, but was placed there by his family," she said. "And prior to that, from March 13, 1985, through April 16, 1985, he was in the Baylor Medical Center. Prior to that, November 1983 through December 1984, he was at another residential mental health treatment facility. And that he was in and out of these facilities over that period of time and had received a certain diagnosis."

The prosecutor took a breath and continued. "The State does not intend to introduce or inquire into the fact that, back in 1982, he was charged with a juvenile offense, subsequently committed to Texas Youth Commission to serve time in one of their facilities. But that was turned over by a Writ of Habeas Corpus and he was subsequently placed on juvenile probation.

"We do not intend to go there," Dawson-Brown said firmly. "We're just trying to go into his background, so the jury can assess his credibility."

Berke Bettis interrupted the prosecutor. "I submit to the court that the bare fact that a person is placed in a residential treatment center, without any judicial adjudication of incompetency, forces that person into making a choice of either having to explain the underlying facts themselves, getting into evidence alleged extraneous wrongdoing or permitting the jury to infer or assume from the fact of such placement, unexplained, that such wrongdoing exists."

The judge peered at the defense attorney. "If I understand your argument correctly, Mr. Bettis, are you arguing that if the defendant didn't explain why he was in a mental health center, the jury would infer that he was there, because he had done something wrong, had committed some crime? I don't know that that necessarily follows. For a person to be in a mental health facility doesn't mean he or she has committed a crime."

Bettis protested, "It certainly means, or allows the jury to draw the inference, that they had engaged in some form of prior misconduct, deviant behavior or other wrong acts."

He hurried on with his argument, insisting that the fact that a person had been placed by a parent in a residential mental health facility was irrelevant, because under the Texas Family Code it is the parents' right to determine the place where their child shall reside. Such placement, Bettis argued, "is extra-judicial in character, is supported by no judicial finding of wrongdoing. It creates a prejudicial effect on the jury. It has such tangential relevance, if any, that the admission of such evidence should be precluded."

"Judge," said Dawson-Brown, "the whole case depends on whether or not this jury believes Chris Ochoa or Richard Danziger. It's come down to credibility. Certainly, this person's history of what he was doing, his mental status, will affect their determination of whether he is telling the truth now."

Bettis had an answer ready. "I bring to the court's attention rule 601 of the Texas Rules of Criminal Evidence, which specifically provides that every person is competent to be a witness except as provided in two sections, one relating to minors and the other to insane persons, who, in the opinion of the court, are in an insane condition when they're called to testify.

"If the court is to permit this type of evidence, it seems to me that under rule 601, in the absence of any offer of proof by the State to have a prior determination of the incompetency of the witness, State is going to have to excuse the jury and conduct an independent examination to determine whether this witness was, in the court's opinion, at the time of the events in question, an insane person. All of this, it seems to me, is so tangential, such an immaterial issue, the presentation of the sort of evidence the prosecution contends for should be prevented by this court in the exercise of its sound discretion of the control of this trial.

"And again, I just point out that the prosecutor herself, in describing what it was she intended to show through this evidence was, among other things, what was his mental state and what was he doing? That has to get into allegations of conduct. It has to fall within the purview of prior misdeeds, prior acts.

"For all these reasons, I must urge on the court that there's no relevance here which outweighs the prejudicial character of this evidence. And, in any case, if the court finds it to be relevant, then there's a predicate under rule 601 I think has to be complied with."

Dawson-Brown protested. "Judge, the State's not alleging that he's incompetent and that we want a hearing and him taken off the stand, because he is not competent to testify. What we're asserting is that this information goes to the jury's determination of his credibility.

"Mr. Bettis and I both have copies of the documents from the mental health facility wherein he received a diagnosis of conduct disorder, socialized aggressive. This was done independently by the doctors there treating Richard Danziger, and they determined that this treatment was necessary. Certainly these diagnoses would be important to the jury to determine his credibility. He has received a diagnosis of a mental illness under the DSM 3 (a psychiatric diagnos-ticians' handbook)."

The judge ended the argument there. "For the time being, I'm going to sustain the objection, and you can go ahead and continue the cross-examination of the witness on other matters. We'll come back to this later."

Dawson-Brown wouldn't give up. "Could I ask this witness if he knows what his mental diagnosis was? He may know."

Bettis objected. "It would be hearsay if he knew, and—"

"I sustained the objection for the time being," the judge said definitively.

He went on, "Now we're going to take a break."

The tense spectators looked grateful.

## Chapter 15

# One Last Gasp

After the twenty-minute recess, Dawson-Brown resumed her cross-examination of Richard Danziger. Coming at it from a different angle, she went over much of the same ground both she and Berke Bettis had covered earlier. Danziger once again assumed his brash pose, sometimes answering her questions directly, sometimes his answers were only tangentially relevant to her questions. Frequently, he took issue with the questions themselves.

At times, Dawson-Brown appeared to be sucked into the contentious dialogue. During it, she asked, "You testified that you were curious about this, that's why you asked the security guard questions."

"Yes, ma'am."

Her face was taut as she spread a half dozen photos on the rail of the witness box—gruesome photos taken during Nancy DePriest's autopsy. One could argue murder in the abstract but seeing photos made the smell, sight and taste of violent death real.

Danziger leaned away. "I didn't do that," Danziger once again insisted.

Dawson-Brown carefully picked up the photos one by one and made a neat stack. "I'm just trying to help you with your curiosity," she said, pausing to let this sink in.

Bettis jumped to his feet. "Judge, I object to the prosecutor's side-bar remarks. If she has questions to pose to the witness, she can pose questions. Stating to the witness, 'I'm just trying to help you with your curiosity' while throwing photographs of the nude body of the victim, the crime of which he is accused, in front of a witness is not posing a question. It is a sidebar remark, and I object to it and ask the court to admonish the prosecutor to restrict herself to permissible lines of inquiry."

Judge Perkins overruled the objection, contending that Dawson-Brown was only responding to a remark the witness had made to her. "It's not proper for that witness to be gratuitously going off and saying things to the lawyers when they're cross-examining him. If he continues to do that, the lawyer's free to answer appropriately."

Seeming to be satisfied, Dawson-Brown continued her cross-examination by asking Danziger about his interrogation by Detective Balagia on November 11, 1988. Danziger's most frequent response was that he didn't say most of the statements Balagia had testified Danziger had said.

He also said the testimony of the security guard he'd spoken to at the Pizza Hut where Nancy was killed was mostly lies. In fact, according to the defendant, every witness who had testified about statements Danziger had made was lying—or twisting his words.

"So everybody up here has lied," Dawson-Brown said, her voice filled with disapproval and dislike.

"Chris did, for sure. Yes," Danziger said in an accusatory manner.

"Is this a conspiracy against you?" she grimaced.

"I doubt it." Danziger tilted his head.

Dawson-Brown paused a moment then pounced. "Why would these people lie?"

"I don't know." He shrugged. "I don't know what's going on in their heads."

Dawson-Brown returned to the subject of Detective Balagia.

"Did you say, 'You don't have any evidence that would link me to the crime'?"

"That's right."

"How are you so sure?"

"Because I wasn't there. That's why." He spoke slowly and deliberately.

"Did you also tell him that 'You're not going to pin a capital murder on me'?"

"Yes, I did."

"He's not lying abut that?"

"No. He isn't."

Dawson-Brown asked about another question Balagia had posed to Danziger. "When Detective Balagia asked you where you acquired such knowledge of evidence in forensics, did you tell him you read a lot and watched TV and you know basic police officer procedures?"

Danziger shook his head again. "He asked me if I watched *Quincy*. I told him yes. Who hasn't watched *Quincy*? That's a stupid question."

"That's not what Detective Balagia—"

Danziger interrupted. "Well, he lied, because he asked me if I watched *Quincy*, and I go 'Yeah.' He goes, 'You're interested in forensics?' I go, 'I'm interested in anything I don't know.' That's what I said."

"So you know about forensics," Dawson-Brown persisted.

"No. I don't. Not really."

She challenged him. "So, did you tell Detective Balagia that or not? Is he lying on this point?"

"Tell him what?"

Appearing frustrated, Dawson-Brown said, "That you had acquired knowledge of evidence of forensics because you read a lot and watch TV and that you know basic police procedure."

"Acquire *what* evidence?" Danziger demanded.

"Knowledge about evidence in forensics."

"I don't get the point that you're trying to state."

Dawson-Brown drew a deep breath. "Detective Balagia said that you, in response to his question, 'Where did you acquire such a knowledge of evidence in forensics?', you responded that you read a lot and watched TV and that you knew basic police procedure."

"No. I didn't know anything about forensics, besides the *Quincy* show. *That* was the question: 'Do you watch *Quincy*?' And I go, 'Yeah.'"

Dawson-Brown looked at her notes. "What he put down here is not what you just said."

"Well, I didn't acquire knowledge of it. Besides watching TV, I never read a book on forensics."

"So once again, Detective Balagia is telling lies."

"That's a lie there."

The prosecutor's probing cross-examination and Danziger's hostile, quick-tempered responses continued going back and forth as Danziger spent three hours on the stand on two separate days. The prosecutor was determined to let the jury see this man from different perspectives as the State did: a cold, unremorseful killer. She left no stone unturned. She asked, "What about the hair they found at the scene?"

He shot her an angry look. "That wasn't my hair. Why didn't you send it to genetics to find out whether it was my hair? Because you knew it would be negative, that's why."

Disbelief flashed in Dawson-Brown's eyes. "Did you hear the doctor testify he needed a root to do that analysis?" Dawson-Brown asked.

"No. I didn't hear that."

"You weren't listening?"

"I don't remember him saying that. I wouldn't doubt if he said that. But I figured genetics could do whatever they wanted with things."

"You didn't think about pubic hairs falling out that day, did you?"

Danziger looked exasperated. "I wasn't there!"

"Where's the gun?" Dawson-Brown demanded abruptly.

"I have no gun."

"Where did you get the gun?" She asked as if she hadn't heard him.

"Never owned a gun."

Switching gears again, Dawson-Brown asked, "Why would Chris tell these lies?"

"Accusing me of the crime?"

"Yes."

"To get out of capital murder, to get out of anything."

"So he came in with this scheme?"

Danziger looked at her quizzically. "Is that all of your question?"

"Uh-huh."

"Yes."

"And on Friday the eleventh, when he told the police it was you who did this and that you had confessed it to him, he was thinking about getting out of capital murder and implicating an innocent man, at that time."

"I really don't know why. It could be any number of things," Danziger said. "I don't know what goes through his head."

"You think you're being framed?"

Danziger gave a disgusted look. "By him, yes."

"And the cops have joined in?" Dawson-Brown sounded very skeptical.

"I didn't say those statements that they stated. No, I didn't." There was a terrible simplicity in his last statement that hung in the air.

Dawson-Brown rushed on to another topic. "It worried you when they took your shoes, didn't it?"

"It didn't worry me. I was wondering some why they took my shoes, yeah."

"Weren't you afraid you might have left a little spot of blood on them?"

"No! I wasn't afraid of a single thing, because *I wasn't there.*"

"You're pretty sure you hadn't left a sample of your semen."

"*I wasn't there* to leave a sample. That's why." His anger was close to feral.

That was Dawson-Brown's final question. The jury and spectators seemed immobile now. The ordeal was finally over. After both sides rested the case, Judge Perkins called a recess until one o'clock in the afternoon.

Jeanette was more than ready for a break. She felt numb. It seemed incredible that this belligerent, argumentative teenager had been one of the killers to savagely take the life of her vibrant, intelligent, loving daughter.

At one o'clock, Judge Perkins addressed the jury, telling them that he would read the charge, then they would hear arguments from the State and the defense in three segments. First, the State would be allowed to open their argument, second, the defense would argue their case and third, the State would be allowed to close the argument. He explained that the State goes first and third in order of argument, because they have the burden of proof.

The judge read the charge to them: Richard Danziger was charged by indictment with the offense of aggravated sexual assault. Then he read the case law that defines what aggravated sexual assault is.

Moving to the next section of the charge, the judge defined the terms "deadly weapon" and "bodily injury."

Then he spent a great deal of time on the law regarding testimony of an accomplice. He told the jury that a conviction cannot be had upon the testimony of an accomplice unless the jury first believes the accomplice's testimony is true and that it shows the defendant is guilty. Even then, he told them, you cannot convict unless the accomplice's testimony is corroborated by other evidence to connect the defendant with the offense charged, and the corroboration is not sufficient if it merely shows the commission of the offense, but it *also must tend to connect the defendant with its commission.*

"You are instructed that Chris Ochoa was an accomplice if any offense was committed," he said. "And you are instructed that you cannot find the defendant guilty upon the testimony of Chris Ochoa unless you first believe that the testimony of the said Chris Ochoa is true and that it shows the defendant is guilty as charged in the indictment. Then, you cannot convict the defendant, Richard Danziger, unless you further believe that there is other evidence in this case, outside the evidence of said Chris Ochoa, tending to connect the defendant with the commission of the offense charged in the indictment. Then from all the evidence you must believe, beyond a reasonable doubt, that the defendant is guilty."

He also addressed the law regarding defense claiming alibi. "If the evidence in this case raises in your minds a reasonable doubt as to the presence of the defendant at the place where the offense was committed, if committed, at the time of the commission thereof, then you will find the defendant 'Not guilty' and say so by your verdict."

In conclusion, the judge reminded the jurors that the burden of proof is on the State. All persons are presumed to be innocent and no person may be convicted unless *each element of the offense* is proved beyond a reasonable doubt.

"Now, bearing in mind the foregoing instructions and definitions, if you find the State has failed to prove each element of the offense beyond a reasonable doubt or if you have a reasonable doubt thereof, you will acquit the defendant and say by your verdict, 'Not guilty.'"

Assistant District Attorney LaRu Woody spoke first for the State. She expanded on each of the arguments the judge had outlined in his charge, assuring the jury the State had met its obligation of proof for each segment. Woody focused on the section regarding an accomplice, honing in on Chris Ochoa's testimony.

"It does not say that there must be independent evidence that, by itself, beyond a reasonable doubt, will prove that Richard Danziger is guilty. It says there must be evidence *outside* Mr. Ochoa's testimony that *tends to connect* Richard Danziger with this crime."

Turning to the issue of the alibi, her voice was taut, "I anticipate the defense will argue that the timing alone made it impossible for Richard Danziger to have committed this offense. If Rhonda had been the alibi the defendant was hoping she would be, we'd not have to resort to their reliance on time. However, let's look at the evidence we have about the time. My recollection is that Todd DePriest last saw Nancy alive at 7:50 in the morning. My recollection is that we have evidence at 9:30 that very same morning that Nancy DePriest was dead. The offense was committed some time in between there.

"Who gave statements that same day? Who discussed time the same day as the offense occurred? Whose time will be the most accurate? My recollection is that Todd DePriest went down that day to the police department and gave a statement. My recollection is that the man who discovered Nancy's body went down that day and gave a statement: 9:30 when he went into the Pizza Hut and found Nancy DePriest lying there; 9:33 when he called."

A shiver ran through the courtroom. She delivered her next words with quiet certainty. "Those are the times I think are the most accurate, that you can most accurately count on. It comes to mind that Richard Danziger didn't allow himself much time to commit this offense. I'd like you to reflect on how this crime was originally planned. Relying on Chris Ochoa's testimony that they planned a robbery the night before at Rhonda's house. This was to be a robbery. They were to go in there at gunpoint and rob the store on I-35 for a quick getaway. My recollection of the evidence is that it started as a simple two-minute robbery. It shouldn't have taken that long. Plenty of time for Richard Danziger to head back to south Austin, hop in bed with Rhonda and get to work on time if need be."

Then Woody returned to the subject of a second person being involved in Nancy DePriest's murder. "There's no doubt Chris Ochoa was an accomplice," she said. "The judge has told you that. We're not denying that. Chris Ochoa sat up there and admitted to you his guilt in this case.

"The next question is, was the testimony of Chris Ochoa true? Not, does Chris Ochoa always tell the truth? I think he'll be the first one to admit to you he lied. He lied and said Richard did it all. He lied that second time when he said he just watched. Then, for some reason he gave up lying. You'll be the judge as to whether or not he lied here the other day. Was Chris Ochoa's testimony true? Not that first statement, not that second or third statement, but was his testimony to you the truth? You saw how that man acted on the stand. You evaluate whether or not his testimony was true.

"And, if true, did that testimony link Richard Danziger? Did it show the guilt of Richard Danziger? You bet it did. He didn't say, 'I did it by myself.' He told you Richard Danziger's every involvement in that case. If that testimony was true, it clearly went to Richard Danziger's guilt. But that's not enough. You must have other evidence that tends to connect the defendant. Not evidence that proves beyond a reasonable doubt, but tends to connect this defendant, and then you take all that evidence to make your decision."

Her tone hardened. "Let's look at some of that evidence that tends to connect the defendant.

"Richard Danziger's pubic hair found in that arcade area.

"Richard Danziger's statement revealing that he knew facts known only to the police or to Nancy's attackers.

"Richard Danziger's statement in front of that jail guard." (That Chris squealed on him.)

She paused a moment letting the jury absorb the three statements. Then she went on. "Any one of those, I believe, would be sufficient corroboration. And I anticipate that those are the very elements the defense counsel are going to attack here in a minute, so I'd like to talk a little bit about each one.

"The hair. That was Richard Danziger's mistake—leaving one hair behind. The testimony will show you that the place was wiped down. The testimony will show you it had been flooded. They weren't even able to lift blood stains from her clothing. That hair was not just any hair. It was a pubic hair.

"I think defense counsel will ask you to disregard it. It was too small. It's broken. It's not an absolute identifier. Juan Rojas didn't make any bones about it on the stand, saying this is not a fingerprint. This is not an absolute identifier. But he did say it was not Nancy DePriest's hair. It was not Chris Ochoa's hair.

"I would suggest to you that the evidence of that hair is vital, that it is important and that it is something that you can take that tends to connect this defendant to this crime.

"Let's look at another piece of evidence: the defendant's statement to the police that the blue apron was found in the sink, that night of November 11. I guess the defendant's suggesting that the police made that all up or they were confused or they were just lying.

"Now, seems to me the police officers charged with the investigation of criminal offenses, specifically homicide, are very cautious people. I guess we are to believe that they wanted to clear this case so badly they would falsely accuse an individual. I guess they're suggesting that their statistics are important, so they had to get this one off the books so they could move on. So they picked the most likely person, Richard Danziger. Those three police officers imputed those words to his mouth that night?

"And why—what was Chris Ochoa's motive to make this up about Richard Danziger? Why in the world would Chris Ochoa have made this up about Richard Danziger? I submit to you that Chris Ochoa did not make this up. I submit to you that Chris Ochoa told you the truth from that witness stand. And there is plenty of evidence that tends to connect this defendant, Richard Danziger, to this offense. And we would ask you to return a guilty verdict."

The jury was quite still as her last words lingered in the air.

Chapter 16

# The Verdict

Jeanette's sisters had told her they would be there to lend her support when the verdict came down. They were seated on either side of her, all three holding hands, listening intently to LaRu Woody's argument. Every time the prosecutor spoke of the horrible events causing Nancy's death, Jeanette squeezed her sisters' hands.

When Berke Bettis stood up to give the defense argument, he ran back through the two hundred plus exhibits that had been introduced during the trial.

Then Bettis proceeded to remind his audience of the law regarding accomplice testimony, as it had been introduced first in the court's charge and again in ADA Woody's argument.

After that, he moved on to the defense claims. "I could stand up here and go back to the testimony of every witness who has testified about their opinions about relative times of the events on that morning. But it wouldn't resolve the question. It seems to me that the issue is hopelessly and insolubly muddled."

Bettis turned slightly and addressed the jury, his deep voice almost sonorous. "Those of us who sit through trials know that it's not uncommon that even two people observing the same phenomenon from different vantage points will have slightly different recollections of when it happened and how it happened. We heard from so many people here that it would be a wonder if you all could achieve any consensus among yourselves about the exact time which any specific event of that terrible morning took place. But what you have to do then is go back to the court's instructions. The judge tells you that if the evidence in this case raises in your mind a reasonable doubt as to the presence of the defendant at the place where the offense was committed, at the time of the commission thereon, then you will find Richard Danziger not guilty and say that by your verdict.

"So it boils down to the testimony of Chris Ochoa, the accomplice, and then the other evidence and whether in your collective minds Ochoa is believable. Even if it is believable, is there other independent evidence which tends to connect Richard with the commission of these atrocities that, taken together as a whole, proves beyond a reasonable doubt he is guilty?

"What about the other evidence, apart from Chris Ochoa's testimony, that tends to connect Richard to the commission of this crime? What about it?" He almost seemed to be asking the question of himself and pausing, he looked from one jury member to another.

Then he went on. "You will get to go back in the jury room and examine every one of these two hundred-plus pieces of evidence. You can look at every garment, every piece of clothing that Richard Danziger owned. You can look at the report; the laboratory of the Department of Public Safety took those, analyzed every spot, went through them with a fine-tooth comb, subjected them to every test science knows how to subject.

"You will recall the testimony of Christopher Ochoa, who said this boy," gesturing toward the defendant, "took the bleeding body of Nancy DePriest under the shoulders and carried her from the place where she was shot, back to where they supposedly together tried to destroy the evidence. Look on each and every one of these pieces of evidence. Look at the only pair of shoes that the boy owned. Look at his shirts. Look at his khaki pants. And remember the testimony of the Texas Department of Public Safety chemist who came before you and told you that in the first analysis performed on this evidence, there were no stains of significance.

"Look at the extent to which the crime scene was taken apart by the police. And recall that there's not a fingerprint to be found.

"Go further. Look through the scientific evidence sent to the laboratories in Atlanta, in California. Recall the testimony of the scientists who are on the forefront of modern forensic investigation, that they found not one shred of physical evidence, not right down to the level of DNA, that links Richard to the story told about him by Chris Ochoa.

"And then recall the testimony of Mr. Rojas who, finally on January 16, of this year, delivered himself of the opinion that one fragment of a pubic hair found at the scene of the crime fifteen months ago was consistent with the specimen freely and voluntarily provided to the police at that time by Richard Danziger, consistent with, but not a fingerprint, said this man, who finally, at the very end of the police investigation, finally came to you with a hair which he admitted he could not even identify."

His voice was grim as he continued. "I suggest to you, in evaluating everything you heard, that it's perfectly plausible to believe Chris Ochoa's testimony in terms of what he said he did and in terms of what the person who acted with him did, at least up to a point. But there are a couple of important differences you might consider. Recall, if you will, that when the police were first investigating the Pizza Hut tragedy, the theory was widely put out to the media and reported that Nancy DePriest must have known her assailant in order for him to be admitted inside. Now, Chris Ochoa has come up with a new version. In order to make it more credible that Richard Danziger was the mastermind of this crime, he suggests that it was Richard who brought the gun and Richard who brought a key. But you've also heard testimony from managers, from cooks, people in the management hierarchy of Pizza Hut, that those keys were controlled. That access to different stores is only by virtue of a master key. That just a couple of weeks before this tragedy occurred, the locks at all the Pizza Huts had been changed, because there was some breach of security.

"And yet, if you want to accept Chris Ochoa's version of what happened, you'd have to believe that somehow Richard Danziger, a cook at another store, obtained a key to the other store or a master key—but without any reason to believe that's possible or likely. I suggest to you that what really happened is set out in Chris's statement, that indeed, Nancy's first words to him were, "What's up, Chris?" That she opened the door to him, a fellow employee whom she knew—and that knowledge cost her her life at his hands. And I suggest that Chris Ochoa and the real accomplice then entered that store and did pretty much everything that Chris Ochoa told you happened there."

Bettis moved on to another inconsistency he said he found in Chris Ochoa's statement. "You recall that when he gave his second statement to the police, with Sergeant Polanco sitting across the table from him, when Sergeant Polanco pulled out his revolver and said, 'Was it a gun like this, with a cylinder like this?'

"Chris said, 'Yeah. That's what it was.' Yes sir. You bet. 'Wasn't an automatic, was it, Chris?' 'No, absolutely not an automatic.'

"Why would he lie about something that's seemingly as inconsequential as that?" Bettis' voice hardened, then he paused, letting the words sink in. "I suggest to you that there is a reason. Because he wanted to keep the police as far away from that gun as possible. And he succeeded to this date. The reason he wanted to keep the police away from that gun was because he knew there was something about that .22 automatic with which he killed Nancy DePriest that could come back to him or come back to the person with whom he really committed the crime.

"In any case, the police proceeded with their investigation. They had the first statement from Chris Ochoa: 'Richard Danziger told me he did it.'

"Here they had a kid who was on felony probation, had a criminal record. Makes him a likely suspect. They concentrated on Richard.

"Now, here we are after fifteen months of investigation. What do they have to support and corroborate that portion of Chris Ochoa's statements that tends to implicate Richard?

"They have the unreported and unwritten recollections of the homicide detectives. Richard thinks they lied. That doesn't seem very reasonable. But it seems certainly plausible from his point of view for him to believe that. I don't think you have to believe the detectives consciously fabricated anything to accept the fact that sometimes what we hear is not what was said, but what we want to hear. That if we want a thing to be true badly enough, our perceptions of reality tend to be what we want them to be.

"It would have been the simplest thing in the world for Sergeant Boardman, for Detective Balagia, for Sergeant Polanco, to have turned on a little tape recorder in that interrogation room and resolve any doubt about what Richard said, when he said it, in what context and in response to what question.

"It would have been the work of a few minutes to get a secretary in there to take it down in dictation and reduce it to typewriting and bring it back and put it in front of him for his signature. If that had happened, there would not be any question. There would not be any doubt about whether Richard said, as many of the witnesses said, it was a small caliber weapon, probably a .22; there would be no doubt if Richard said, 'The sink in the women's restroom was clogged up with a blue apron flooding the premises and causing the evidence to be washed away.' Or if Richard really said the back sink was clogged up with *something*.

"But that wasn't done. And that isn't resolved.

"What other corroboration is there? It's Rhonda's belated recollection the year before that she had to move her car seat up. You all heard her testimony. If you feel that the recollection is such a strong circumstance tending to connect Richard to the commission of this offense as to remove any reasonable doubt, then, of course, you must find him guilty."

Bettis paused a moment. "It is inconceivable to me that you could do so.

"And then, as far as scientific evidence, we have a fragment of pubic hair consistent with Richard Danziger.

"All those exhibits. All those tests. Not one drop of blood." There was a terrible, telling simplicity in those three sentences as if they were connected.

Now Bettis looked each juror in the eye. "Chris Ochoa stands before you, by his own admission guilty of many terrible crimes. There is nothing you can do that will undo what he has done or that will bring Nancy back. She is gone. But you can do something by following your oaths as jurors and by careful deliberation. You can prevent another horror from being perpetrated by Chris Ochoa. You have it within your sole power to prevent the horror of an innocent man being convicted on the testimony of that human being.

"You've given a tremendous amount of dedication to the job which you had to do up to now. And I ask you not to abandon that sense of dedication as you go back in the jury room to deliberate.

"Richard has waited fifteen months for your verdict. So do not rush to judgment. I believe that if you will go back there and discuss the facts of this case, unclouded by the emotion that the tragedy of Nancy's death injects into those facts, that a careful consideration of all those facts will leave you with a reasonable doubt. Then you will go back to the court's charge and you will find that, based on that reasonable doubt, you must return a verdict of not guilty.

"God's speed to you all in your deliberations."

Claire Dawson-Brown gave the State's final argument. From the prosecution's viewpoint she retraced the ground covered in the judge's charge, in ADA Woody's first argument and the closing argument by defense attorney Berke Bettis.

Then she pounded on the testimony of Chris Ochoa. "Every one of you in this courtroom, if you believe Chris Ochoa, you can find the defendant guilty beyond a reasonable doubt—just on that alone. That gets you beyond a reasonable doubt hurdle. Except the law requires you to find some evidence that tends to connect Richard Danziger. I want each of you to understand that.

"Let's attack the police," she continued building on the tension already in the courtroom. "They're lying; they're fabricating; they want to solve this crime so bad they're hearing things, these trained investigators, they're hearing things that aren't being said.

"*Certainly,* if they're going to hear things that aren't being said, wouldn't they hear Richard Danziger say, 'I *was* there' and just report that? Wouldn't they make up something better?

"And the fact that they didn't take a written statement that night, are you going to punish them? 'No, police officers, we want you to write it down next time. Even though we believe that's what was told to you, we're going to find this man not guilty, this rapist, because we want you to learn that lesson.'

"If you think they got up there and perjured themselves just so they could get a conviction on an innocent man, then we're all in big trouble.

"There was an attack on the fact that none of this physical evidence links Richard Danziger. The statement was made here in the courtroom this afternoon that every shred of Richard Danziger's clothes was analyzed.

"There's no evidence of that. There's no testimony that this is every shred of Richard Danziger's clothes. You think he's keeping his bloody clothes for the police to find two weeks later? Those bloody clothes are in the same place where that gun is, some place where we'll never find them. The place Richard Danziger did not reveal to Chris Ochoa. Richard Danziger is no dummy."

Turning to Chris Ochoa's confession, she said, watching the jury closely, "Look at the details of the crime. When Chris was talking about how they bound and gagged Nancy, when they took her to the arcade area, how her shirt was taken from her legs where it had been used as a ligament and thrown off on Richard. Remember where her shirt was found? Right in that doorway by the arcade.

"Now are you going to believe the police sat and coached him on all those details so once again we could convict an innocent man? Is that what you're to believe? That's what the defense is asserting.

"Ladies and gentleman, you can tell from the evidence, just as Sergeant Polanco did, he had that hunch, that gut feeling, it took two people to commit this crime. This is not a one-person crime. The things that were done to Nancy DePriest, the movement of her body throughout that restaurant, moving her around after she had been shot, washed off and slippery, that 120-pound lifeless body, is not something that you would expect one person to do and certainly not Chris Ochoa. You know he had someone with him and he's always told you who it was.

"What it gets down to is you have to make a decision from your heart, from your gut, based upon whom you believe. I was in the same courtroom with you this morning. And you *know*; you know the truth. You just need to tell him. Thank you."

Judge Perkins addressed the jurors, "Ladies and gentlemen of the jury, you may now retire to the jury room to consider your verdict." It was 2:44 in the afternoon.

As the jurors filed out of the courtroom, he turned to the gallery and warned that when the verdict was returned, there was to be no display of emotion, no outburst of joy or wailing of despair. Jeanette and her sisters walked slowly out of the courtroom, ready for a break from the oppressive atmosphere that had pervaded the courtroom for so many days.

In her mind, though, Jeanette could not get away from the trial. She replayed Ochoa's testimony. He seemed to know every minute, excruciating detail. He must have been present when her daughter died. It was beyond her comprehension that someone—anyone—could admit to committing such a horrendous act, such an atrocity, if he had not actually done it.

Jeanette and her sisters went to find a place where they could talk not too far from the courtroom. She had no idea how long the jury might deliberate, but she knew she wanted to be in that room when the jurors returned. Media people clustered around her. They wanted to interview her. She shook her head no but promised she would give a statement after the verdict was in.

One young woman walked up to her and told Jeanette she worked for a radio news program, "I don't want to bother you, but here's my card. Please give me a call when you feel like talking. I would like to talk to you about your daughter." Then the woman walked away.

Jeanette was so startled, she didn't even notice what the woman looked like, but she was touched that the woman wanted to talk about Nancy, not just about the gruesome details of her death.

Time inched by, but still, Jeanette was a little surprised when a bailiff came to get her at five o'clock, because the jury was coming back. "It hasn't been very long," she said to the man. "Is that good or bad?"

He shook his head. "I don't know."

With her sisters, Jeanette took her customary seat behind the prosecution table. Once again the sisters clasped hands, watching the jurors file in. Jeanette literally held her breath until the jury finally got situated, ready to render its verdict.

One woman juror caught Jeanette's eye for just an instant before she took her seat in the jury box, gave her a smile so brief it was barely noticeable and gave an imperceptible nod of her head. Immediately, Jeanette knew. She knew the verdict before it was read and it was all she could do to contain her relief that the men whom she believed had so brutally raped and tortured her daughter would pay for their savage actions.

When the jury foreman announced that Richard Danziger had been found guilty of aggravated sexual assault, Jeanette thought she couldn't hold in her emotions any longer. Judge Perkins told the jury that the defendant had asked that, in the event they rendered a guilty verdict, they also assess punishment. Therefore, they were dismissed for the night and would come back the following morning at ten o'clock. At that time Judge Perkins would again give them the charge, and the State and defense would be allowed to argue before the jury once more, before the same twelve people who had found Richard Danziger guilty of sexually assaulting Nancy DePriest. The same jury would decide his punishment.

With her sisters, Jeanette went out for dinner, but she never could remember what she ate. They rehashed the day's events at the trial and Jeanette talked about her impressions throughout the trial. When they got back to the hotel, she pleaded exhaustion and went to her room. She waited for Jim's nightly call.

When she told him about the guilty verdict, he and she supported each other in their pain and relief. Again though, as he had every night she had been in Austin, Jim encouraged her to have hope, try to feel love in her heart so there would be no room for hate or anger or revenge. Knowing those negative emotions would consume her if she let them, she promised him she would try to let them go. After his call, she gratefully crawled between the cool, clean sheets and fell into a restless sleep.

*Then she saw Nancy and her heart began to pound. The picture was dark except for a bright circle that spotlighted her beautiful daughter, who was nude, on her knees on a cold tile floor, looking up at her mother with terrified eyes. A hand holding a gun pressed it against the back of Nancy's head. Her hands were drawn tightly behind her, restrained. She was crying, begging for her life. "Please don't hurt me. I have a baby, please, no don't. Mama. Help me, please help me!"*

The sound of the gunshot catapulted Jeanette, screaming, from her pillow. She was drenched in sweat, her heart still pounding furiously. Jeanette closed her eyes and tried to recover the vision. She couldn't tell whether it was in a restaurant or not. Only Nancy was vivid. And the hand holding the gun. Nancy! Everything else was dark. Nancy needed her help. What could she have done to prevent those awful things from happening to her daughter? She was her mother. She should have been able to prevent this. She should have kept her daughter close, never let her get married and move away. Oh, God, what had she done? A few lines from the Bible popped into her head. She didn't remember them exactly word for word, but they said something about the sins of the parents being visited upon children. Had Nancy died because of Jeanette's past? *Stop it!* She scolded herself. *That's completely irrational.* Still, she couldn't escape that burdensome feeling.

Finally, her terror subsided, leaving her with an overwhelming sadness that was like an unbearable physical pain stabbing every cell in her body.

Unable to go back to sleep, Jeanette stayed awake through the night thinking of Nancy.

The punishment phase of Richard Danziger's trial got underway promptly at 10:00 A.M. the next morning, February 2, 1990. The jurors listened attentively as Dawson-Brown asked for life imprisonment for the man they had decreed guilty of aggravated sexual assault, and Berke Bettis urged them to show mercy to this young man—this teenager—who had so much of his life yet ahead of him. When they had finished, Judge Perkins sent the jury to deliberate once more, this time deciding on how much time Richard

Danziger would spend in prison.

The death penalty was not an option and Jeanette was glad. Taking Danziger's life would not bring Nancy back to her and she believed a lifetime in prison would be worse punishment than death. After the jury had left the courtroom, Jeanette, her sisters and a few other observers went out into the corridor. She wished they could go out to the patio area where she had gone during breaks in the proceedings, but she had no idea how long the jury would be out and she didn't want to be that far away. She and her sisters were discussing what to do, whether they should go anywhere, when the bailiff approached her.

"The jury's coming back," he told her.

Astonished, Jeanette gasped. "So soon? It's been about five minutes!"

"Seven and a half, actually," the bailiff said.

They rushed back into the courtroom and took their customary seats. When the rustle of whispers and papers had stopped, the jurors entered the box and Judge Perkins asked for their decision.

"Life in prison." Richard Danziger would have plenty of time to reflect on what the jury and she believed he had done to Nancy DePriest.

Since Chris Ochoa had been given a life term as a condition of his plea bargain, Jeanette felt justice had been served. A life for a life. A life of knowing and reliving all the monstrous acts they had performed seemed a fitting punishment.

Judge Perkins thanked the jurors for their service and adjourned. Immediately, a bailiff walked up to Jeanette and told her the jurors wanted to meet with her. She agreed to go with him to the jury room. She wanted to thank each of them personally for their work, for making what she thought was the right decision. She knew, as it had been for her, this had to have been an exhausting, soul-rending experience for them, listening to all of the horrible details of Nancy's brutal death, weighing the testimony and then having the future of a young man in their hands.

Jeanette hesitated a moment at the door and looked at the twelve people gathered there, waiting quietly for her. Walking in, it seemed the most natural thing in the world for her to open her arms to the one nearest and draw her close in a warm embrace. When Jeanette did that, tears began to flow out of her eyes and down her face. When she drew back, she saw tears in the other woman's eyes as well. She hugged each of them in turn and by the time she had embraced the last one, everyone was crying. She could tell they were compassionate people and they thought they'd done the right thing. She said she would be forever grateful to them.

After she met with the jury, Jeanette went outside the courthouse and met with the press. She told reporters justice had been done. She assured them as she had herself. "God will have the final word."

"You know they will be eligible for parole in fifteen years," one reporter said.

"Yes. I know that," she answered. "And I will be back here to fight any parole for them. Every time they come up for parole, I will be here."

Chapter 17

# Peaceful Interval

Her sisters had to leave for home before Jeanette finished talking with the press and her interview with the young radio reporter. When she finally did get in her car and started home, it had started to rain. Somewhere outside of Austin, the storm became so heavy her ancient windshield wipers could barely keep up with the torrent. The car crept along and she had to fight to stay alert. Jeanette was tired; she hadn't slept much after the nightmare. And she wanted to get home. To be with Jim, who could comfort her and talk to her as no one else ever had or ever could.

A couple of hours later, the old car began to lose power. It sputtered and she barely had time to pull to the side of the road before the motor died completely. She buried her face in her hands and cried. This was too much. What was she going to do now?

Eventually, a compassionate motorist came along and helped her get the car going again, and she was on her way. Still, it was night before she reached home. Jim was at work and she let herself into the empty house and switched on the lights. Her heart seemed to leap as she looked into the living room. There, hanging on the wall, was Nancy's almost life-size photograph. The one the photographer had

given Jeanette for Nancy's funeral. She had not had the money to have
the picture framed the way she thought it deserved, so she had kept it
packed away. She walked across the room, looked into her daughter's
smiling eyes and ran her fingers reverently along the side of the frame.
Jim had done this. She knew instantly. It was so like him. Tears of love
and gratitude rushed to her eyes. *Thank God for Jim*, she thought. *Thank
God for sending me this man who understands me so well and always knows just
what to do and say.*

So her life, post-Nancy's death, had finally begun. Most days, she
could hardly function. She couldn't sleep without medication and even
then she was subjected, night after night, to the horrifying dream of
Nancy on her knees begging Jeanette for help. Every night she woke
up screaming, and Jim cradled her in his arms, held her close and
talked softly, reassuringly, to her until she fell asleep again.

From that first night, when they had talked all night long, both
had known they would be together. It was as if they had known each
other always. During the next few months, they'd had more serious
talks about what was ahead of them if they married. Jim had never
been married before, so they knew it would be a huge step for him.
For Jeanette, too, because she had never felt so committed to anyone
before.

Jim and Jeanette had delayed making wedding plans until after
the Danziger trial. In the spring of 1990, they decided they needed to
get on with their lives. The flurry of wedding planning helped to take
the edge off Jeanette's emotions, to a degree. She hadn't had a real
wedding before and she wanted this to be a special time for both of
them.

The date was set: June 23, 1990. The place: Pine Springs Baptist
Church. Two of Jim's sisters, along with his nieces and nephews, came
from New York. Jeanette's family came. Her stepfather would give her
away. The moment she got to the church, she realized she had
forgotten Jim's sister's corsage. Jim was in the groom's room, pacing,

so Jeanette's stepfather was dispatched to get the flowers. By the time he returned, Jim and the best men were pale and anxious.

Meanwhile the veil refused to stay on Jeanette's head, so someone rustled up some paper clips for her. But the three-year-old flower girl stole the show when she refused to step out into the aisle to strew her petals. She had done beautifully during rehearsal, but when her big moment came, she froze.

Nevertheless, they got through the ceremony, with smiles, a few tears and choking voices as they repeated their vows. After the ceremony, the guests drove to a lake house that belonged to a friend and the party began. When festivities were at their peak, Jim and Jeanette Popp drove away to begin their honeymoon.

For two weeks, it was as if Jeanette was in another world. They had decided on a long road trip to several neighboring states, and she saw beautiful scenery and breathtaking sights she hadn't seen before. She and Jim had time to talk about their future and what a wonderful life they were having. Even the nightmares faded during those two weeks. To Jeanette, it was as if she and Jim had been together forever and that whole other life before Jim had never happened. She had never been that other person. She was with him always. She didn't think of that other life, how it used to be. Not even about how bad her childhood had been. Those things didn't relate to her anymore. This was her life, now. *This has always been my life,* she thought.

Too soon, the honeymoon trip was over and it was time for real life. The couple began to put into place the plans they had been making. They both decided to go to school, Jeanette to become a medical assistant and Jim to DeVry University. Despite their happiness at being together, Jeanette's nightmares returned, but less frequently. Jeanette still suffered from depression and anxiety and still went through long periods when she was angry and short-tempered. They moved to a Fort Worth suburb and both got good jobs, she in a medical clinic and Jim with an oil field equipment company. Four years after Nancy's death, Jeanette was doing her internship at a medical clinic in Fort Worth. She told her doctor she thought something was seriously wrong with her. He counseled with her and ran a battery of tests, including an electrocardiogram, and discovered she had valvular heart disease. The doctor prescribed antidepressants and anti-anxiety medication. Within a week, she felt like a new person. Jim marveled at the transformation.

It was like a miracle. She could deal with the memories of Nancy without falling apart, without being angry. She was more in control of herself, of her emotions and her reactions. Still, occasionally, thoughts of suicide crossed her mind, but she never focused on those thoughts, because of Jim.

Jeanette still thought of her daughter throughout the day, every day. Every morning when she woke up, the first thing she did, while she was still lying in bed, was offer a prayer for Nancy and tell her daughter, "Good morning." Some days, she told Nancy about her plans for the day.

When Jeanette thought about Chris Ochoa and Richard Danziger, she hoped they were reaping the crop they had sown. She could picture Ochoa in a tiny cell in that hot little area of Texas called Tennessee County, the door closed to the outside world, all alone. She'd heard about the horrors of some Texas prisons. Of body bags rolling down the hallway. Of inmates getting stabbed and strangled. Of riots, where prisoners went wild and guards used brute force to control them. Sometimes, when prisoners were killing each other, the entire prison would be locked down. A lockdown in the summer could be ghastly, unspeakably hot, because there was no air conditioning. Sometimes inmates threw water from their toilets onto the floor, then lay down it, to see if they could cool off. Three days in a cell without a shower, wearing the same sticky, smelly clothes.

It was what Ochoa and Danziger deserved, Jeanette thought, believing they were being justly punished for Nancy's brutal murder.

Had she at that point had any inkling of the bitter truth, all the pain which finally seemed to be diminishing would have resurged again, only more virulently.

Chapter 18

# In Limbo

The hell of Tennessee County prison was nothing compared to the personal hell of Richard Danziger.

From Travis County Jail, he was transferred to the Clemens Facility, a maximum-security prison in Amarillo, Texas, filled with Texas's most dangerous and violent offenders. Just a year later, a violent inmate wearing steel-toed boots attacked Danziger from behind and kicked him repeatedly in the head. An investigation showed the attacker mistook Danziger for another prisoner. He was beaten by mistake.

The attack left Danziger helpless, unconscious and lying in a pool of his own blood. He was barely alive when he arrived at a local hospital more than an hour later. There, Danziger survived brain surgery, but his life would never be the same. The doctor had to remove a portion of his brain, leaving him with mobility impairments, slurred speech, poor memory and a proneness to seizures.

After three weeks in the hospital, he was returned to the Texas Department of Criminal Justice (TDCJ) and he was moved from facility to facility over the next few years. Despite his obvious physical and mental disabilities, TDCJ prison officials placed him back in the general population. He repeatedly suffered from seizures and often fell off his bunk onto the concrete. Because his mobility and memory were severely impaired, Richard could not find his way around the prison; guards and inmates often found him lost and crying in a corner. After a year of this, prison officials sought psychological care for the inmate and doctors were able to identify his seizure disorder and prescribe medication.

Late in 1992, he was admitted to crisis management for attempted suicide. TDCJ reports indicated that despite his obvious mental and physical limitations, the TDCJ staff allowed Danziger to self-administer his medications. Consequently, the reports continued to note that he often failed or refused to take his medications and as a consequence suffered from seizures, hallucinations and depression. TDCJ reports also indicated that when staff monitored his medication, Danziger's seizures and hallucinations were controlled. By March 1996, TDCJ records showed he was not receiving proper medication and two months later, he experienced multiple seizures, associated with violent vomiting. Staff notes stated that his physical condition was flat, almost frozen, with no facial expression or eye contact.

A few months later, TDCJ staff found Richard with dried blood and lacerations on his face and a large bruise on his forehead. Records indicated that he had not received medications for four days. After he was given proper medication, his condition improved and he was discharged from crisis management. The discharge report states: *"It is important to note that continued medication compliance is necessary if this patient is to remain in his present state of good remission."*

Yet, his medication status still was not monitored and six months later, he was found in his cell, unresponsive, his clothes soaked in urine and perspiration. The report states that Danziger had not showered, eaten or left his cell for several days. A report the following day said he had not bathed for thirty days and was actively hallucinating.

Apparently, he refused to shower, because he feared the other prisoners would get him alone in the shower and assault him.

In March of 1997, Richard Danziger was moved to the Skyview psychiatric prison in Rusk, Texas.

Jeanette had wanted the killers of her daughter to suffer for the rest of their lives. Nevertheless, if she'd known what was happening to Richard Danziger, her steely resolve might have softened. She wanted the killers' punishment to be within their minds and hearts; she wanted them to think about the life that they took and feel remorse until their own lives ended.

At this point, she didn't know more than that the men being punished had been judged guilty of her daughter's savage death. And she, like the jury, had believed Ochoa's confession and the evidence presented at the trial. Still, even believing Danziger to be guilty, she had no desire for him to endure the physical and mental brutality that certainly must have been sheer torture.

# Chapter 19

# Another Confession?

By 1996, Jeanette was no longer in touch with law enforcement officials in Austin or anyone from the Travis County law enforcement community. She thought she was through with that part of her life. She had no way of knowing she was far from finished with it.

On February 5, an inmate in another TDCJ prison sat down with a pen and some lined notebook paper and began to write a letter, filled with misspelled words and lacking much punctuation, but surprisingly well thought-out and logical. It was addressed to the editor of Austin's daily newspaper:

*Dear Editor,*

*My name is Achim Josef Marino, and I am an inmate in the Texas Prison Systems McConnell Unit at Beeville, Texas. In October of 1988, I shot and killed Nancy Lena Dupriest at the Pizza Hut at Reinli Lane in Austin, Texas. In 1990, while in the Travis County Jail, I heard that two men by the name of Dansinger and Ochoa were convicted for the above offence. I recently became a Christian. When I got out of jail on June 23, 1988, I was possessed by a spirit which came to me one morning in Germany in the mid-sixties. I had just woken up when I felt a overwhelming sense of dread and fear. A serpent dragon type animal rose up out of the floor of my room and looked at me for a second or two, then receded back into the floor. I was so scared that I could not move. Finally, I unfroze and went to my Aunt Elka's room and stood near her while she and my Uncle Jack slept. Moments later, she woke up and screamed and cursed at me to leave the room. During those early years my mother and my aunt treated me with what I perceived as hatred and contempt.*

*From that day forward, I changed for the worse. Days later, I tried to kill my mother by decapitating her with these heavy wooden shutters. In those days, buildings in Germany had massive wooden shutters. They were operated by a belt pull with a sharp metal serrated catch. However, if you pulled the belt down and then held the metal catch, when you let go of the belt, the shutters would then crash down in a loud boom. One day, I saw my mother leaning out of the window and I walked up behind her and let the shutters loose on her, intending to kill her. However, she managed to pull her head in before the shutters could get down. I grew up hating and fearing both my mother and my aunt.*

*I came to the U.S. in 1967. In 1971, a Kansas juvenile judge had me committed to the Martin Schools on Stassney Lane in Austin, Texas for mentally disturbed kids. I was 12 years old. When I was 16, the Martin Schools had to let me go because of lack of funding. In 1976, I went to the Austin State Hospital for a 14 day mental evaluation, but due to my experience at Martin School, I was able to fake my way through the evaluation and get released.*

*In 1982, I went to Texas prison. In May of 1983, I got out. Ten days after I got out, I was arrested for armed robbery. I went back to prison with a fifteen year sentence. I was on psychotropic medication at this time.*

*At first, I was on the Coffield Unit and it was a blood bath. There was no law there. People were being stabbed and dieing all over. I withdrew within myself and just lived a fantasy life in my head. When I got out in 1988, I hated people in general, and women in particular. I was delusionary and came out thinking that in life anything goes. I didn't believe in good or evil, nor God or the Devil. I didn't know the difference anyway.*

*While at Coffield, I got locked up and was kept on the 4th floor of U-Wing. Inmates were burning their mattresses and the guards wouldn't put out the fires. The cotton stuffing would smolder and smoke like crazy, despite being drenched by water. I almost smothered to death numerous times. But no help came. Since then, I remember my past life only in a shadowy sense.*

*In 1988, when I killed Nancy Dupriest, I killed her for two reasons. I didn't want another man having sex with her after me, and I wanted to absorb her life force because I thought I would get better. I wanted to become superior, stronger, physicly and mentaly. When I was in prison I use to read all these fantasy/fiction novels. They had all of these supernatural ritualistic books going around then. I grew up believing every-thing on television, etc., too. The charactors in these books would kill just like eating and breathing. In one book, I read about these psychic vampires from space that could do supernatural stuff after killing someone. And others, just like it. I lived in my head and in these books from 1983 to 1988. Sometimes I'd read three books in one day.*

*The Texas prison system is an evil cesspool. The inmates and guards are all subhuman. You can come in a car thief, but you'll come out a murderer. Emotionally damaged people should not be allowed down here. What ever the problems were, they'll be ten times worse. Particularly a immature and deranged personality. At any rate, I have three reasons for coming to the newspaper. Number one, my conscience and my faith dictate that I come clean and get Dansinger and Ochoa acquitted. I can't bring Nancy Dupriest back, but at least I can try to help those two innocent men. I know that my destiny is the death penalty. But at least my conscience will be a little clearer, but not much.*

*The second reason for this letter is that I believe that I am going to be killed by inmates sometime this week. Prison officials denied my request for protective custody and put me right back into the area of the prison where the inmates who will kill me are. So therefore, for Dansinger and Ochoa sake, I needed to put this on paper, even though by itself, it probably would not help them.*

*Which brings me to my third reason. I have physical evidence from the Pizza Hut, including the keys and money bags. I am afraid that the police will balk at admitting their error and destroy or lose the evidence to cover up their error. I want the newspaper to contact Dansinger and Ochoa's attorneys and set up a meeting between us all so that I can make sure that the police are watched and accompanied when they go and get those items. I use to watch the talk shows every day on television in my cell on Ramsey I. I saw where the authorities balked at releasing innocent people from prison even though the guilty party stepped forward.*

Marino's confession must have sounded to the people at the newspaper like the ramblings of a delusional individual.

*In closing, this world is nothing but a pre-planned distraction, vice, etc. Things are not as they appear. We have all been deceived, mislead and manipulated by the master con, the devil. Crime, racial hatred, religious hatred, class hatred, political hatred are all tools used by the devil to distract us from the truth. . .*

*I hope you will mediate this situation in the interest of justice.*
*Respectfully Yours,*
*Achim J. Marino*
*cc:Elizabeth Watson, Austin Police Department*
*Susan Maldonado, Austin A.C.L.U.*

Apparently neither the editors at the newspaper nor the chief of the Austin Police Department considered the letter a serious confession. Innocent people confessed to crimes all the time. This was just another crackpot. The letter was filed appropriately and life moved on. It wasn't taken seriously so police officials didn't think Jeanette Popp should be told that someone else had confessed to murdering her daughter.

Two years later, on February 17, 1998, Achim Joe Marino wrote a second letter to authorities, going into more detail about his life of crime and his murder of Nancy DePriest. This time he addressed it to the top law enforcement officer in Texas, then-governor George W. Bush:

*Re: Murder Confession.*
*Dear Governor Bush Sir:*
*My name is Achim Josef Marino, and I am currently confined in the McConnell Unit of the TDCJ, serving three life sentences plus three ten-year sentences, for crimes committed at Austin, Texas in late 1988 and 1990. While in Austin in 1988, I also robbed, raped and shot a 20-year-old women at the Pizza Hut at Reinli*

*Lane. This was in late October of 1988, after purchasing the murder weapon via the newspaper's classified section. The womens name was Nancy Lena Dupriest, and I have not been convicted for this crime. Approximately a month after this crime, I was arrested in El Paso, Texas, where the murder weapon was confiscated by the El Paso police department. . .At the time of my arrest, I had the keys as well as two currency bags from the Pizza Hut with the name of Pizza Hut's bank on the bag, in my possession and which remained in my personal property in the county jail for approximately 14 months. A friend in El Paso picked up my personal property after I was transferred to TDCJ for parole violation. She later took these items to my parents home, where they remain to this day. . .*

*. . . In 1990, after I was re-paroled by TDCJ, I was once again arrested in Austin, Texas for robbery, on approximately 3-30-90. While in the county jail, I was told by my cell mate that two men named Dansinger and Ochoa had been convicted for that crime. I told him at that time that they had gotten the wrong people, that I knew the guy who had done it. He then told me that Dansinger and Ochoa had pled guilty to the murder.*

*Governor Bush, Sir, I do not know these men, nor why they pled guilty to a crime they never committed. I can only assume that they must have been facing a capital murder trial with a poor chance of acquittal, but I tell you this, sir, I did this awfull crime and I was alone.*

*Early last year, I wrote the Editor of a Texas newspaper, Chief Elizabeth Watson of the A.P.D. and Ms. Susan Maldonado of the Austin office of the A.C.L.U., confessing to this crime because I believed that I was about to be killed here at the prison, and therefore I wanted to clear my conscience somewhat in regards to the lives of Dansinger, Ochoa and their loved ones. However, the confessions I'd made to these people were ultimately ignored.*

*Now, I make this confession for a different reason. My life is no longer in danger, but my conscience still sickens me. I cannot help Nancy Lena Dupriest or her family, but at least I can attempt to make amends to Dansinger and Ochoa and their loved ones by doing my Christian duty and come clean about this terrible crime, a crime which has been enlarged and magnified by the arrest and conviction of two innocent men. Additionally, I have had a spiritual awakening and conversion, resulting in me becoming a Christian. This is a direct result of joining the Alcoholics*

*Anonymous/Narcotics Anonymous Twelve Step Program, some 21 months ago, and whose 12 steps and guiding principles caused me to have a spiritual awakening,* which ultimately lead me to the answer, Jesus Christ, His Father our Creator, the Holy Spirit, and of course, this confession. The Christian life-style and value system demands that I do this, even at the loss of my life, which I'm fully prepared to lose and expect to loose. I'm deeply sickened, disgusted and mortified for the crime I have committed, as well as my entire past life. I grieve for Nancy Lena Dupriest, her loved ones, as well as those of Dansinger and Ochoa, and also my family. Prior to my Christian conversion and healing, *I was insane.* Nevertheless, there can be no excuses for my crime, because I knew exactly what I was doing. I'm prepared to pay the price for my actions, Governor Bush, Sir. A copy of this letter/confession to you will also be sent to Ronny Earle of the Travis County District Attorney's Office. *I wish to respectfully remind you that in the event that you all decide to once again ignore this confession, that you all are legally and morally obligated to contact Dansinger and Ochoa's attorneys and families concerning this confession.* Thank you. God bless you and your family.

> Yours in Jesus Christ,
> Achim J. Marino

A spokesman for Governor Bush's office relayed that a governor receives about fourteen hundred letters from prisoners each year and, although the spokesman couldn't remember ever receiving another murder confession by letter, he was sure it had not been brought to the governor's attention. More likely, it was given to the governor's general counsel and criminal justice staff. Regardless of who saw the letter, no one responded to it nor did anyone from the governor's office follow up on the letter with the Austin Police Department, Travis County District Attorney or, as Marino had suggested in his letter, either Richard Danziger, Chris Ochoa or their attorneys.

It did not seem necessary, the governor's spokesman said, because Marino had written in his letter that he had already written his allegations to those law enforcement entities.

A month or so after receiving Marino's second letter, the Austin police did institute an investigation in the matter. Apparently, the investigators were acting on the presumption that Marino could have been at the crime scene, along with Danziger and Ochoa. The investigation turned up exactly what Marino had said it would. At his parents' house in El Paso, police found keys to the Pizza Hut and bank bags that had belonged to the store. Then they turned up the gun in the property department of the El Paso police.

Eventually, an Austin police officer and a Texas Ranger went to the prison unit where Chris Ochoa was incarcerated and told him there was another man out there who said he was with Ochoa and Danziger when they killed Nancy DePriest. They did not tell him Marino had written letters to law enforcement officials and the governor's office. Ochoa denied knowing Achim "Joe" Marino. Ochoa said he had never met him and Marino had not been with Danziger and Ochoa when Nancy DePriest was killed.

After listening to the two men's startling disclosures, Ochoa asked, "What if I call Barry Scheck?" Scheck and Peter Neufeld were generating a great deal of publicity for the Innocence Project at the Cardoza School of Law, which they co-founded and co-directed. The Innocence Project is a national litigation and public policy organization dedicated to exonerating wrongfully convicted people through DNA testing and reforming the criminal justice system to prevent further injustices.

When Ochoa posed this question, the police officer gave him a level gaze. "I wouldn't do that if I were you," he said. "You're gonna make it worse for yourself."

# Chapter 20

# The Real Thing

Soon the revelation had taken on a momentum of its own. In August of 2000, Achim Josef Marino was brought to Austin where he made a formal confession in the death of Nancy DePriest. The twenty-one-page document, written in his own hand, covered the things he had written in his letters—and much more:

> My name is Achim Josef Marino and I am a West German national currently serving three concurrent aggravated life sentences in the Texas Department of Criminal Justice, stemming from the 1990 convictions in Travis County, Austin, Texas, in regards to offenses which were committed in both 1988 and 1990. Additionally, I also was serving three concurrent ten year sentences, concurrently with the aforementioned three life sentences stemming from 1990 convictions in Travis County, Austin, Texas...
>
> However, those ten year sentences discharged on 30 May 2000. My parole eligibility date is 30 May 2005...
>
> On 9 December 1999, the Board of Immigration Appeal in Falls Church, Virginia, issued a Final order of Deportation in my case; therefore affirming the order to return me to Germany. As a result, on or about 30 May 2005, due to severe overcrowding problems within the TDCJ and based upon TDCJ precedent set in the

*last ninety days in foreign national inmate cases, I would have received a semi-automatic parole to my country of West Germany. In light of the above facts, the following murder confession, by Achim Josef Marino in regard to the victim twenty-year-old Nancy Lena Dupriest, who was robbed, raped and murdered on or about October/November 1988. . .should be given great weight.*

*. . .On 21 October 1988, I purchased a Ruger .22 caliber semi-automatic pistol with ammunition from a individual I had called on the phone, after seeing his add in the* Austin American Statesman. . .

The confession explained why Marino was driving the borrowed beige four-door automobile. Then the confession continued. . .*I gained entrance to the store on Riverside by deception, telling two males that I was there to do a safety check on their pressurized beverage lines. However, <u>I was there to rob them.</u> Nevertheless, they were suspicious of me and kept a close guard on me to the point where I could not get my gun out of my carryall bag. I then went through the motions of the inspection, and then left. The men saw me get into my car and leave.*

*I then drove to the Pizza Hut on Reinli Lane and gained entrance by the same deception as at the other store. I parked the car south of the Pizza Hut, in their parking lot. I gained entrance through the west facing door by knocking on the door. A young blond women around twenty years of age, unlocked the door and allowed me in. She escorted me to the southeast corner of the store to show me the oxygen tanks and pressurized lines. She then left me. <u>She was wearing no shoes at the time, but I saw nylons on her feet. She also had dark pants, a apron and a pullover shirt on. After she left, I heard the telephone ring and a conversation.</u>*

*<u>I then removed my weapon from my carry-all, went to the woman and ordered her to the men's bathroom (about five or so feet north of the wall telephone).</u>. . .I saw the woman's shoes on the floor by the table she was working at, where a large machine with metal rollers was being used by her to flatten small dough balls into pizza shells. (The men's bathroom is located north of the west side entrance.) After going inside I handcuffed her hands behind her back. I bought three pairs of handcuffs in Austin a week or so before. I then told her I was going to remove her clothing and have sex with her.*

*She looked at me and said, "Please don't. Please don't hurt me."*

*I removed her apron, her pants and her panties, then rolled her pullover shirt and bra over her head. I then escorted her to the southwest corner of the store, where I placed several aprons I found on the floor. I then told the women to lay down on the floor. I entered her vagina with my penis, laying on top of her. I sucked her nipples and sucked her neck at her right side. I orgasmed. I then asked her to go back to the men's room. As she turned her back, I picked up my gun and followed her to the bathroom, where I told her to get under the bathroom counter. I told her that I needed to handcuff her to the drain pipes under the counter, so that I could escape. As she turned her back to me under the counter, I shot her in the back of the head once, on her left side. She fell to the floor and did not move. I then tried to locate the used shell ejected from my gun, but could not find it. I searched everywhere in there, but could not find it. I then turned on the water in the bathroom sinks and closed the drains, in order to flood the restroom out. (The reason I wanted the spent shell was because I had loaded the clip with my bare hands.)*

*I then dragged the woman out of the men's restroom by her feet, to the lobby just a few feet north of the west side door. I flipped her over on her stomach and removed my handcuffs from her, removing her bra and pullover shirt from behind her, off her arms. (I may have done this prior to dragging her into the lobby, but I don't think so. It has been twelve years and I have a damaged memory, due to drug abuse.) I searched her and the clothes for my missing shell but never recovered it. I then wiped the surfaces of the doors, etc., with my blue bandanna, to remove my fingerprints. After that, I pushed my carry-all with one or two Pizza Hut leather money bags and small baggies full of change, nickels, dimes and quarters, etc. Prior to taking the woman to the men's room the first time to undress her and cuff her, I made her open the safe for me, which is located by the south door of the pizza hut and then I took her to the men's restroom. At any rate, after I packed my carry-all, in which I also placed Pizza Huts keys, I unlocked the west side door and left. I do not remember locking this door, though I may have.*

*. . . When I left Pizza Hut that day, Nancy Lena Dupriest was laying on her stomach, five to ten feet north of the west entrance, her head pointing west, her feet pointing east.*

Next, Marino told of going to a friend's home and stopping at a gas station to fill up his car's tank, for which he paid with the change from the Pizza Hut—about twelve dollars in all. He said he also gave his friend ten dollars in cash from the robbery. Then he detailed his actions for the next several days, traveling with friends to Houston and then to El Paso. He lived there with a woman friend until November 26, 1988, when they had an argument at the bus station, in which he threatened to shoot her. Later that day, El Paso police arrested him. He had his carry-all bag with him and the police discovered a Ruger .22 caliber semi-automatic, three pairs of handcuffs, Pizza Hut keys and leather money bags.

In Marino's confession, he recounted his spiritual experience in which he became a Christian, as well as his supernatural experience in Germany when he was a child. In giving his legal history, he said that from 1975 to early 1995, he used PCP, cocaine, weed and alcohol, as well as paper acid.

*Because of my mental maladies, depending on whether I was normal or psychotic, I might have either good trips or bad trips. When I was released in June of 1988, I was psychotic on a continuous basis, without drug use. I did not think or know that it was wrong to rob, rape or kill, etc. Further, I was required by the voices and Abbadon to perform a sacrifice to them. This was the mental state I was in when I got out of prison in 1988 and the rest is history.*

*. . .I wrote the first murder confession, because I believed that two innocent men, Ochoa and Dansinger, had been convicted for the robbery, rape and murder of Nancy Lena Dupriest. As a Christian, I had a duty to act at once. That confession was ignored. Two years later . . . I wrote the second confession in a Christian attempt to make amends and to exonerate innocent persons convicted for my evil offense. I do not know, nor have I ever met, Ochoa or Dansinger. Further, on the day that I committed these crimes. . .I acted alone.*

*. . .Let's face it, I got away with this crime, and after Ochoa and Dansinger got convicted, I was home free. Further, because of TDCJ overcrowding and the emergency release of foreign national inmates who have "Final order of deportation," I would have*

been "outta here" by no later than 30 May 2005. This statement therefore is credible.

Respectfully Submitted,
Achim J. Marino
22 August 2000

## Chapter 21

# Another Nightmare

Every morning when Jeanette Popp awoke, her first thought was of her daughter, Nancy. In that waking instant each day, she lay with her eyes closed and said a prayer for Nancy. Today was a little different. It was October 24, 2000. Exactly twelve years to the day since Nancy was killed. She said her prayer for Nancy and gave thanks to God for Jim Popp, her wonderful husband of ten years, the man Jeanette was convinced God had sent to save her.

Now, twelve years after Nancy's death, she could think of the way Nancy had lived more than of the way she had died. At times Jeanette smiled at the memory of her daughter, vital, alive, happy. And she breathed a prayer of thanksgiving that the recurrent nightmare, in which Nancy had begged Jeanette to help her, came rarely now.

Jeanette's reverie was shattered by the sound of the telephone loudly ringing. She glanced at the clock. Just after seven.

"Jeanette!" Her brother-in-law, speaking rapidly, almost incoherently. "You need to turn on the TV," he said. "There's something about Nancy on one of the morning shows."

"What?" she demanded. "What about Nancy?"

"Turn on the television," he said again, talking about what he had seen and heard, talking so fast it was almost incomprehensible to her. "They're talking about Nancy's death and the men convicted and another man who's apparently confessed."

"Confessed what?" Confused, Jeanette fumbled with the TV remote control and found the channel her brother-in-law had mentioned. She saw the face of Ronnie Earle, District Attorney of Travis County, telling a national television audience that Richard Danziger and Christopher Ochoa probably were not guilty of raping and murdering her daughter.

She was stunned. Ochoa had confessed and Danziger had been found guilty and she had sat through that entire, horrible ordeal of a trial and heard the confession. And now, Earle was saying they might not be guilty?

She sat in shocked disbelief, still holding the phone to her ear, hardly comprehending Earle's words. A third man, named Marino, also a prison inmate, had confessed to the killing. Had been confessing for four years. Now, the Austin Police Department and the District Attorney's office had opened an investigation. At the request of attorneys from the Wisconsin Innocence Project, Ochoa's DNA had been tested against samples from the DePriest case, and those tests indicated he was telling the truth when he said he did not rape her. The name Achim Josef Marino was completely unfamiliar to Jeanette. Who was this Marino and how did he figure in her daughter's death? Throughout most of the segment and after she turned off the TV, she sat slumped in sorrow, tears running down her cheeks.

Then a sudden rush of anger coursed through her, almost overwhelming in its intensity. Hadn't she heard, with her own ears, Ochoa testifying that they were guilty of repeatedly raping Nancy and murdering her? "If they want to let those two killers go free, it will be over my dead body," she said aloud. "I won't allow this to happen."

Then another thought flashed through her mind like a rocket blasting through space. For twelve years, she had lived with nightmarish visions of Nancy being repeatedly raped and sodomized, begging for her life. What if Ochoa had *not* told the truth? What if Nancy's attack had not been as brutal, as dehumanizing, as she had thought all these years? Jeanette had to know the truth of what had happened to her daughter. She took a deep breath, picked up the phone again and called the office of the Travis County District Attorney.

Ronnie Earle was not there, of course. He was telling the awful story about Nancy's death and the two men prosecuted on national television. Jeanette was shunted around until an Assistant District Attorney, who gave her name as Rosemary Lehmberg, picked up the phone. Jeanette identified herself to the woman and demanded to know why she hadn't been informed about what had been happening.

"I'm sorry you weren't notified," Lehmberg said. "We have been keeping your son-in-law apprised of the situation."

"Well, he didn't tell me and I think it is your responsibility to let me know."

"Perhaps," Lehmberg murmured. "But please, don't jump to conclusions, Mrs. Popp."

Jeanette asked whether Marino's DNA had been compared with samples taken from Nancy's body. Rosemary told her it had. "We performed the tests and Marino definitely assaulted your daughter."

"What about DNA from Ochoa and Danziger?" Jeanette asked. "Did you run tests on theirs, too?"

"Yes, we did," Rosemary stated. Silence built between the two women.

"Well?" Jeanette demanded.

"We can't find their DNA."

For a moment, Jeanette was speechless. What did this mean, was it lost? The Assistant DA just said it had been tested. Jeanette shook her head in bewilderment. "What do you mean, you can't find their DNA?"

According to the Assistant DA, it was their theory that Marino raped Nancy last and covered up their DNA.

Jeanette's anger flared again. "Excuse me!" she snapped. "You are not talking to a child. If there are three DNA samples, there are three DNA samples. I don't care who went last. If you did a vaginal swab, you got them all. If there was only one sample, then only one man raped my daughter! If one man raped Nancy, then Christopher Ochoa's story of repeated attacks on my daughter is not true."

Lehmberg gave no answer to Jeanette's anguished words. But after more sharp prodding from Jeanette, Lehmberg revealed that Marino had also told authorities where to find a gun that had been tested against the brass casing found at the scene and it was definitely the murder weapon. He also told them where to find Nancy's keys to the Pizza Hut where she was killed. Along with those items were bank bags bearing the name of the bank where Pizza Hut had its account. Marino said he had taken the bags when he robbed the store before assaulting Nancy. These things had been found at his parents' house two years earlier.

"Two years?" Jeanette cried in astonishment. Thinking her heart would surely break, she asked again: "The District Attorney's office has known about this for two years? And they never told anyone? They did nothing about the two men rotting in jail? They never told me?"

Lehmberg said no more on the subject.

Lehmberg then told Jeanette about the two confessions Achim Josef Marino had written. Even though Jeanette begged her, the assistant DA refused to tell Jeanette what the confessions contained, except that Marino said he had raped and killed Nancy.

Jeanette took a deep, heavy breath and exhaled slowly, trying to maintain some semblance of composure. "How long has your department been looking for a link between Marino and these two men?" she wanted to know.

There was a long, heavy moment before the woman answered.

"Four years."

Jeanette's heart seemed as if it would burst. Why, if they had known about this confession for four years, wasn't something done about it? What kind of justice was that?

So many dark thoughts flew through Jeanette's mind, she couldn't sort them out. Why had the District Attorney's office waited so long to investigate this apparent miscarriage of justice? Why had they spent so many years trying to establish that Marino, Danziger and Ochoa knew each other? That all three were involved in Nancy's death? Did they really believe that scenario was possible or were they just resistant to the truth—that the Austin Police Department and their own office had sent two innocent men to prison for life?

"Then you're not likely to find a link, are you?" Jeanette said tautly. Lehmberg didn't answer that question. Jeanette didn't think she had gotten the whole story from Lehmberg, but she didn't know what to do to get it. The woman kept returning to the subject of a link between Marino and the convicted men. Jeanette felt at this point there was none. Finally Jeanette ended the call. She sat there stunned. Then she remembered something she had heard Earle say on the television show. He'd said that Ochoa was being represented by the Wisconsin Innocence Project.

Immediately, Jeanette sat down at her computer and sent the Innocence Project an email. *I am Nancy DePriest's mother*, she wrote. *And I want to talk to you.*

While she waited for a response from Wisconsin, Jeanette went online and discovered that the case actually was under review and that Ochoa and Danziger were likely to be set free.

Soon she came on an article that had appeared in the *Washington Post* a week earlier. The reporter apparently had interviewed Ochoa's attorneys, as well as attorneys and others who had been involved in the prosecution of Ochoa and Danziger. Through the newspaper story, Jeanette found out that several years earlier, Achim Josef Marino had mailed a confession to Texas officials, including then-governor George W. Bush, whose office did not follow up on the letter. It was only recently that law enforcement officials gave the matter a high priority, after professors and students from the Wisconsin Innocence Project began looking into the case. According to Ochoa's attorneys, the story went on: "the re-examination of the case is yielding a tale of Texas's tough law and order system gone awry—a system Bush, in his Republican presidential campaign, repeatedly has described as fair, efficient and loaded with safeguards."

The *Post* story quoted a Bush spokesman as saying the governor's office did not follow up on the letter it received in February 1998, because in it Marino said he had already written to Austin's police chief and the District Attorney.

If Marino had not mentioned those other letters, the spokesman said, "we would have referred it to the most appropriate agency." He said it was highly unlikely that Bush was even told about the letter.

As Jeanette read on and on, sadness and pain gripped her. It seemed that instead of justice for her daughter, all that had been gained was two more tragic victims.

"The governor's office doesn't investigate cases," the spokesman said. He released a copy of the letter from the governor's office files. In the letter, Marino told authorities where to find the keys and money bags that he said he stole from the Pizza Hut.

The story went on to say that, according to Ochoa's attorneys, by the time that letter was sent to Bush, Austin police, acting on an earlier Marino letter, had found the keys and money bags in April 1996. Yet for four years, for reasons that are unclear, no action was taken to free the two men. To those attorneys, the two men's case history offered disturbing examples of the abuses and mistakes that can occur in the criminal justice process, including the failure of authorities to rectify an injustice after evidence of it first surfaced in Marino's letter.

Barry Scheck, co-founder of the Innocence Project at the Cardoza School of Law in New York, who was working with the Wisconsin advocates to gain freedom for the two men, boldly stated, "Nobody can tell me that in this case, the death penalty element was not uniquely corruptive. Ochoa confessed, because they threatened to execute him."

The *Post* reporter had also talked to Berke Bettis, Richard Danziger's attorney at his trial. "Frankly, I'd like to throttle Ochoa," Bettis said. "He got on the witness stand and took my client and he sent him to the joint, where Danziger got the crap beat out of him—ruined his life. It was a damn cowardly, miserable thing to do.

"Maybe I'm just trying to be vicariously angry for Danziger, because I don't know if he's even capable of being angry on his own anymore."

Bettis said about Chris Ochoa's witness-stand performance, "He convinced me. By the time the trial was over, I had no reason to doubt that my client was guilty."

According to Ochoa's Austin attorney, William Allison, his client was able to testify in great detail about the murder, because homicide detectives had filled his head with information during the interrogation. "They showed him crime scene photos, they showed him autopsy photos, they showed him everything," Allison said. "Every fact that Ochoa had came from the police, because he had no facts himself."

Jeanette began to search the web and newspaper files. She had to know the whole truth, know all that had not been told to her about Nancy's death and killer. In an online story on Salon.com, Jeanette found out that District Judge Robert Perkins, who had presided at Danziger's trial, said that Ochoa's testimony was very compelling and "any jury hearing that testimony would have found those two guys guilty." The judge was particularly taken by the amount of firsthand details Ochoa divulged in addition to his emotional testimony.

Ochoa's attorneys were now insisting that the investigators on the case had forced their client to lie in his confession and testimony. "He was made to feel he was doomed one way or the other. His doom could either be death or it could be life in prison," an Innocence Project lawyer said.

Allison said the police provided Ochoa with a plausible story coupled with significant facts from the crime scene. "There isn't any way he would have known the facts about the case unless they told him," Allison said. He believed the police "violated every rule of taking down a statement that you can violate. The invocation of asking for a lawyer should have stopped the interrogation at that point." Allison also suspected that Ochoa was given case information during his interrogations and that a critical tape recording of the interrogation, occurring just prior to the confession, had mysteriously disappeared.

The Salon.com story also quoted Rhonda Shore, Richard Danziger's former girlfriend, as saying her examination with the same detectives was "the most horrific, the most horrible experience I've ever been through in my life. I had nightmares about this forever." She said that in addition to threats of having her children taken from her, the detectives also attempted to connect her to the murder. "They threatened that if Richard gets out he's going to hunt me down and kill me like he did Nancy DePriest. They told me Richard had told Chris that I'm the one who supplied the gun. Another time they said, 'Your boyfriend's holding her head and you're the one who pulled the trigger for your little love interest.'"

As Jeanette read on, she learned to her horror that Ochoa had spent those twelve years in two medium security units, first at Coffield Prison near Tennessee Colony and then at the state prison in Huntsville. Ochoa's uncle said that at first his nephew was "shocked" and "really didn't know how to handle" his incarceration. The uncle feared Ochoa was giving up hope as he slipped into a depression. "He thought he was going to die there. I kept telling him to keep his faith up, to try to keep positive thoughts in mind."

Ochoa's uncle and his mother were quoted as saying that while in prison, Ochoa maintained good relations with the wardens and received sufficient jobs while also obtaining two college diplomas in business administration and in computer science.

According to his attorneys, Ochoa told his uncle, "They made me confess and how am I going to prove my innocence now? It's my word against theirs."

Jeanette was already incredulous and exhausted from her research and resurging pain when she came on another story, this one in the *New York Times*, reported on the release of a Texas prisoner, convicted by the Travis County District Attorney, who had just been freed based on DNA evidence. In commenting on the release, District Attorney Ronnie Earle said that this was a great tragedy for both the wrongly convicted man and the community. "Austin has always prided itself on its values and there is no higher value than justice," he said.

Earle also announced that as a result of this, his office had started reexamining more than four hundred convictions to see if other miscarriages of justice could be corrected through DNA testing. These cases were convictions prior to when DNA testing technology became available in 1994. Cases to be reviewed included any involving a continuing claim of innocence, a questionable identity of the suspect or an outcome that could be affected by DNA evidence.

Barry Scheck was working with Earle on the structure and methods of the review panel.

Scheck said the fact that Texas law did not require DNA testing after a conviction made the review panel in Travis County noteworthy. The panel was unique in both the investigation and the prosecutors' approach.

"This shows that there are prosecutors who are willing to seek the truth and correct injustices, no matter how embarrassing it might be," Scheck told the *Times*. "That's an important principle."

Meanwhile, Texas State Senators Rodney Ellis and David Sibley, a Democrat and a Republican, were preparing to introduce legislation in January that would require such access to DNA testing.

After digesting all the new information she could find about her daughter's death, Ochoa, Danziger and the probable real killer, Jeanette was even more anxious to talk to the people in Wisconsin. After what seemed like eons to Jeanette, but which actually was only a couple of days, they returned her email and set up a conference call with her the following day. Unable to rest or sleep, she thought the moment for the phone call would never come. But it did. First, the lawyers for the project apologized profusely for causing Jeanette to have to relive Nancy's murder, the most horrendous event of Jeanette's life. She accepted the apology, grateful that the men were sensitive enough to understand how traumatic this new investigation could be for her. Her next thought wasn't so charitable. She felt Ronnie Earle should be the one apologizing. For at least four years, he hadn't told her what was happening so she accepted that Ochoa's story of the humiliation and torture of her daughter was true when it wasn't.

"I almost had a heart attack when I got your email," one of the men told her. "I thought you were going to give us all sorts of problems."

Jeanette assured him that causing problems was not her intention. She just wanted to get the real truth from them. "I need to know what you know," she said.

For two hours they talked, telling her what they had learned to that point.

First, they told her that the medical examiner for Travis County had recently amended the autopsy report he performed on Nancy. Now, the man was saying he was mistaken about Nancy being sodomized. The rectal tearing had been caused by a procedure done at the hospital, while she was still on the respirator.

The law professors told her of Achim Josef Marino's letters, the first of which was written in 1996, confessing to the crime. There also was a sixteen-page letter Marino had sent to then-governor George W. Bush, whose office said he wasn't legally obligated to pass the letter on to the proper authorities. The letter had gathered dust in the files of the governor's office for four years.

Then, there was the formal confession given to police in August of 2000. According to Ochoa's new lawyers, Ochoa had told them that Austin homicide detectives had coerced a false confession from him, breaking him psychologically, then force-feeding him details of the murder that only the actual killer would know. That coerced confession was then used to convict Danziger.

The lawyers promised to send her copies of the amended autopsy report, Marino's letters and his confession, as well as a summary of Danziger's trial transcript. These arrived the following day. Soon thereafter, the group sent Jeanette the complete trial transcript.

Jeanette wanted to know what they had done to help bring freedom to Christopher Ochoa and Richard Danziger. And they told her. She breathed a heavy sigh of relief.

A few days later, Barry Scheck called Jeanette, thanking her for believing in what the Wisconsin Innocence Project was doing.

"I just want to know what I can do to help," she told him.

"What we need most right now," he told her, "is publicity. The public needs to know what has happened to these two innocent men. The public needs to put pressure on Austin law enforcement officials to set them free."

"What can I do?" she asked.

"Go to the media. The newspapers. TV. Radio. Tell them what has happened and make a plea to Ronnie Earle to free those men."

Jeanette agreed. "I'm going to do just that." But before she embarked on that path, she wrote a letter to Chris Ochoa, pledging to help him gain his freedom:

*Dear Chris,*

*I hope it's o.k. if I call you Chris. My name is Jeanette Popp. I am Nancy's mother. I don't know exactly how to start. There are no words to express my sorrow at all the horrible things that have happened to you. I cannot imagine the fear you must* have felt that would make you believe that the confession was the only way to save your life. I have only found out about all this on October 24, 2000. I was so shocked, I really didn't know what to do or what to think. I now believe with all my heart that you and Richard are innocent. I can never make up to you and your family for what you have suffered.

I do want you to know I will do anything I can to hasten your release. I have been in touch with your attorneys and told them I want very much to help you and Richard. I feel so guilty. The loss of Nancy was completely devastating to my life. But now, if in some way I can help the two of you, maybe it will help me. Two wrongs never make a right. What happened to Nancy was wrong and then what has happened to you has only made it worse. Nancy would want me to do everything in my power to right this wrong. I have told the D.A. that my family and I want them to rush this up as quickly as possible. I have told her that I believe in your innocence. I hope it helps. To your family, I can only say I am so very sorry. I pray for all of you each night. That God will watch over you, keep you safe from any further persecution and bless you with a speedy release and a new and happy life. If there is anything I can do for you or your family, please let me know. I would like very much to meet you, if that would be agreeable to you. I feel I need to see you face to face and tell you how sorry I am. May God bless and keep you all the days of your life.

Sincerely,
Jeanette Popp

Next, keeping her word to attorney Barry Scheck to contact as many news sources as she could, Jeanette first called her local newspaper, the *Azle News*. The editor immediately sent a reporter to interview her and they spent several hours together.

Later, seeing the story, Jeanette felt the reporter had conveyed not only what she said but also how she felt.

The reporter recounted Jeanette's account of Nancy's death, Chris Ochoa's confession and Richard Danziger's conviction for sexual assault. Then he summarized the confessions made by Achim Josef Marino and told about the lawyers who had been working for

Chris Ochoa's release since the fall of 1998. They had begun their work after Ochoa had written the Wisconsin Innocence Project, a group at the University of Wisconsin that focuses on the use of DNA evidence to overturn murder convictions.

The newspaper piece pointed out that Danziger and Ochoa might be exonerated by the use of recent scientific advances in DNA testing. Although DNA testing was available in 1988, the story said, it didn't have the discriminating powers that had now become available.

The article referred to Jeanette's call to Rosemary Lehmberg, the Travis County Assistant District Attorney who was working on the case. She had told Jeanette they had two specific rounds of DNA tests done. A California doctor had tested a DNA sample from the crime to see if DNA was present from the two convicted men. It was not found.

Another recent DNA test indicated that Achim Marino's DNA was present, but those results had not yet been officially announced.

A third test was being done that might shed more light on the situation, Lehmberg had told Jeanette. Some hair from the crime scene had been sent to another lab for mitochondrial DNA testing. Her office was looking to have the results back within two weeks and they were hoping to announce the results at that time.

According to the article, the District Attorney's office was having the weapon Marino claimed to have used tested by a ballistics expert.

And, wrote the reporter, lawyers for Ochoa had stated that although he confessed to the murder, it was coerced by police. The story quoted one of the law students working on the case as saying, "The police held rather long interrogations of twelve hours apiece. They made him feel that they had him and that if he didn't confess, he would get the death penalty. They told him that Danziger had confessed, then they tapped him on the arm and told him that was where the needle would go (for lethal injection)."

Ochoa's lawyers also cited recent news reports indicating the detective who interviewed Ochoa was fired years later for giving perjured testimony.

Jeanette was quoted as saying, "The new DNA evidence and scenarios are entirely possible, as Danziger proclaimed his innocence throughout the trial." She said she was absolutely certain Ochoa was intimidated by the police, because she remembered him at the trial as being timid and mild, seeming like a person who could be influenced by others.

A moving statement from Jeanette concluded the article: "I don't want Nancy to be forgotten in all of this. She is very important to me in my life. At the same time, don't forget Ochoa's and Danziger's families. There are three mothers and three children involved here. I can't bring my child back, but I will do everything in my power to bring their sons back."

Other newspapers as well as broadcast media picked up the story. Jeanette became a media maven as the situation gained a great deal of publicity in the next weeks. Not enough to satisfy Jeanette, however, because she hoped that the two men would be free by Christmas, able to enjoy the holidays with their families. It didn't happen.

However, there was some news that both encouraged Jeanette and fed her fury over the injustice that had been done, not only to Chris Ochoa and Richard Danziger, but to herself and her daughter as well.

On December 22, a Texas newspaper reported that Austin Chief of Police Stanly L. Knee called in Texas Rangers and the United States Attorney's office to help the police review whether officer misconduct contributed to the wrongful conviction of Chris Ochoa and Richard Danziger. In announcing the unprecedented investigation, Knee said there was insufficient evidence to link the two men to Nancy's murder.

Jeanette couldn't believe her eyes as she read on and the article pointed out that Knee's conclusion came almost five years after Achim Marino confessed to the crime and amid mounting evidence, including DNA analysis, that Ochoa and Danziger were wrongly convicted.

Knee said that two rangers would assist a team of Austin officers under Assistant Chief James Fealy in reconstructing the twelve-year-old investigation to determine whether homicide detectives violated policy or broke any laws. The team's report was expected in about five weeks, he said, and would be given to him and then reviewed by federal prosecutors. The key question for the panel reviewing the investigation was whether Ochoa's confession was obtained illegally or whether he lied about killing Nancy DePriest, for some reason known only to himself.

Knee insisted that his department had nothing at that time to indicate any misconduct by any police officer. However, Jeanette felt that when the chief can't tell you how two people can be sent to prison for several years without any evidence to connect them to the crime, he needs to look into it.

One of the officers under investigation, now in the office of professional standards, would not comment; an attorney for the second man said the officer did nothing wrong. The third officer had died in the interim.

Travis County prosecutors had already scrutinized the police department's small homicide unit for alleged shoddy work and allegations of coercing confessions. The county probe included cases from 1986 to 1992, but did not include the DePriest case.

At that time, the DA's office looked at allegations of officers posing as state child caseworkers and immigration officials and threatening suspects and witnesses that their children would be taken by the State or their families would get deported.

No criminal charges were instituted as a result of the District Attorney's investigation, but the police department increased the number of homicide detectives, increased funding for forensics and improved training on how to interview suspects.

The same homicide department was again under intense scrutiny and Knee, who was hired as chief in 1997, said, "I thought it best to bring in two investigators who had never been associated with the homicide unit."

Defense lawyers were going to ask District Judge Bob Perkins to overturn Ochoa's conviction on January 16. Danziger's lawyers would ask for a similar hearing, but first wanted to arrange for his care, since he had serious brain damage as a result of the severe beating in prison more than a decade earlier.

The situation was hard for Jeanette to accept, but she already knew from Ochoa's attorneys that there were problems with the police interrogations of Ochoa. As a child, Jeanette had been taught that policemen are our friends. If she was ever in trouble, she should find the nearest police officer. She should never doubt anything a police officer told her. The police were the good guys. She could believe what they said. She could trust them. They would protect her and keep her safe. There had never been any reason for Jeanette to harbor the slightest suspicion that police officers could lie and coerce others to lie as well. Until now.

Now that Jeanette knew the date for Ochoa's hearing, she made plans to attend, with the blessing of his attorneys. Producers for the *Nightline* television show asked to interview her prior to the hearing and she agreed to meet them in Austin, where they were filming the show in a hotel.

Jeanette was sitting in the hotel lobby, waiting to be called for her interview, when a woman in a dark suit approached her. "Are you Jeanette Popp?" the woman asked.

"Yes, I am."

The woman offered her hand. "I'm Rosemary Lehmberg. We've talked before."

Jeanette shook hands and said she remembered their phone conversation two months earlier.

"What are you doing here?" Lehmberg asked.

"I'm here to do the *Nightline* show," Jeanette answered. "I guess you already know that, though."

"What are you going to tell them?"

Jeanette, deciding she should be on the same footing with the other woman, stood up. "I'm going to tell them about the horrible injustice that has been done here."

"Are you planning to be here for Ochoa's hearing next week?" Lehmberg asked.

"Yes, I am," Jeanette said firmly.

"Fine. We'll book all your travel arrangements, take care of your hotel and we will brief you before court."

Jeanette raised her eyebrows quizzically. "That isn't necessary. All my arrangements have been made. Thank you very much, though."

"By whom?" Lehmberg asked.

"By Barry Scheck."

"I see." Then she told Jeanette she needed to report to the District Attorney's office before going to court.

Taken back, Jeanette stammered. "No. I—I don't have to. No," she said more firmly. "I won't." She turned and walked away.

## Chapter 22

# The Hearing

Jeanette got ready for Chris Ochoa's hearing with mixed feelings. She was excited that he was, more than likely, going to become a free man. At the same time, she was fearful as well. What could she say to comfort this man who had lost not only his freedom, but also his youth and his dreams to a flawed legal system? Intellectually, she knew it was not her fault that Chris had languished in prison for more than a decade. Nevertheless, she felt somehow guilty, maybe because she had felt so strongly that justice for her daughter had been done when he and Richard Danziger had been sent to prison. She had believed with all her heart that he was guilty. She had *wanted* to believe he was guilty. That was the only way she had been able to cope with the loss of her daughter. So now she didn't know how to face him or what to say to him.

And how was she going to face his mother? A woman whose grief must have been as intense as her own? Yet Jeanette felt she had to be there to do and say what she could. Surely Nancy would have wanted this.

Outside the door to the courtroom, she took a deep breath. She would tell them how sorry she was that they had all suffered such a horrendous injustice. For now, that was all she could do.

Inside the room, she was met by Bill Allison, the Austin attorney who was representing Chris, along with Lester Pray, Keith Findley and Rhonda Klein of the Wisconsin Innocence Project and Barry Scheck. They greeted her warmly. Then Allison led her to a row of seats immediately behind the plaintiff's table and introduced her to Chris Ochoa's mother. Jeanette looked at the older woman, noting the dark eyes still filled with sadness, even today when her son would become a free man. Perhaps, Jeanette thought, the woman had felt hopeless for so long, it was difficult, if not impossible, to summon any hope. Jeanette took both her hands firmly in her own.

"I am so, so sorry for what has happened to your family," Jeanette choked out, tears burning her eyes.

The woman nodded and tears began to trickle down her cheeks. For a moment the two mothers stood, clasping hands, lost in the enormity of the moment. Then they embraced, their tears mingling as their cheeks touched. Afterward they sat down, side by side, still holding hands.

To court observers, it might have seemed strange to see the two mothers in that first row, one waiting to welcome her wrongly imprisoned son to freedom, the other one still grieving for the daughter she would never see again.

For the first time, Jeanette noticed that Rosemary Lehmberg had entered the room and was standing beside a table across the aisle with other people, presumably her associates from the District Attorney's office. Jeanette knew one of the men with Lehmberg must be Bryan Case, the Assistant District Attorney who would be representing their department that day. Lehmberg abruptly turned and came toward Jeanette.

Leaning over the railing that separated the spectators from the participants, she said, "Well, I see you made it."

Jeanette nodded. "Yes, I did. And I had a very pleasant trip."

Nodding but saying nothing more, Lehmberg strode back to her group.

A stir among the attorneys drew Jeanette's attention and she saw a side door open and Christopher Ochoa being escorted into the room. He stopped at the table to greet his attorneys, but his gaze was on his mother. Bill Allison motioned Ochoa to be seated and the group of attorneys sat at the table with him.

A bailiff entered and announced the appearance of Judge Bob Perkins, the same judge who had presided over Richard Danziger's trial and the same one who had pronounced a life sentence for Chris Ochoa over a decade before.

The first order of business was to enter into the record the Stipulation of Evidence to which both Chris Ochoa's attorneys and Bryan Case for the District Attorney's office had agreed. This section stated that if various witnesses from the Austin Police Department, the Travis County Sheriff's Office, the Texas Department of Public Safety's DNA Crime Lab, Chris Ochoa and the Texas Department of Corrections Institutional Division were called to testify in the hearing, they would truthfully testify under oath and introduce documentation and other reliable evidence to establish certain facts. Beginning with the first questioning of Christopher Ochoa until the present day, these facts were entered into the record.

An Application for Writ of Habeas Corpus for Christopher Ochoa was entered next.

When it came time for the Findings of Fact and Conclusions of Law, Jeanette's rapt attention was riveted on them from the beginning revelations.

The first fact was that the applicant, Christopher Ochoa, was brought to the Austin Police Department Headquarters on November 11, 1988, for questioning in the capital murder of Nancy DePriest in Austin, Texas, which had occurred in Austin on October 24, 1988. On November 11, 1988, Chris Ochoa was twenty-two years old and had never before been in police custody.

Jeanette's aching mind could hardly digest the number of disturbing clues which should have prompted the police to question their veracity.

The second fact was that on the morning of November 11, 1988, Sergeant Bruce Boardman was dispatched to the place where Ochoa worked in order to bring him in for questioning. Ochoa was briefly questioned by Sergeant Boardman before being turned over to Sergeant Hector Polanco and Detective Ed Balagia in the homicide unit. The two investigators then interrogated Chris Ochoa for the remainder of Friday, November 11, and all day Monday, November 14, 1988, until ten o'clock that night. Chris Ochoa initially insisted he had no involvement in the offense. Over the course of these two days of questioning, Ochoa produced two written statements, each typed by one of the officers, but each signed by Christopher Ochoa. In the first statement, Ochoa said Richard Danziger admitted to him he was the lone perpetrator of the capital murder of Nancy DePriest. The second, a more lengthy and detailed statement, admitted participation in the robbery, rape and murder of Nancy DePriest, but stated that Richard Danziger had shot her.

Another fact: Saturday and Sunday, November 12 and 13, 1988, the Austin Police Department rented a room for Ochoa at a hotel on Town Lake in Austin, Texas, and told him not to leave. According to Ochoa, he was told that, because of his cooperation against Richard Danziger, there was a chance that Danziger might try to come after him. Christopher Ochoa did as he was told.

More disclosures: Officers from the homicide unit picked up Ochoa from the hotel early Monday morning and began questioning him at the homicide detail. A tape recording exists of Ochoa being questioned from noon until 1:00 P.M. that day. During this interview, Ochoa was recorded as stating that he went to the Pizza Hut with Richard Danziger, but that he remained across the street, leaving when he heard a shot coming from inside the store. The tape-recorded interview exists and had been transcribed prior to the 1990 trial.

Then, between 1:00 P.M. and 5:00 P.M., further tape-recorded interviewing took place. This tape recording does not now exist and did not exist at the time of the 1990 trial.

The next was that Chris Ochoa gave a tape-recorded statement to Lieutenant Manuel Fuentes of the Austin Police Department and Texas Ranger Sal Abrero on August 29, 2000, at the Texas Department of Criminal Justice, Institutional Division's Wynne Unit in Huntsville, Texas. In this interview, Ochoa made seven statements. Now it was sure that they had been not false but true.

The first statement was that Ochoa said one of his interrogators told him he was going to get "the needle" if he did not cooperate. Ochoa understood this to mean the death penalty.

Second, according to the statement, the detective told Ochoa that he was "fresh meat" and that he was going to put Ochoa "downstairs" where other inmates were going to "have (him)." Chris understood this to mean he was going to be raped.

Third, Chris asked for a lawyer but was told by an unidentified female officer that he was not entitled to a lawyer until he was charged with a crime.

Fourth, Chris was told that Richard Danziger was in the next room "fixing to talk" and that if he did not talk first, Richard was going to talk. Chris understood this to mean that Richard would be the one to get the benefit of cooperating with the police.

Fifth, Ochoa stated that during the afternoon of the interrogation on Monday, November 14, 1988, Detective Balagia said to Chris, "I'm tired of you." The detective then picked up a chair and threw it at him. The chair went over his head and bounced off the wall; the detective caught it before it hit Chris in the head. Chris thought the officers were going to beat him up.

Sixth, Chris said that all of the operative facts of the crime that he recited in his statements came from the Austin Police Department officers who were questioning him. These facts were either supplied to him directly by autopsy photos and discussions of the crime scene or through corrections when he said something that did not comport with known facts.

Seventh, the interrogation on the afternoon of November 14, 1988, was being tape-recorded. However, at some point in the questioning, the officers got frustrated at Chris for his stuttering and his inability to remember the facts correctly. They had been stopping the tape, talking with him about his "mistakes, then turning the tape back on and continuing. Finally, they shut off the tape recorder and began typing the second statement."

Jeanette turned pale as other revelations were now piled on the already shocking disclosures: On March 7, 1989, a third and final written statement was given to the Austin Police Department after Chris showed "deception" on a polygraph question about whether or not Richard Danziger shot Nancy DePriest. The polygraph examination was given at the Travis County District Attorney's office. This third statement changed Chris's assertion in his second statement that Richard Danziger shot Nancy DePriest and stated that he, Christopher Ochoa, was the shooter.

Fact: In the fulfillment of the terms of a plea agreement that he would not be exposed to the death penalty, Chris pled guilty to first degree felony murder on May 5, 1989, before the Honorable Robert Perkins in the 331 District Court for Travis County, Texas. The sentencing was postponed.

Fact: Richard Danziger was tried before a jury commencing on January 23, 1990, Honorable Robert Perkins presiding. As required under the terms of the plea agreement, Chris Ochoa testified as a witness for the State. His testimony was generally consistent with his confessions of November 14, 1988, and March 7, 1989. The jury found Danziger guilty of the only offense charged in the indictment, aggravated sexual assault. He was sentenced to life in prison.

Fact: On March 6, 1990, Chris was sentenced by the Honorable Bob Perkins to life in prison.

Fact: The Austin Police Department and the Travis County District Attorney's office received letters from a Texas prison inmate named Achim Josef Marino confessing to the murder, sexual assault and robbery of Nancy DePriest. Subsequently, Achim Marino gave videotaped statements to the Austin Police Department and an Austin television station in addition to a handwritten statement. In his statements, he stated that in the summer of 1990, while in Travis County Jail on other charges, he became aware that two people had been convicted of the Pizza Hut murder. Marino did not act on this knowledge until 1996, when, motivated by a religious conversion, he wrote a confession to the crime stating that he did not believe Chris Ochoa or Richard Danziger should be incarcerated for a crime that he alone committed. Marino stated he was aware that he was confessing to a crime for which he could be punished by death. He stated that he had never met and did not know Richard Danziger or Chris Ochoa. He further stated that the police would be able to find corroborating evidence at his parents' home in El Paso, Texas, including the bank bag he took from the Pizza Hut at the time of the crime, the handcuffs used to bind DePriest and the .22 caliber Ruger with which he shot her.

Fact: The District Attorney's office and the Austin Police Department conducted an extensive investigation of Marino's claims. Police officers traveled to El Paso, Texas, and retrieved the named items from Achim Marino's parents' house and the El Paso Police Department. While most of the items Marino said would be at his parents' house were there, the gun was in the custody of the El Paso Police Department, which had arrested Marino with this weapon in a bus station in El Paso in 1988. The reinvestigation established that all of these items were indeed used in or taken from the restaurant where the rape, robbery and murder of Nancy DePriest occurred.

Fact: In his confessions, Achim Marino stated that when he was arrested in El Paso in 1988 he possessed the pistol that he used to kill Nancy DePriest and that this pistol was at his parents' house in El

Paso. At the scene of the murder, a shell casing was found on the floor underneath the body of Nancy DePriest. In December 2000, tool markings tests conducted by a private laboratory conclusively determined that this shell casing found at the murder scene came from the same gun Marino said was the murder weapon—the same weapon that was taken from him by police in El Paso in 1988.

Jeanette's head ached as the recitation of facts went on and on. How could this miscarriage of justice have happened?

Fact: At the request of the Travis County District Attorney's office, DNA testing was conducted on semen from vaginal swabs taken from Nancy DePriest. Testing was conducted in the summer and fall of 2000 by the Texas Department of Public Safety Crime Laboratory and an independent laboratory, Forensic Science Associates of Richmond, California. This testing conclusively showed that DNA taken from the semen matched the DNA of Achim Josef Marino. The DNA testing also conclusively *excluded* Christopher Ochoa and Richard Danziger as donors of the semen. Further, mitochondrial DNA testing was performed on a pubic hair that was found at the scene and entered into evidence during the 1990 trial. While testimony at trial indicated that the pubic hair was consistent with Richard Danziger's pubic hair, the mitochondrial DNA tests conducted in December 2000 *conclusively excluded* Richard Danziger as being the contributor of that hair. In addition, no other physical evidence, such as fingerprints, hair, blood or other material, placed either Richard Danziger or Chris Ochoa at the scene of the crime and no physical evidence from the restaurant or the victim was ever found in the possession of or on the person of Richard Danziger or Chris Ochoa or their belongings.

Fact: The District Attorney's office and the Austin Police Department conducted an extensive investigation to determine whether any link ever existed between Achim Josef Marino and Chris Ochoa or Richard Danziger. This investigation revealed no connection between Marino and either Chris or Richard Danziger. Ochoa confirmed that he did not know and had never met Achim Marino. Achim Josef Marino confirmed that he had never met either Christopher Ochoa or Richard Danziger. Richard Danziger had confirmed that he did not know Marino.

For twelve long years, Jeanette had been haunted by visions of her daughter being repeatedly and brutally raped by two subhuman beings. Now that was about to change.

Fact: One of the things that Christopher Ochoa "confessed" in his statements to the officers during his interrogations on November 14, 1988, and March 7, 1989, was that both he and Richard Danziger sodomized Nancy DePriest. As described by Chris Ochoa in those confessions, sodomy meant anal intercourse. At the time Ochoa made these written statements, it was the opinion of the Travis County Medical Examiner, Roberto Bayardo, M. D., pursuant to the autopsy that he personally performed on Nancy DePriest, that she had been anally assaulted. Dr. Bayardo so testified in the trial of Richard Danziger. On November 22, 2000, Dr. Bayardo filed an addendum to his original autopsy report. The addendum states that at the time of the autopsy, he was not aware of crucial details surrounding Nancy DePriest's hospitalization on October 24, 1988. Along with re-examination of photographs taken in the hospital and at autopsy, the new information led him to conclude that the anal and rectal injuries he observed at autopsy were caused by the insertion of a rectal thermometer probe while Nancy DePriest was in the hospital awaiting organ donation and were not the result of rectal or anal sexual assault. Achim Marino unequivocally denied that he anally assaulted DePriest.

Jeanette choked back tears as she listened to this fact. Now her vision of Nancy's final minutes could be altered substantially. Maybe her daughter hadn't suffered as horribly as she had believed.

Achim Josef Marino's confessions were further corroborated by information Jeanette had not heard before and facts that had not been revealed at trial:

First, investigations in 1988 and 1989 revealed that Nancy was most likely killed between 8:00 and 9:00 on the morning of October 24, 1988. Police officers took a statement from a woman who was driving south on Interstate 35 heading to work. She passed the restaurant where Nancy was killed at 8:15 A.M. and, glancing to her left, observed a man in his twenties standing at the west side entrance to the Pizza Hut. He was carrying what appeared to be a small toolbox by the handles, was dressed in a blue shirt and blue pants and appeared to be a workman knocking at the door. Achim Marino, in his statements, said that he gained entry through the west door by posing as a repairman carrying a small satchel and that he was wearing a blue work shirt and blue jeans. Chris Ochoa, in his statements, claimed to have entered through the east side door with a key. The west side door could not be opened from the outside with a key; it could only be opened from the inside.

Second, police officers took a statement in 1988 from a woman who was walking to work and passed by the restaurant during the relevant time period. She reported seeing a large yellow car parked behind the building on its south side. Achim Josef Marino states that on the morning of the murder he was driving a friend's car, which was beige-colored. He stated that he parked it behind the building on the south side.

Third, Emergency Medical Technicians testified at trial that they found Nancy DePriest lying on her back with her hands behind her. Turning her over, they found her brassiere loosely wrapped around her wrists and lower arms. Christopher Ochoa's November fourteenth statement claimed that he had used DePriest's brassiere to tie her hands together before she was sexually assaulted. At trial, marks on her wrists were identified as ligature marks, consistent with a brassiere binding the wrists together. Achim Josef Marino, in his statements, said he used a pair of handcuffs to bind Nancy's hands together. He stated that he put the handcuffs on her while she was standing up, then disrobed her by pulling her shirt and brassiere up, over and then behind her head. He escorted her to the back room, put aprons on the floor, upon which he sexually assaulted her, and then escorted her back to the restroom before shooting her in the back of the head while she knelt in response to his directions. Marino stated that he pulled her out of the restroom to look for the cartridge expelled from the gun and flooded the floor in a hurried attempt to remove possible fingerprints on the cartridge after being unable to find it. He then removed the handcuffs from Nancy and took them with him. In August 2000, the parallel marks roughly 1/8 inches apart left by the handcuffs on a live person were compared to the marks photographed at the hospital on October 24, 1988. From lay opinion, the marks were identical.

Concluding the Statement of Facts was the declaration that Christopher Ochoa and Richard Danziger had spent more than twelve years in jail and prison. Both the Travis County District Attorney's office and the Austin Police Department joined Christopher Ochoa in his assertion that he is innocent of the robbery, sexual assault and murder of Nancy DePriest and urged his release from custody.

Then Judge Perkins noted: "The court is of the opinion that the newly discovered evidence would have convinced a jury of the applicant's innocence.

"The court is further of the opinion that the applicant has shown more than his probable innocence, he has unquestionably shown his actual innocence.

"The applicant has proven by clear and convincing evidence that no rational juror could have found him guilty in light of the newly available confessions of Achim Josef Marino and the DNA evidence.

"Applicant has proven by clear and convincing evidence that he would not have been convicted of this offense had DNA testing and the Marino confessions been available at his plea in 1990.

"The State has agreed that had the newly discovered DNA test been available at the time of the investigation, during 1988 and 1989, no charges would have been filed against him."

At the end of the hearing, Judge Perkins granted Christopher Ochoa's petition and he was released on personal bond while the court order was being reviewed by the Texas Court of Criminal Appeals. Judge Perkins assured Chris he expected no problems with the appeals court.

A wave of relief washed through the room when Judge Perkins uttered his final words, freeing Christopher Ochoa. The euphoria was palpable among Chris's lawyers, his family and definitely in Jeanette. At last she knew the truth. Nancy had not been subjected to all the brutal indignities Chris had testified to at the trial. Yes, her daughter was dead. Yes, it was still a tragedy, but Jeanette drew comfort from feeling that, perhaps, Nancy's ordeal had been over quickly, with a minimum of pain and only a brief moment of fear. Marino had said in his confession that he had not told Nancy he was going to kill her. Jeanette's mind and grieving heart renewed the hope now that Nancy had not had to face her attacker knowing death was coming swiftly and surely.

Chris hugged his attorneys and shook hands with the prosecutors and with Judge Perkins. Then the crowd around the free man parted to allow his mother, crying, hands outstretched, to reach her son. After a long embrace, during which tears of mother and son flowed, Chris gently withdrew, turned to Jeanette and hugged her as well. "I have a little gift for you," she said. "Could we have a moment of privacy sometime?" He nodded, but before they could leave the courtroom, Jeanette saw a woman in the back of the courtroom who looked familiar to her. Their eyes met and when the woman started walking toward her, Jeanette recognized her as Rhonda Shore, Richard Danziger's girlfriend.

Rhonda held her hand out to Jeanette, who took it in both her own. "I am so, so sorry," Rhonda said. "I was so afraid. The police told me if I didn't say what they wanted me to, they could make it look like I was there with Richard when your daughter was killed. Then they said they would have Child Protective Services take my kids away. I couldn't do anything else."

Jeanette nodded. "I understand. But it has been so hard on everyone."

The woman nodded miserably and seemed unable to say more or turn away, until someone touched Jeanette's arm and said she and Chris could have five minutes to talk in a nearby room, if they hurried. So the mother of the murder victim and man who'd been misjudged guilty of the crime left the courtroom.

They were led to a small room and cautioned that they had only about five minutes before they had to move on to the luncheon that had been planned to celebrate Chris's victory. After lunch, they would participate in a press conference to be held at the Texas State Capitol building.

Jeanette handed Chris the gift she'd brought, a small, handmade wooden chest, and told him how sorry she was that he had been forced to endure such unspeakable agony for the past twelve years.

He looked at her, his eyes moist with unshed tears. "I am so sorry I wasn't strong enough to stand up to the police. I was terrified after hours and hours with the police." He said he thought if he didn't do what they told him to do, they would kill him. He also said he didn't want to implicate Richard Danziger, but for the scenario the detectives had painted, they needed two people.

He told her he thought that when he got away from the police and got a public defender, he would tell his attorney the truth. And he did, but the lawyer did not believe him.

Studying Chris, Jeanette could understand how a timid, naïve, terrified young man had simply gone into survival mode and ended up in a situation he couldn't control.

All through lunch, Jeanette was nervous, unable to eat, wishing she could be with Jim for a moment, overwhelmed by all that was happening. She was about to participate in a giant press conference and she was trembling with apprehension. The *Nightline* staff had been polite and considerate, had made her feel comfortable, completely at ease. Her story had flowed forth so easily, she hardly knew she was being interviewed. Now, she was faced with the prospect of television reporters, live cameras, all manner of questions she wasn't sure she could answer and she felt almost ill. Chris, a novice at this himself, kept patting her on the back and reassuring her everything would be all right. She would be great.

When the group assembled at the Capitol to talk to the media, it is difficult to say who was the greater person of interest: Chris Ochoa or Jeanette Popp. Certainly, Chris's story of false arrest and innocence was of national interest, but of almost as much interest was this woman, the mother of the murder victim, who had done everything she could to help set Ochoa free. Such a situation was almost unheard of.

As the cameras rolled, Chris first apologized to his onetime roommate, Richard Danziger, for testimony that led to Richard's wrongful conviction. "I am sorry. I feel guilty about what happened to Richard Danziger," he said. "I feel very badly for not having had the courage to stand up to the police." All those present were most likely aware that Richard's release had been delayed because of the permanent head injuries he sustained early in his confinement in prison as a result of a brutal beating by another inmate.

"I want to convey a message to all the innocent men in prison to not give up hope, to not give up, because there are people who care," Chris said, referring to Barry Scheck and John Pray of the Wisconsin Innocence Project.

Chris told the media he blamed Austin police for pressuring him into his 1988 confession, saying the death penalty was held over his head as he was pushed to admit his involvement. "If they had done their job right, we wouldn't have gone through this," he said, calling on the department to apologize for its actions.

Austin Assistant Police Chief Fealy told the press that a police detective and a Texas Ranger had been reinvestigating the case for two years and merited some credit for the information that came to light clearing the two men. He also mentioned that the review team appointed by the chief of police was looking at the case from start to finish, to "see if there are things that can be learned about the incident to keep it from ever happening again."

Fealy said the review team would issue a report on its findings shortly. He declined to comment about the detective who obtained Chris's confession.

"What Chris's release, and the release of these other men and women, proves is that the way we try and sentence people in this country is desperately flawed," said John Pray. "For every one of these men for whom there is DNA to test, there are dozens of men and women who are denied access to DNA testing, for whom the evidence has been lost or destroyed or for whom DNA is not available as evidence."

When it was her turn to speak, Jeanette looked around the room for a moment or two, then pushed aside the papers she held. "I had a speech all written out," she said, "but I'm not going to use it.

"As all of you know, on October 24, 1988, my daughter, Nancy DePriest, was brutally raped and murdered in Austin. The police said it was a horrible, heinous crime. And I agree. In late 1988, another horrible, heinous crime was in progress, the wrongful imprisonment of Christopher Ochoa and Richard Danziger. It was then compounded in 1990 when they were wrongly convicted.

"I was going to stand up here and thank all these wonderful people, but everybody has already done that for me and it's been an honor to be associated with them. They are wonderful. I'm sure that every day Christopher Ochoa must have prayed for a miracle and it came in the form of the Innocence Project and these gentlemen and ladies.

"I didn't learn about any of this until October 24, 2000, which was the twelfth anniversary of my daughter's death. I learned of it by watching a television show. I was skeptical. *I had been in that courtroom. I heard the evidence. I heard Christopher.* So I wanted answers. And the more answers I got, the more frustrated I became with the judicial system. The cruelty of the lies that were told to me about the injuries sustained by my daughter has given me horrible nightmares for twelve years. *Sodomy—something that never happened. Begging for her life—something she did not do.* For a police officer to tell me those things and let me believe them for twelve years is unforgivable. And I don't think I'm quite as forgiving yet as Christopher, but I'm learning from him. I certainly hope that I can do that someday.

"There are so many things I have wanted to say. However, I'm not used to all this. You guys have been really wonderful—very polite, not pushy. You've let me take my time and get used to all this fuss. I've had so many compliments the past few days, I'm probably going to go home with a big head. These things are not true. I'm not a remarkable person. I'm not a different person. I'm just like anybody else. I'm just like you. I come from a little town called Azle, Texas, with a big family. I've gone through a tragedy. I have learned from that tragedy.

"And, after much prayer and discussion with my family, I made the decision to do all I could to aid Christopher and Richard in their releases. It was something I had to do. If you don't stand for something, you're going to fall for anything. I have to stand up and say, 'This is wrong.' It's horrible. It's going on all over the United States. We've got to stop this. And the only way that's going to happen is through the voice of the people. I ask the public now, and the media especially—you have such a loud voice—in loving memory of my daughter, it is my wish that the death penalty be abolished in the state of Texas so that it can no longer be used as a threat to coerce confessions from the innocent. Life is a God-given gift. He gives it and only He should take it. I don't believe that anyone can be so positive that they can take another person's life.

"So, in memory of my daughter, please join us—the Innocence

Project—in the freeing of innocent people, the abolition of the death penalty in Texas and across the nation. And perhaps, in doing this, my beautiful baby will not have died in vain."

At the conclusion of the press conference, Chris and his attorneys called for passage of four criminal justice bills that were currently before the Texas Legislature. Those measures would require post-conviction DNA testing in Texas, better legal representation for indigent persons charged with crimes, improved compensation for those who were wrongly imprisoned and the creation of innocence commissions to examine cases similar to Chris's and Richard's.

"We have to fix the system," Chris said. "Under the system we have, I came close to losing my life."

When he was asked what he would do now that he was out of prison, Chris said he would return to El Paso to find a job and enroll in college to seek a bachelor's degree in business administration.

"I am also going to go to a church in El Paso, where my grand-mother took me when I was little and taught me to pray."

One of the dozens of people who congratulated Jeanette and Chris after the press conference was over was Scott Cobb, president of the Texas Moratorium Network, a recently formed grassroots non-profit organization with the primary goal of mobilizing statewide support for a moratorium on executions. TMN was founded in 2000 by several people who had been involved in what became known as *The March on the Mansion* held in Austin on October 15, 2000, to protest capital punishment in Texas under then-governor George W. Bush.

Cobb held Jeanette's hands and looked into her eyes a long time. "We need you so much," he said. "Yours is such an overwhelming story, one that everyone should hear."

Ever since Jeanette had learned of the monumental mistake the criminal justice system in Austin had made, her horror had been growing. It was hard to imagine the tragedies suffered by Chris Ochoa and Richard Danziger, but thinking of all she had learned from attor-neys who had participated in releasing Chris, she knew it could have been worse. Much worse. Given Texas's penchant for capital punishment, it certainly could have meant the death of both men. Impulsively, Jeanette asked Scott what she could do to help his group in their fight against the death penalty. In answer, he invited her to go to dinner with him and some of his colleagues and he would explain what they were trying to do and what she could do to help. He told her the group was made up of volunteers who were not reimbursed for any of their time and effort, not even for their expenses. Some of them had been touched by violence, but some of them had not. They were simply committed to their work to abolish the death penalty.

Scott and his friends told her that she could speak to the committees of the Texas Legislature when they began considering the measures Chris had mentioned during the press conference; TMN was also advocating in favor of legislation that would enact a moratorium on executions. She promised she would do that and anything else she could do to help eliminate the death penalty. Without even realizing it, she had begun to walk the path to activism that would take her all across the country, make her known nationally and abroad and lead her into some of the most fulfilling years of her life.

Chapter 23

# What the Review
# Team Found

Less than a week later, the Review Team Report, written by
Assistant Chief Fealy, on the 1988 DePriest Investigation was
delivered to Chief Stanley Knee:

*On January 2, 2001, I convened the Nancy DePriest Homicide Review Team,
as directed by the chief of police,* Fealy wrote. *The mission of the team was to review
the Austin Police Department investigation of the 1988 murder of Nancy DePriest.
The team was made up of five members of the Austin Police Department and two
rangers from the Texas Department of Public Safety. None of the detectives on the team
had been involved in the original investigation. Detective Manuel Fuentes, who had
been the Austin police officer to interview Chris Ochoa in prison in 1998 and who
had led the investigation that ultimately cleared Chris's name, was a member of the
group, however.*

The report stated that the review of the investigation was
complete and briefly summarized the case:

*On October 24, 1988, Nancy DePriest was found brutally murdered at her
place of employment, the Pizza Hut restaurant. A subsequent investigation eventually
focused on two suspects—Christopher Ochoa and Richard Danziger. Ochoa confessed
to the crime and named Danziger as an accomplice in the case. Both were imprisoned*

*for their part in this crime.*

In February of 1996, a Texas Department of Corrections inmate, Achim Josef Marino, confessed to being the sole person responsible for Nancy DePriest's death. After an extensive four-year investigation by the Austin Police Department, Marino's confession was found to be valid. Investigators found no evidence linking Ochoa and Danziger to the crime against DePriest other than Ochoa's confession. In August 2000, Ochoa recanted his confession after almost twelve years and several opportunities to do so to police and prosecutors. He now alleges that the confession was coerced; he implies that the original detectives provided him the details for his confession.

Fealy wrote, *Our main goal as a review team was to find answers to these two questions:*

*First, how were two apparently innocent people convicted of the murder and aggravated sexual assault of Nancy DePriest? Second, were any Austin Police Department policies or criminal statutes violated during this investigation?*

*The review conducted was based solely on the documentation relating to this case. No interviews were conducted during the review. The review team was provided access to:*

*The case offense report*
*Witness statements*
*Written confessions*
*Audiotaped statements and confessions*
*Court transcripts*
*Forensic reports*
*Crime scene photos*
*Contents of the case file*

According to the report, the original investigation was flawed in three main areas:

*Investigative leads and techniques*
*Confessions and statements*
*Documentation*

The report continued:

*In many instances commonly accepted, logical investigative techniques were not used by detectives in the original 1988 investigation of the case. Case detectives formed inaccurate conclusions about the circumstances of the crime, resulting in notable misinterpretations of the crime scene. Other mistakes apparently occurred, because of these misinterpretations.*

*An apparent failure to use available resources, such as computer searches and alerting other agencies about the modus operandi of the crime, did not allow detectives access to information that might have led to the early identification of legitimate suspects in the beginning stages of this investigation. In fact, some review team members found reason to believe that the true perpetrator of the crime, Achim Marino, could have possibly become a suspect prior to his 1996 confession if available investigative resources had been efficiently used. Other leads were evident early in the investigation, but no documentation exists to indicate that these leads were followed up on.*

*Several suspects were identified early in the investigation based on detectives' belief that these people knew facts known only to the police or the perpetrator. Two such individuals were arrested, and later cleared, prior to the arrest of Danziger and Ochoa. Detectives continued to rely on their belief that Danziger and Ochoa knew facts that could only be known to the police or the perpetrator even after it should have been apparent that at least some of these same facts were known to the public at large and, most specifically, Pizza Hut employees. Both Danziger and Ochoa were Pizza Hut employees at the time of their arrest. The review team believed that it is probable that some of these facts that Ochoa included in his confession came from his interaction with homicide detectives and from his contact with other Pizza Hut employees.*

*Inconsistencies surrounding when statements were recorded or written caused concerns for the review team. Documentation about what Danziger said to the police "does not exist." One detective did record in his supplementary report some of the conversation that occurred; however, there is no documentation of any efforts to get a formal statement from him.*

*Confessions and statements also became areas of concern for the review team. The three confessions given by Chris Ochoa were key factors in the case against both Ochoa* and Danziger. The review team believes that the lack of any evidentiary corroboration of Ochoa's confession poses major concerns. The review team identified several problems centering around the written confessions and the single audio-taped interview with Ochoa. There are instances in the taped interview with Ochoa where he gave details of the crime that detectives should have known were inaccurate. We know that conversations took place between investigators and Ochoa after the taped interview and before investigators took Ochoa's typed confession. The review team noticed that the inaccurate details Ochoa mentioned in the taped interview were corrected by the time the typed confession occurred. There is no documentation to indicate how this transpired. Ochoa now claims that he did not read his confession before signing it.

There are also substantial indications in his typed confessions that Ochoa provided detectives with details of the crime that only the police or the perpetrator would know. Some details centered on erroneous conclusions made by investigators about what happened at the crime scene.

The review team believes Ochoa used details gleaned from police investigators or the media in his confessions.

Statements from witnesses may have been impacted by some of the same deficiencies mentioned above. Multiple statements taken from some witnesses spread over a lengthy time period presented a confusing array of information. Suggestive questioning on the part of detectives appears to have affected at least one witness statement. It also appears that some witnesses who should have been interviewed never were.

A general lack of documentation permeates this case, Fealy wrote. Standard investigative techniques for documentation do not appear to have been followed consistently in this case. Some detectives described the process of taking statements and confessions in a rather sketchy manner in supplementary reports. At other times, documentation of interviews conducted with suspects were not included in the offense report at all. There is no documentation that clearly indicates whether or not Richard Danziger was ever offered the opportunity to give a formal statement.

Early suspects (other than Ochoa and Danziger) were interviewed and, in some cases, arrested, without sufficient documentation of the process involved in eliminating them as suspects in the crime. In attempts to track down documents and evidence, the review team found that some items are missing. Limited documentation of what *happened to these items makes it difficult to track who released what to which agency. We think that these items may have been lost during the trial process, but the documentation does not exist to confirm or deny this belief.*

*Another problem was noted by the team. Investigators often submitted supplementary reports long after the events occurred, leaving open the possibility that these reports weren't written in a timely manner. Failing to document events in a timely manner often results in inaccurate reporting because details become harder to remember as memories fade.*

*Strong indications that investigators supplied Ochoa with information about the circumstances of the crime and later allowed him to include this information in confessions were found. We could not claim with certainty that investigators intentionally fed information to Ochoa, nor could we prove this was done inadvertently. We also found no evidence to confirm Ochoa's allegations of coercion. Because of the lack of documentation of the many hours of conversation, interviews, and interrogations with Ochoa, coercion is difficult to substantiate or refute.*

*In conjunction with this review, team members studied research on false confessions. It appears that Christopher Ochoa fits the profile of an individual who gives false confessions. Although this type of research may not have been as available in 1988 as it is now, a multitude of indicators exist that should have flagged his confession as potentially false.*

*In answer to the second question, the review of documentation did not reveal any direct evidence of departmental violations by homicide investigators other than violations that might have occurred during Ochoa's interviews and interrogations. For this reason, the review team feels that an investigation into the events surrounding these interviews and interrogations is warranted.*

*For reasons I've presented above, the review team recommends to you that the Austin Police Department's Internal Affairs Division investigate the circumstances surrounding this 1988 investigation. We also recommend that the U.S. Attorney's Office conduct a review of circumstances surrounding Ochoa's confessions.*

*I feel you should also know about a few positive facets of this case. The reinvestigation of this homicide case by the current APD homicide unit, particularly Detective Manuel Fuentes and Texas Ranger Sal Abreo, was conducted to the highest professional standards. This reinvestigation led to the truth.*

The picture painted was of an investigation that was flawed from the beginning and got worse day by day, ending with the conviction of two innocent men. Although the review cast much of the blame for the botched investigation on the detectives working the case and the mistakes they made that could have been avoided, it did not accuse the detectives assigned to the case of intentional wrongdoing.

Chapter 24

# Where Do We Go From Here?

Reactions to the report were mixed. Some were shocked. Others outraged. Still others, complacent or resigned. Many people thought that it would be highly unlikely that an internal review would chastise overzealous officers for deliberate misconduct which contributed to a miscarriage of justice that resulted in so many broken lives. The excuses were many. After so many years, memories had faded, evidence was misplaced, life had gone on as usual—except for Ochoa and Danziger. Finally, it had been recognized and reported that interrogation techniques and records had been flawed and, ostensibly, steps were being taken to see that, in the future, accurate records of interviews and interrogations would be kept.

Richard Danziger, too, would have his day in court. First, a month long evaluation was conducted to decide what kind of care he would need upon his release. He might need permanent institutionalization, said his attorney, David Sheppard, who was appointed only two weeks before Chris Ochoa's hearing. According to Sheppard, his client talked about the case and grasped what was happening. In mid-March 2001, two months after Chris Ochoa was released, Richard Danziger walked out of a treatment center a free man except for an appearance before a judge, which would take place the following week.

"They done me bad twice," Danziger said. "They convicted me wrongly and they kicked my head in." He spoke in an unaffected tone, sometimes slurring his words.

David Sheppard wanted his client to receive more evaluation and treatment at the rehabilitation center where he had been sent in January, but the state money to keep him there was about to run out. Danziger would have to move into a group facility. His short-term memory frequently failed, Sheppard said, and he was easily distracted. He could put food on a stove and forget to return. Or he could forget to take the medication to prevent his damaging seizures, as he had so many times when he was held in the jail's general population, before he was finally sent to a psychiatric unit. Unless the state agreed to provide more money, said Sheppard, Danziger, against his doctor's recommendation, would probably go to Florida to live with his sister.

The chances of the state of Texas paying for any more care for Danziger were very slim. Wrongly convicted Texans were entitled to a maximum of twenty-five thousand dollars for pain and suffering and medical expenses from the state. To receive the money, Danziger would have to sue and meet the law's conditions, which included obtaining a pardon for a crime he didn't commit.

That compensation law had been passed in 1985, before the advances in DNA testing that now are helping wrongly convicted inmates prove their innocence.

When Danziger was released, Texas had paid only two wrongly convicted Texans, for a total of $50,969.86, according to figures from the state comptroller's office. Four others were awaiting compensation, both of whom had been found guilty of aggravated rape. "They spent twenty-nine years in prison between them, and they're getting twenty-five thousand dollars each," said their attorney. "Obviously, this is inadequate."

Already, though, such cases had spurred the Texas Legislature to take another look at the rules for paying wrongly convicted people.

Seven bills were being considered during the current legislative session, most aimed at increasing or eliminating the State cap on damages. Several would loosen the restrictions on suing the State.

One lawmaker, Senator Rodney Ellis, proposed a bill that would compensate wrongly convicted people for lost wages, counseling, medical expenses, attorneys' fees and twenty-five thousand dollars for each year incarcerated. "If the State makes a mistake, the State has a responsibility to help people put their lives back in order," he said.

Danziger's sister, distressed about her brother's condition, spoke of his problems as a child. She said he was diagnosed as hyperactive as a boy, roaring around Beeville on his skateboard and dirt bike, bringing home wounded animals to care for them. When his parents divorced in 1982, Richard stayed with his mother and that was when trouble began, the sister said. She said her mother was very strict and repeatedly packed Richard off to treatment centers when she felt she was losing control of him.

Danziger said he wanted to travel and live on his own. "I don't want to be an object of pity," he said. "It makes my head weak." Even as he spoke, his family and perhaps he himself were aware he probably could never live independently.

Jeanette was just as heartbroken over Richard's condition as she had been about Ochoa's incarceration. It was appalling that two innocent young men could have their lives so thoroughly devastated. And she was determined to help stop such miscarriages of justice and change the laws to protect those who were wrongly charged. Scott Cobb of the Texas Moratorium Network, who kept in touch with her, encouraged her to join the group, which she did. Cobb also arranged to get her on the list of those who testify before the two legislative committees he had spoken to her about. In each committee meeting, she told the story of her daughter's death, told of the wrongful conviction of Chris Ochoa and Richard Danziger and asked the legislators to approve the measures they were considering.

"It was the most emotional hearing I have ever been to in my life," said Houston State Representative Harold Dutton, who sponsored the legislation. "I was drained, exhausted for the rest of the day."

The bill never made it out of the house committee, but in Jeanette, capital punishment foes had found the compassionate face and voice of a victim to include in their fight, one who, because of her heart and the intensity of her emotions, could reach people most others never could.

A few weeks later, Texas Governor Rick Perry signed into law a bill authored by Senator Robert Duncan of Lubbock, requiring DNA testing for certain convicted felons to remove doubts about their guilt or innocence. The State would pay for the tests, the cost of which was estimated at about fifty thousand dollars a year. The law also required prosecutors to preserve biological evidence obtained at a crime scene, consequently making it easier for the wrongly convicted to prove their innocence. Prior to the new law, convicted felons had to obtain a court order if they wanted DNA testing.

"We've already learned this session that we have persons who were convicted in error," Senator Duncan said. "New technology and advancements in DNA for biological evidence could indeed provide the key that could unlock the door for those folks."

Jeanette and her friends in the Texas Moratorium Network, although pleased with the passage of the bill, thought that was not enough. More was needed to balance the scales of justice between powerful prosecutors and poor defendants. Another bill currently being considered in the legislature was called the Texas Fair Defense Act, meant to address concerns about defendants who could not afford to hire attorneys.

"The harsh reality is, poor defendants get a poor defense in Texas," said Senator Rodney Ellis, author of this legislation. Ellis's bill would require that a lawyer be appointed within four days of a person's arrest in large counties, such as Travis County, and within six days for smaller counties, those with populations of less than two hundred fifty thousand.

Disparities in the approach to indigent defense varied from county to county, as well as from courtroom to courtroom, according to a study by the Texas Appleseed Fair Defense Project. Texas was one of only four states that provided no state funding for indigent defense and ranked second to last in the nation in per-capita spending on indigent criminal defense. This amounted to less than five dollars per capita.

Horror stories were told about ineffective court-appointed attorneys. It was said some fell asleep during trial. The most alarming stories, though, were of defense attorneys persuading innocent defendants to accept plea bargains, regardless of their claims of innocence.

All told, seven bills concerning the rights of persons accused of violent crimes were introduced in the legislature that session, including one that would provide for a two year moratorium on executions. They didn't all make it through the process, but the fact they were even being considered was deemed a victory. And those that did pass were cause for celebration among defenders of victims' rights.

Amid the publicity about Chris and Richard, and the unprecedented actions by the state legislature, it was as if Achim Marino was forgotten by everyone except Jeanette Popp. Again, the District Attorney's office was not keeping her in the loop, but then she read in a Texas newspaper that he was indicted on evidence showing that he raped and killed her daughter. Jeanette decided she wanted to talk to him. She wanted to ask him herself what had happened in the last moments of Nancy's life.

After Chris was released, he and Jeanette began receiving requests from both national and state television and radio shows for them to make appearances. For the next several months, they made the talk show circuit, traveled across the country, from California to New York City to Wisconsin to El Paso. They went on *Nightline, Good Morning America* and *The View* among others. The incongruity and the humility they both exhibited and their heart made the appearances of the aggrieved mother and the exonerated murderer powerful.

They received no pay for their appearances on the shows, but their expenses were paid. Jeanette and Chris joked that they could quickly get used to staying in fine hotels, eating in fancy restaurants and being driven around the cities in limousines.

Though she felt these appearances were important to advancing the cause they both fervently believed in, for a while it seemed to Jeanette she was traveling more than she was home. When she had talked to Jim about her taking up this cause that had seized her attention and her emotions, they agreed she would quit her job so she could be free to advocate for changing Texas law. They were doing well. Jim had been at the same job for twelve years and they had built their home themselves. Their life together was good. And Jim understood that Jeanette had to do this one thing, to make sure justice and not injustice was the outcome of Nancy's tragic death.

On the trips for their appearances, Jeanette found Chris interesting, knowledgeable and extremely shy. They frequently sat together, holding hands before going on camera. Although, at times he now was an outspoken crusader, at others Jeanette felt he was still a frightened kid.

Once, while they were standing on a street curb at the airport waiting to check their luggage in for a flight to another appearance, a police car pulled up. Jeanette watched Chris begin to shake, perspiration dripping down his face. When the police officer got out of the car, she thought Chris was going to bolt. She took his arm. "It's okay, Chris," she said. "It's okay. He's not here for you." Chris looked terrified and she could understand why, considering his experience with law enforcement.

Wherever they did appearances, one question was always asked, and it was the most difficult for Chris to answer: Why did you confess to this killing?

"I don't know," he said over and over again, to every questioner. "I was so scared. If you've never been in that situation, you don't know what you're going to do. You can sit there and say, 'I would never ever confess to something I didn't do.' But you just don't know."

When he was asked about how he felt about the legal system in light of his experience with it, he did have an answer. "It's not the greatest system in the world, but it's what we have."

Then, Chris told his audiences how moved he was by all the people who had helped him. He never failed to give credit to his attorneys, to the Innocence Project and to Jeanette. Her heart was touched by the sweetness of his attitude and demeanor as he talked about those who fought for his release.

When Chris told Jeanette he was going back to El Paso to be with his family and get back in school, she knew she would miss him, miss his support, but she promised herself she would keep on going. As long as people wanted to hear Nancy's story, her brutal death and the miscarriage of justice in the imprisonment of two innocent men, the struggle for their release, she would tell it to finally achieve justice for Nancy and to change the law.

Jeanette followed those same instincts she had in her relationship with the Innocence Project and the Texas Moratorium Network. As she told her story, she tried to persuade other Texans of the wrongs in the Texas system, of other possible innocent men and women jailed and to right the wrongs they needed to fix.

Soon she was elected chairperson of TMN, and she used that pulpit to coax, plead and bully the people of Texas into listening to her and those she represented. She posted a notice on the TMN website, called Moratorium at Our Request. In it, she retold her tragic experiences, reminding her readers of Richard Danziger who had been serving the life sentence the State of Texas gave him—"for Richard Danziger is a prisoner of his own mind." She included in the piece the major points which she hammered home over and over again in the next years:

- The death penalty in the State of Texas is seriously flawed.
- It executes juvenile offenders and people with mental retardation.
- It snubs its nose at the rehabilitated.
- It doesn't care if a person is a future danger to society or not.
- It doesn't care if a person has had incompetent representation.
- It doesn't even know the guilty from the innocent.

Jeanette continues: "It can't, you see. It's only a killing machine. The busiest one in the United States. It's breaking international laws few others would dare to break. Killing children and the mentally retarded by record numbers. Shouldn't this killing machine also receive the ultimate sentence? After all, we know beyond a reasonable doubt it will continue to kill. How do we stop this indiscriminate killing?

"A MORATORIUM NOW!

"Let us take two years to contemplate where this system has gone so wrong. Prosecutorial misconduct, police brutality, false testimony, mistaken eyewitnesses, junk science, sleeping lawyers, black offenders being tried by all-white juries. This is not a jury of their peers. If we allow this, we must also allow all black juries to hear cases of an accused white person. We must have justice for all, rich or poor, black or white, the accused and the innocent. We must demand a judicial system that saves the innocent and properly punishes the criminal.

"I cannot believe we are so bloodthirsty that we can't wait two years to have an execution. Are we afraid we'll go through some type of withdrawal? Or are we afraid of what we'll find? Have we executed innocents? Probably. If not, at the rate we're progressing, we most certainly will.

"Can't we temper our justice with a little mercy? Maybe some forgiveness thrown in would be nice. We don't have to become murderers to stop murderers.

"Please, in loving memory of Nancy DePriest, my daughter, I beg you to help me stop executions so real justice can be done."

# Chapter 25

# The Eyes
# of a Murderer

Jeanette's requests to meet with Achim Josef Marino had, so far, met with silence and her letters to him were unanswered. Both Marino's attorney, Larry Sauer, and Bryan Case of the District Attorney's office were adamantly resistant to the idea.

Then, she got a telephone call from Bryan Case. He said he would allow her to see Marino if she agreed to try and persuade Marino to take the plea bargain the District Attorney's office was offering—that the DA would take the death penalty off the table if Marino would plead guilty to murder and aggravated robbery in exchange for two life sentences. By accepting this plea, Marino would avoid the death penalty and the District Attorney's office would not have to conduct a trial.

Jeanette told Case she had been waiting a year to talk to Marino and she would beg him to take the plea, if his attorney would allow her access to him.

That same day, Marino's attorney, Larry Sauer, called and asked her if she could come to Austin to speak to his client. Marino was being brought to the Travis County Jail and had a question for Jeanette: Did she want him to live or die?

Sauer told her Marino was weighing the offer from the District Attorney's office, for him to plead guilty to murder and aggravated robbery in exchange for two life sentences. Jeanette had been thinking all along that she could not bear sitting through another trial. She could not survive more hours and days and weeks of listening to the awful things that had been done to her daughter. She didn't think she could live through that nightmare again.

Even more pressing for Jeanette than the need to avoid a trial was her conviction that it would be morally and spiritually wrong for the State to take Marino's life. She wanted to tell him that. She told Sauer she would come, but she had some questions for Marino and she wanted to be assured he would answer them. There were no promises, but there was no reason to think Marino would not respond to her questions, according to Sauer.

Scott Cobb accompanied Jeanette to the Travis County Jail. As they stood in front, Scott took her arm and they stopped on the concrete steps. "Jeanette, are you sure you can do this?"

She gazed at him levelly. "You know, Scott, for almost a year, I've been preaching forgiveness, preaching against the death penalty. Now I've got to know if I can actually do it."

Scott nodded and they went inside, where they were searched. She was advised she couldn't take anything into the room that was glass, so her compact was removed from her purse. They walked into a small, plain conference room with windows on all sides, containing a long table and four chairs. She and Scott sat together on one side of the table and he clasped her hand. Larry Sauer came in and introduced himself, then sat on the same side of the table. Jeanette watched him covertly. He didn't look like any of the attorneys she had met so far. He was dressed casually and wore his long gray-white hair pulled back into a ponytail. He greeted Jeanette and Scott, but said nothing else.

Two guards escorted Marino in and Jeanette could not tear her eyes away from this frightening looking man, dressed in an orange jumpsuit, wearing tattoos up and down his arms and one on his chest. *Prison tattoos,* Jeanette thought. She knew what he was and what he was capable of, but it was as if he mesmerized her, as a cobra hypnotizes its prey. He wasn't tall, but sturdy looking, with piercing blue eyes that reminded her of blued steel. He looked directly into her eyes and she felt as if he was looking through her rather than at her, as if he could see her very soul. He sat down across from her, and she felt a shudder run through her. This was the second hardest thing she had ever done, to sit across the table from this man who had murdered her daughter and look into his cold blue eyes. There was not a flicker of emotion as those eyes met hers, nothing visible on his face, not even curiosity.

Jeanette spoke first, in the steadiest voice she could muster. "Mr. Marino, could you answer some questions for me?"

"Yes, ma'am."

"Did my daughter fight you?"

"No. She didn't."

"Did she say anything?"

"Yes. She said, 'Don't hurt me.' That's all she ever said."

Jeanette let her breath out slowly. "Did you hit her? Did you beat her?"

"No. I didn't." For an instant, Jeanette thought he sounded insulted, as if she could dare ask such a question.

"Did you rape her?" Jeanette choked.

"Yes."

"More than once?"

"No. I didn't."

For some reason, Jeanette believed him. He had proven he had killed Nancy; why would he lie about the details?

"Did she know you were going to kill her?" she asked.

"No. I handcuffed her under the bathroom sink. I told her I was giving myself time to get away. She turned away from me and I shot her. Then I took the handcuffs off."

For a moment, Jeanette couldn't go on. Silence fell heavily upon the room. Sauer had not spoken or participated in the conversation in any way and he too remained silent. Marino just stared at her with those piercing blue eyes.

Finally, Jeanette spoke. "Mr. Marino, you know I don't want you to be executed?"

"I've heard that," he answered stoically.

"It's the truth. I don't want you to die."

He shook his head. "Mrs. Popp, I'd rather be executed than spend the rest of my life in a Texas prison."

Jeanette approached it from another angle. "Mr. Marino, it's my understanding that you are now a born-again Christian?"

He replied that he was, but there was no change in his eyes or demeanor.

"You realize, of course, that what you're asking for is assisted suicide?"

"I guess," he admitted.

"If you really are a born-again Christian, there are still good things you could do with your life to make up for the bad things you've done. You can minister to other inmates—men who need spiritual guidance. You're obviously very concerned about prison conditions. You could work to make things better. You could still do something with your life."

He stared at her with that unwavering blue gaze and said nothing.

"I want you to plead guilty to my daughter's murder and take the two consecutive life sentences. Can you do this for me? I don't think I can go through another trial. I don't think I could stand it. And I really do not want to take the risk that you will be executed."

"I don't understand that," Marino said, surprising Jeanette a little.

Jeanette marshaled her thoughts. She had gone over in her mind what she would say to this man, but now words didn't come. She took a deep breath and told herself she had to go on. Finally she said, "Mr. Marino, I don't know if we serve the same God, but my God says

'Thou shalt not kill.' And I can't be a part of killing you, no matter what you've done. Do you understand that I've forgiven you for what you've done?"

He shrugged. "I've heard that."

"Please, please, take this plea bargain."

"I want a trial," he insisted. "I want to tell my side."

"Mr. Marino, please don't make me go through that again."

"I'm sorry, Mrs. Popp."

Jeanette sighed and leaned back in her chair. "All right, Mr. Marino." She hesitated a moment, then said, "Could I ask you another question? Can you tell me why you killed Nancy?

"You've raped and robbed other people. Why did you kill my daughter?"

His attitude seemed to change subtly, he seemed to be almost respectful as he answered her.

"Ma'am, it wasn't her in particular. I stopped at another place before I got to her, but there were too many people in that place. So I went down the street and found your daughter. I used to be a Satan worshipper and I was having horrible headaches and hearing voices. My Satanic advisors told me that if I made a human sacrifice, the headaches and voices would go away."

"So you killed my daughter to make the headaches and the voices in your head go away?"

"Yes."

"Did it work?"

"No," he admitted.

"Do you know *why* it didn't work?" Jeanette demanded. "Because you can't send an angel to Satan."

He kept that distant blue gaze on her, but said nothing more.

After the guards took Marino out of the room, Jeanette was trembling and breathing rapidly. She realized how shaken she was by the confrontation. Scott helped her from the chair and guided her toward the door with a firm hand on her back. Outside, they were met by a dozen reporters who had been told of the meeting by the TMN and another anti-death penalty group, Murder Victims' Families for Reconciliation.

Scott was the first to address the group of press and anti-death penalty supporters. "Today, I was honored to be in the room when Jeanette Popp met with the man, Achim Josef Marino, who has confessed to murdering her daughter, Nancy DePriest. Jeanette is the bravest person I have ever met. She is the most loving person. Today, Jeanette has done us all a great service. She has done something that only someone as strong as she is could possibly do. First, she has created space for all the innocent victims involved in this case to heal. That means a space for her to heal herself and also space for the two innocent men, Christopher Ochoa and Richard Danziger, who spent years in prison for a crime they did not commit, to heal.

"But she has also given us, the people of Texas, a great gift. She has created a space for us, the people of Texas, to speak rationally and honestly about the death penalty. Her courage as a mother of a murder victim has made it possible for all of us to be able to question the way the death penalty is administered in Texas—without having to worry that we are disrespecting the victims of crime. As the mother of a murder victim, she has demonstrated that it is okay to speak out against the death penalty. She has fought for the last year to make sure that people know that there is an alternative to revenge, there is an alternative to the death penalty. People often ask, what would you do if your child was murdered? Would you want revenge? Would you want the murderer to be executed? Jeanette has given us her answer. She sat face-to-face today with the person who killed her daughter and she said that she wanted to save his life. She told him that she did not want him to receive the death penalty, despite the horrible crime that he has committed." He paused to let his words be absorbed.

Then he went on, his voice firm, taut. "I heard Jeanette back in March when she came to Austin to testify in front of a legislative committee here in the capitol in favor of a moratorium on executions.

After hearing her powerful testimony and the testimony of two innocent men who spent years on Texas's death row before being released, two committees of the Texas legislature voted in favor of a moratorium. Later, another moratorium bill received fifty-three votes on the floor of the Texas House of Representatives. Jeanette's story is powerful. She has suffered enormously, because the death penalty was used as a threat to wrongfully send two innocent men to prison for the murder of her daughter.

"During that testimony, she told the story of the murder of her daughter in 1988 here in Austin. Two men, Christopher Ochoa and Richard Danziger, spent twelve years in prison for that crime, but they were innocent. They had been convicted, because the Austin Police Department coerced a false confession from Chris by threatening him with the death penalty. Jeanette can talk more about how the Austin Police Department cooked up a gruesome story about what had happened to Nancy. It was a horrific tale, but it was completely fictional. The police were convinced that Ochoa and Danziger had committed the crime together and, in exchange for avoiding a death sentence, Ochoa had to take Richard Danziger down with him. That was part of the plea bargain. 'He had to testify against Danziger,' said one of Chris's lawyers from the Wisconsin Innocence Project, which took up the case after receiving a letter from Chris and determined that he indeed was innocent. From the very beginning, Richard Danziger maintained his innocence and early this year, the state of Texas agreed and set him free. When Christopher Ochoa was exonerated for the murder of Nancy and released from prison, Jeanette said that she did not want the District Attorney, Ronnie Earle, to seek the death penalty against Marino."

His voice rose. "Jeanette said she was going to save the life of Achim Josef Marino and today she took another great step toward achieving that goal.

"That is the story that Jeanette told three legislative committees last spring. If everyone in the legislature had been able to hear

Jeanette's testimony, instead of just the members of those committees, then I am sure the moratorium bills would have passed. Jeanette has created space for us to debate the death penalty, so let's do just that."

Again he paused as though reflecting and then he went on, voicing his obviously deep convictions. "Across this nation, ninety-eight innocent people have been released from death row since the death penalty was reinstated in the 1970s. Twenty-one of those innocent people have been released just since 1999. The death penalty runs the risk of executing innocent people. A large reason why innocent people wind up on death row is because of the kind of coerced confessions and other police misconduct that resulted in Christopher Ochoa's and Richard Danziger's convictions.

"The death penalty is too expensive. According to one study in Texas, a death penalty case costs an average of $2.3 million, about three times the cost of imprisoning someone in a single cell at the highest security level for forty years (*Dallas Morning News*, March 8, 1992). By pressuring the District Attorney not to seek the death penalty against Marino, Jeanette has saved the taxpayers of Travis County perhaps a million dollars. Yet, the District Attorney would not even pay for her expenses today to come down and talk to Marino.

"Last summer, Governor Perry surrounded himself with a few victims of crime in order to give himself political cover when he vetoed a bill that would have banned the execution of people with mental retardation. I challenge him next time to stand next to Jeanette and sign that bill. This year, the governors of Florida, Arizona, Connecticut, North Carolina and Missouri signed bills banning the execution of people with mental retardation. Texas should be on that list next time. I also invite the governor to stand next to Jeanette next time and sign a bill to ban the execution of people under the age of eighteen who commit crimes. Texas leads the world in executing juveniles."

Then he focused on his aims. "Most importantly, I invite Governor Perry and all the candidates in next year's elections to endorse a moratorium on executions, so that we can appoint a commission to comprehensively study the administration of the death penalty. A moratorium is an issue that will win votes for politicians in next year's election. A moratorium is not about whether you are morally opposed to the death penalty. It is about fairness. It is about whether you believe the state of Texas has a death penalty system that protects innocent people from being executed and that protects African-Americans and other minorities from being disproportionately sentenced to death. Almost 67 percent of the people on Texas's death row are minorities, 43 percent are African-Americans, despite the fact that they comprise only about 11.5 percent of the population of Texas.

"We also need a moratorium on executions while we decide whether juries should be given the option of sentencing people to life without parole as an alternative to the death penalty. Already, polls indicate that support for the death penalty drops below 50 percent if people are asked about alternatives, such as life without parole."

His speech ended with moving words: "People often ask how you can favor a moratorium or how can you be against the death penalty. Don't you care about the victims of crime? My answer is to point to Jeanette and say, Jeanette, I love you. Thank you for your courage."

Jeanette had spotted an Assistant District Attorney a few feet away and, while Scott was speaking, made her way toward him.

He recognized her, of course, and nodded a cool greeting. Over the past year, everyone in the Travis County District Attorney's office had become very well acquainted with Jeanette Popp because of her increased activism against the death penalty. It seemed as if everywhere she went, she drew the media and she was vocal, singling out and criticizing the Austin and Travis County law enforcement officials, because of what she perceived as corruption and conspiracy to clear cases and put people in jail—or execute them if the case seemed to warrant the death penalty.

Jeanette told the ADA what had happened in the meeting with Marino, that he was adamant about going to trial and telling his side of the story. She said he'd told her he'd prefer to die rather than spend the rest of his life in prison. She asked the ADA if he could get his office to take the death penalty off the table.

He said he would speak to District Attorney Ronnie Earle about doing that and then he would get back to her with an answer.

Turning to the reporters when Scott had finished his speech, Jeanette said, "The saving of this man's life is the most important thing to me at this time. I will not dishonor my daughter with the taking of another life in her name."

She told the reporters she had learned from Marino the real details of Nancy's death. "What actually happened was not as bad as my nightmares and certainly not as bad as I was led to believe in the beginning. I think I can go on now.

"I have forgiven Marino," she said. "But I am still furious that the Austin Police Department coerced a false confession from Chris."

She concluded with a plea. "I am asking the people of Travis County to please, in memory of my daughter and on my behalf, please call the District Attorney's office and protest the death penalty in this case. Please keep my daughter's memory from being stained with this man's blood. Don't let them kill for us."

A week later, she learned that District Attorney Earle would not ask for the death penalty in Marino's trial, which probably would be held sometime the following year. She will never know whether it was her actions and words or whether it was some other consideration that affected Earle's decision. Whatever caused Earle to decide against the death penalty, Jeanette felt he did the right thing, she told her supporters. And with that, she was satisfied.

## Chapter 26

# Facing
# Another Trial

Jeanette had learned that Achim Marino's trial had been set for October 7, 2002, and every day she awoke dreading it. A few days before the trial was to start, Bryan Case called and asked if she would consider talking to Marino again. The Assistant District Attorney wanted to see if Jeanette could persuade him to change his mind and accept the plea that still was on the table. She had read in the newspapers that Marino was so determined to stand trial that he had written a letter to a Texas newspaper in which he said he decided to plead not guilty by reason of insanity.

"Originally, I had intended to accept a state plea bargain solely to spare Jeanette Popp and her family and friends the trauma and the pain of a subsequent murder trial," he wrote. "However, because I am a former mentally ill person who was also subject to direct demonic influences . . . I cannot morally or in good conscience plead guilty to the murder of Nancy Lena DePriest, and the reason for my change of heart can be summed up in two words. Andrea Yates."

Yates was a Houston mother who had drowned her five small children in the bathtub the previous summer and her trial had already been held. A Houston jury had rejected the death penalty in her case and sentenced Yates to life in prison.

Marino wrote, "After Yates' sentence was reported to the media, 'normal' society inundated both talk and non-talk formatted radio with calls clamoring for vengeance and Yates' blood. The vast majority of normal society is passively hostile toward the mentally ill, and if given the chance, such as during jury service, will injure such a person at the first opportunity."

In his letter, Marino also said he hoped his case would expose flaws in the way the Texas criminal justice system deals with mentally ill defendants.

To be found not guilty by reason of insanity, a defendant must have a severe mental disease or defect that prevented him from knowing right from wrong at the time of the crime. A court-appointed psychiatrist had already examined Marino and determined that the man's mental illness fell short of criminal insanity. In his report to Judge Bob Perkins, the psychiatrist wrote, "Mr. Marino may have suffered from bipolar disorder at the time of the offense, but he knew that his conduct was wrong and illegal. He set out to murder someone, gained the cooperation of his victim by guile, robbed her, sexually assaulted her and murdered her. Fearing detection, he spent a great deal of effort trying to locate the spent shell casing. All of this strongly indicates that he knew it was illegal and wrong."

Jeanette agreed with the psychiatrist. She did not believe for a moment that Marino was insane, but she felt he was not rational either. She would never forget how he had sat quietly and looked her in the eyes and told her exactly what he had done to her daughter and why he had done it. To her, that was not insanity.

She didn't understand why Case thought she could influence Marino at this point, since she had obviously failed the first time, but she agreed to meet with Marino. She asked Marino's attorney, Larry Sauer, if she could videotape the conversation. She wanted to share it with groups such as the TMN and Murder Victims' Families for Reconciliation, who could show it to victims' families, so they could get a sense of what it was like to visit with the murderer of a loved one. Marino agreed to the taping. His attorney agreed. It never occurred to Jeanette that she would need permission from the District Attorney.

A crowd had gathered at the jail before she went in—the press, members of TMN, including Scott Cobb who would go in with her—to give her support when she talked to Marino. When she told them she would be taping the conversation, the press asked if she would give them copies. She told them she didn't think she could. It might violate Marino's privacy rights.

While she was speaking, Scott Cobb's cell phone rang. It was Bryan Case, who told him, in no uncertain terms, that the meeting was off. She couldn't tape any conversation with Marino. Scott passed the phone to Jeanette and those listening heard only her part of the conversation. She asked why he was canceling the meeting.

This added to her growing anxiety about Marino's trial. She absolutely did not want to go through that trauma again. However, once again she felt she had to be there. This time she hoped real justice for her daughter would be done.

In his opening statement, Bryan Case told the jury, "Nancy DePriest didn't know it, but the minute she opened that door, she was literally a dead woman walking."

In her heart, Jeanette knew that was true. She sat in the front row, holding an unframed five by seven inch photo of Nancy, and sobbed as she listened to the prosecution build its case once more.

In his opening statement, defense attorney Larry Sauer asked the jury of eight women and four men to scrutinize police officers' testimonies against Marino, reminding them that another jury wrongly convicted Richard Danziger of the crime after hearing much of the same evidence.

"You need to look at everything with a very critical eye," he said.

The majority of the three-day trial was taken up by the defendant's testimony in his own behalf. It was clairvoyance, he said, or second sight. Starting in his childhood, Marino said, spirits surrounded him, giving him special knowledge and demanding sacrifices, such as the brutal death of Nancy DePriest. When he spoke her name, he didn't flinch or show any emotion. He looked straight out at his    attorney or down at his hands, but never at the jury. He spoke almost clinically, as if he were talking about another person rather than himself.

For the better part of two days, Marino sat in the witness box, rambling, talking about the voices in his head. What they told him to do. About Andrea Yates' trial. He talked about everything except what he had done to Nancy. Jeanette just wished they would get this over with.

Finally, they did. The case was sent to the jury Thursday morning and, four hours later, they returned with their decision.

The jury found Achim Josef Marino was sane and understood what he was doing when he raped and killed Nancy DePriest. In convicting Marino of capital murder, jurors brushed aside the claims of defense attorneys that Marino was insane and Marino's own testimony that he acted under the spell of demonic spirits.

Marino received an automatic sentence of life in prison. Bryan Case said Marino "should never see the light of day." This life sentence would be added to three life sentences Marino was already serving for aggravated robberies. In 2005, he would become eligible for parole for those crimes and then would begin serving his life sentence for killing Nancy DePriest.

Under Texas law at that time, Marino would have to serve fifteen years of the life sentence for capital murder before becoming eligible for parole.

Victims' family members in Texas are allowed to speak to the court after sentencing. When the time came, Jeanette slowly walked to the witness box, holding the picture of Nancy smiling, her blonde hair glowing, her blue eyes sparkling.

"My daughter has been gone for fourteen years and it's like it was just yesterday," she said. She held up the photo of Nancy so the jurors could see it. "Nancy was a beautiful girl. This is how I remember her. This is how I want you to remember her."

She thanked Bryan Case and his assistant for what they had done to ensure justice for Nancy. By now Jeanette was sobbing heavily, but she turned to Marino.

"May God have mercy on your soul," she said softly.

Once again, reporters were waiting for her outside the courtroom. Jeanette had only one thing to say to them, because now finally it was done. The nightmare was over at last.

"The important thing is, justice has been served," she said. "He's not going to die. But he will not be on the streets again."

## Chapter 27

# Stop the
# Executions

Jeanette continued to speak out against the death penalty as requests by the dozens poured in for her to appear at groups all over.

Years earlier, some death penalty supporters had figured out an easy way to dismiss their opponents. Rather than debate them point by point, they tended to equate opposition to the death penalty with sympathy for criminals. However, death penalty advocates couldn't fling that accusation at Jeanette. For her, violent crime isn't an abstraction, it is an emotional scar that will never go away. For her, the death penalty isn't something that affects someone else, it's a matter of personal anguish.

Certainly, if anyone had a right to want revenge, to seek an eye for an eye, Jeanette did. Instead, she became a crusader for the abolition of the death penalty. Jeanette was featured at the Texas Moratorium Network's march after she joined the group. She made an impressive figure though she didn't present herself as a polished speaker in a power suit. Her long curly blonde hair pulled back in a low ponytail, she looked like anyone's mother in her pink, short sleeved knit shirt, blue jeans and white tennis shoes.

That day, in an unaffected Texas drawl, she sincerely spoke to the crowd about her heartfelt devotion to God and about the importance of being tough on criminals.

She posed an effective argument that capital punishment is wrong for reasons that go beyond cases of mistaken identity, junk science and flaws in the judicial system.

"By the time we get around to executing the person who committed the crime, they're not the same person anymore," she said. For a few moments, her words hung in the air.

"Nancy and I always agreed we were against the death penalty," she told a press conference afterwards. "After Nancy died, I never felt that killing the killer would serve justice. The only feelings I had were of such deep emptiness that still has not been filled. She just took part of me with her. And I was suicidal right after my daughter's death. It took me a while to come out of that depression, but I never had that 'I want somebody to die for this' attitude. I certainly had no love for her killer, but I never had the need for revenge. I think a lot of that is because I have had such great family support. I had my faith in God that all things happen for a reason."

Jeanette spoke earnestly of how she became an activist against the death penalty, because she was so disturbed that the lives of Chris Ochoa and Richard Danziger had been shattered for a crime they didn't commit.

"Now there were two more victims and their families instead of just my daughter and her family. And I've met other people who have been on death row for crimes they didn't commit, and I thought, 'My God, this is not an isolated case.' This is happening over and over again. And I decided I wasn't going to stand still anymore. This has got to stop."

The partisan crowd devoured her every word.

Accepting every opportunity to present her position, she spoke at city councils, universities, high schools, churches, rallies and marches, gaining confidence with each telling.

Unlike other victims who sought closure through the execution of a loved one's murderer, she spoke of forgiveness and reconciliation, of not staining her daughter's memory by killing in her name. All who heard her could tell that she wasn't a paid lobbyist with an agenda, she was simply a mother who found the issue thrust upon her after the child she loved was killed.

As her activities drew more and more publicity, she began getting many emails a week. Most agreed with her view, offering her encouragement and support. Some, though, were filled with hate. A few were especially hurtful, telling her in every sort of manner that if she had really loved her daughter, she would want to see the killer die.

On a visit to a group in El Paso, Jeanette gave her talk and asked for their support for a moratorium on the death penalty. Afterward, Jeanette told the audience in the chamber that she would take questions. One woman, her voice trembling, tears choking her to the point she could barely speak, asked Jeanette, "How can you do this?"

The woman said her own daughter had been murdered. "She was only three years old," the mother sobbed brokenly. "I want the man who did this to die. How can you not feel the same way? Didn't you love your daughter?"

In the face of such grief and distress, Jeanette was stabbed with sorrow for that mother. She understood, moreover, that the grieving woman wasn't being cruel or inhumane to Jeanette. She just wanted what she felt was justice for the death of her daughter and she thought the only justice was in making her daughter's killer pay the price by executing him.

"Yes, I loved my daughter," Jeanette told the woman. "I still love my daughter. But God says we are not to take the life of another, and I think it would dishonor my daughter if I asked for her killer to be executed. Vengeance is mine, sayeth the Lord."

Jeanette thought her heart would break, because she knew there was no way she could make the woman understand that executing her tiny daughter's killer would not bring peace to her heart. Weeping, the woman found her way back to her seat. Jeanette watched her with sadness, but Jeanette felt she had spoken her truth and that was all she could do.

Meeting grieving victims such as this young mother challenged Jeanette's belief system from time to time. When she heard of innocent children who had been murdered for no reason at all, raped, tortured, bludgeoned, dropped off bridges, she sometimes thought, *I could kill that man myself.* But deep down she knew she really couldn't, although she well understood the pain and rage the families of such victims felt.

Some people were more angry than puzzled by her stance, but Jeanette knew that presenting her viewpoint and telling her story to those who opposed was even more important than speaking to sympathizers. When she was asked to speak to a university seminar, the participants of which were primarily police officers, she didn't hesitate.

"I am not trying to insult you," she told them as she began her presentation. "It is not my intention to put all police officers in the same basket. I don't think all policemen are bad. I'm just going to tell you about one I know about."

Then she told the story of her daughter's brutal murder, Chris Ochoa's coerced confession and the terrible miscarriage of justice perpetrated by law enforcement officials. She could tell the officers were uncomfortable, but most were silent. Except for one man, who began abusing her verbally, calling her names and making threats against her. Finally, she gave him a choice. Sit down and shut up. Or leave. He left.

Her experiences as she met other activists and other families of victims reinforced her conviction that the death penalty was wrong. There were too many instances of innocent people being condemned and even the guilty sometimes were mentally ill. She became friends with one member of Murder Victims' Families for Reconciliation whose brother was on death row and after more than a decade, the date for his execution had been set.

Jeanette's friend told her his brother was guilty of the crime of which he had been convicted. He had admitted his guilt. But, her friend said, his brother had experienced mental problems all his life. His family had tried to get help for him when he was just a boy, then again when he was a teenager, but because of a bureaucratic system, he had fallen through the cracks. No one could or would help this family with their child.

When her friend told her the story, Jeanette remembered a court psychiatrist who had once told her, "You can be mentally ill without being legally insane."

*So sad, but all too true,* she thought as she listened to her friend talk about his brother. When he finished, he asked Jeanette if she would come to the prison with him and his family on the day of the execution, which was set for six o'clock in the evening. She agreed, and they went at ten o'clock in the morning to a building near the death house where families could wait for the time of execution. Her friend introduced Jeanette to his sister and his mother. The older woman looked worn and haggard. As they waited together, Jeanette found opportunities to sit with the woman, just the two of them, so they could talk.

The woman said her son had told her how Jeanette lost her daughter. They talked about Nancy for a while and about Jeanette's work with TMN. At length, the woman said, "You know, they've been killing my son every night for the last ten years and I have not been able to do a single thing to save him. I've lain in bed every night for ten years, trying to figure out a way to save my son. Because I know he's going to be murdered.

"I know they're going to do it.

"I know how they're going to do it.

"But I can't stop it."

Jeanette just nodded silently, hoping this mother understood how much she empathized with her suffering, but she had no answer. In her opinion, there was no answer for state sanctioned murder.

The hours passed and the time drew near when this man she didn't even know, but whose plight had touched her so deeply, would be executed. Nearing the time for the appointed execution, Jeanette watched her friend support his mother with his arm around her shoulder as they trudged toward the building where they would wait out the final minutes of the son and brother's life. Jeanette joined the large crowd of demonstrators who had gathered at the wall surrounding the compound that contains the buildings of execution. A huge clock was secured to the wall of the death chamber and the crowd watched it. At one minute before six o'clock, several of the watchers knelt in prayer for the man who was about to die.

A few minutes later, people began walking out of the building enveloped in a somber, silent hush. No one spoke. No one looked at another. Jeanette's friend hurried over and embraced her, tears running down his cheeks. Over his shoulder, she could see his mother, running as fast as she could toward her car.

"Where's your mom going?" Jeanette asked.

He drew away and wiped his cheeks with the backs of his hands. "They wouldn't let her touch my brother, to tell him goodbye. She wants to get to the funeral home and hold him while his body is still warm."

Staring towards the mother, Jeanette just shook her head, trying to dispel her sad, frustrating thoughts and in that moment a new realization came, which she would later introduce into her speeches. *They think they don't create more victims when they do this? Look at that woman! She has been horribly victimized by our judicial system. And has been for years. She was tortured for years. And that's what they do. These people love their family members who are going to be executed and they are tortured with that nightmare of the approaching death for years and years. Children grow up knowing that in ten years or twelve years, Daddy is going to die. Mommy is going to be executed. What kind of a life can that be for them? Those are the other victims. The unrecognized victims. The victims no one knows about. The victims no one talks about. Until you've met them and seen their pain, you don't understand that these mothers, these families are feeling the same pain, the same agony of loss that others felt at the loss of their loved ones.*

Later she sadly proclaimed to her audiences, "We love our children, no matter what they do. Love doesn't change. It's not supposed to. So why would we make someone else feel such grief and loss?

"If you could save someone's life, wouldn't you? Wouldn't any normal person? We can save lives by stopping the death penalty."

When some people began to call Jeanette a "bleeding heart liberal", saying it as if compassion were an obscene word, her reply always was: "I'd rather have a bleeding heart than none at all. I don't want people who do these abominable things to go unpunished. I want them to suffer the most horrible things they could suffer. For my daughter's murder, I want Marino to lie on his hard bunk in his prison cell night after night, wondering if another inmate is going to rape him as he raped Nancy. I want him to be scared every day for the rest of his life, as Nancy must have been."

Yet, for those who insisted they "wanted murderers like Marino to suffer" through lethal injection, Jeanette replied, "Lethal injection is quick. It's over within a few minutes and it's done. They're gone. No suffering for them."

For Jeanette, one of the primary reasons we should do away with executions is what they do to the victims, as well as the killers, kidnappers and rapists. She tells audiences wherever she speaks across the country, "Even though you, as a parent, wife, child of the person in that chamber, stand there and watch the execution, all that hate and rage and anger that you have directed at that person for so long does not die with that person. Where's it going to go? It's going toward yourself, your family, your co-workers, your friends. It will destroy your life—literally eat you alive. When I started thinking about executing Marino, I realized that and I couldn't do that to my husband. I couldn't do that to myself. My daughter would be absolutely furious." She smiles and then she tries to lighten the mood to give them the flavor of the wonderful, lighthearted daughter she lost. "She'd probably come down here and start slapping me around with her halo!"

Chapter 28

# Restitution

Jeanette felt strongly that Chris and Richard should be compensated by the criminal justice system for all they had suffered during the twelve years they were wrongly imprisoned for a crime they didn't commit. So, she was pleased when she heard, in early November of 2002, that both Chris Ochoa and Richard Danziger filed separate lawsuits in federal court against three Austin Police Department homicide investigators. Danziger's sister filed suit on his behalf, asking for fifty million dollars in punitive damages and fifty million dollars in compensation. Chris Ochoa asked for fifty million dollars in punitive damages and twenty million dollars in compensation.

The lawsuits cited illegal acts, including making threats of violence against them and fabricating a confession from Chris Ochoa as well as hiding or destroying exculpatory evidence. In talking of the three detectives involved, Chris Ochoa's attorney, Bill Allison, said with feeling, "They went beyond anything that's acceptable, by anyone's standards."

In addition to naming the three investigators as individuals, the lawsuits named the detectives' supervisors as well as the city of Austin, contending that the department failed to provide adequate training and monitoring of homicide investigators in 1988. Attorneys for both men said other defendants might be added later.

The lawsuits raised new questions about a bleak chapter in the history of the Austin Police Department. The suit claimed that illegal techniques used in interrogations led to the convictions of the two men and were rampant at the time. Attorneys for both Ochoa and Danziger said the detectives' techniques led to false confessions in other cases, including one by another suspect in the same case in which Ochoa and Danziger were convicted.

Danziger's sister, acting on his behalf, also hired attorneys to sue the Texas Department of Criminal Justice, contending that prison officials violated his constitutional rights by providing "grossly deficient" medical care. That lawsuit described in excruciating detail Danziger's suffering in prison, where he had seizures, repeatedly attempted suicide and sometimes hid in the corner, crying.

"At every step, the story gets worse and worse," one of Danziger's attorneys said. "As time went on, it seems that the system failed to an even greater degree."

In support of the men's claims, the lawsuits also cited the Austin Police Department's own investigation into the homicide unit the previous year. That investigation, which consisted of a review of cases from 1986 to 1992, reported a lack of training and supervision, among a host of other problems.

Attorneys for both men pointed out that the trial judge in the case, Judge Bob Perkins, had concluded in 2001 that investigators had fed information to Chris.

Danziger's lawsuit alleged that the police department had acted too slowly on Achim Marino's confession and had let Chris and Richard languish in prison.

Even before the lawsuits were filed, lawyers for both men had advised the city of Austin of their intention to sue. Attorneys for the city told them they felt the city was not liable. At least one member of the city council disagreed, calling Richard's case "the most troubling thing I've had to deal with in my years on the council." He continued, "Ultimately, the justice system broke down in this case. And the city of Austin is part of that justice system."

Richard's attorneys said he needed a lifetime of care, including round-the-clock supervision. His sister said that, if left alone, he would forget to take the medication to control his seizures. He might even forget to eat. She said they were asking for money not only to pay for his care, but also to "make sure that nothing like this ever happens to anyone else."

Eight months of negotiation passed before the Austin city council made its decision regarding Richard Danziger's lawsuit. In June of 2003, the city and Danziger's attorneys reached an agreement, and it was finalized at a city council meeting on July 18, 2003.

Under the terms of the settlement, Danziger received nine million dollars, an unprecedented award, which apparently was one of the largest in the country for a wrong conviction. Danziger's attorney remarked in the press conference that followed, "I want to commend the city attorney, the city council and the city manager for stepping to the plate and taking responsibility and doing the right thing. This will enable Richard to be taken care of for the rest of his life, and we're very happy with this settlement."

When questioned by reporters, he stated that his law firm would receive one third of the settlement amount.

Chris Ochoa did not receive anything in that action. Bill Allison, Chris's attorney, was still engaged in mediation with the city for a proposed settlement. City attorneys and staff had recommended a 5.5 million dollar settlement, but the city council contended that was too much money. It wasn't until November of that year that the council abruptly changed its decision and awarded Chris 5.3 million dollars, just slightly less than staff had recommended months earlier. The settlement required Chris to pay Richard $500,000.

One council member commented that the city's case was strong, but became weaker as the council received new evidence outlining concerns about the way police officers investigated suspects and got confessions. He would not elaborate on his statement, but said the information came from the police department. He said, "The evidence presented to the council relating to patterns and practices at that time was very troubling and substantially increased our risk at trial. It showed internal concern within the police department about the way the police department was handling some of its cases."

Another factor contributing to the council's about-face could have been Richard Danziger's lawsuit against Travis County, seeking damages for the time he remained in prison after Achim Marino first confessed in letters to the police and a Texas newspaper. The suit reminded Travis County that Danziger had remained in prison four more years before DNA evidence cleared him. Travis County awarded him $950,000, said the county judge, because, "I think the average juror probably would have awarded him more. Seldom do you find a defendant who is completely innocent. And he claimed his innocence from the beginning."

The city attorney in charge of the settlement said only that his office was not aware of certain facts as it prepared the case, but became aware of them later and that influenced the legal advice they gave to the council. He said, in his judgment, there was a very high likelihood that the city would lose the lawsuit.

Jeanette hoped the money could ease the paths of the two men—helping Chris back into the mainstream and giving Richard as much peace and pleasure as it was possible for him to enjoy in his injured mental and emotional conditions.

Chapter 29

# One Step Forward, Two Steps Back

By 2004, Jeanette had traveled thousands of miles each year for three years. She had given hundreds of speeches and talked to hundreds of other families of murder victims. She had presented her position to law enforcers, the criminal justice system, churches, civic groups, schools and universities, trying to persuade them to find a better way to deal with violence than perpetrating more violence.

Many of the people she met supported her, including a growing number of state legislators. Not enough, though, to change the law, she discovered. She had been hopeful—even if naïve when it came to government—in 2001 when she joined TMN. Seven bills had been introduced in that session of the legislature which addressed the rights of people accused of violent crime. One bill included easier access to DNA testing by those already convicted, which the state's new governor, Rick Perry, had quickly signed into law.

There had been high enthusiasm for the passage of other bills, according to those lawmakers who were sympathetic to TMN's position. They had hoped that with a new governor, they would be able to address some of the wrongs in the current law regarding the criminal justice system.

During the years when George W. Bush was governor, many lawmakers felt there was no way they would get more progressive legislation past their staunch law and order governor who stood squarely behind the death penalty. For that reason, they didn't even introduce such legislation. Now that Bush was United States president, though, and they had a new governor, they were optimistic things would change in the echoing halls of the state capitol.

It was not to be in 2001, however. There were still many law and order, frontier justice types who wouldn't even consider postponing executions for two years in order to review cases.

One act by the new governor was extremely upsetting to Jeanette, as well as to her lawmaker friends, and to her it indicated that Texas might not have completely severed the cord to the position of their former governor. On the last day of the session, Governor Perry, as former Governor Bush had done before him, vetoed a bill that would have barred the death penalty for convicted killers who are mentally retarded. He had waited until the last minute to reject the measure.

Under the bill, if jurors determined that a convicted killer was mentally retarded, the defendant would have been sentenced to life in prison. Since there is no life without parole provision in Texas law, the defendant would have been eligible for parole in forty years.

After he vetoed the bill, the governor told reporters, "This legislation is not about whether to execute mentally retarded murderers. It's about who determines whether a defendant is mentally retarded in the Texas justice system. Texas juries should be allowed to make those decisions on a case-by-case basis. Taking the death penalty decisions away from jurors in such cases is basically telling the citizens of this state, 'We don't trust you.'" Perry also said, "We do not execute mentally retarded murderers (in Texas) today, but there is no statute barring the practice."

Supporters of the bill stated there were several prisoners currently on Texas's death row who fit the generally accepted definition of mentally retarded. Former Governor Bush had vetoed a similar claim during his tenure as Texas governor, yet it was highly probable that several people executed during those years fit the criteria for mentally retarded.

Senator Ellis, the main supporter of the bill, said, "Governor Perry had a historic opportunity to show the world that we are not only tough on crime but fair and compassionate, as well. He missed the opportunity."

In doing so, Perry challenged a nationwide trend toward protecting mentally retarded killers from execution since this would constitute, in the opinion of many, cruel and unusual punishment, because they do not have the ability to distinguish wrong from right. Mentally retarded killers also are exempt from execution in the federal justice system. And only a few days earlier, Governor Jeb Bush of Florida signed a bill similar to the one Perry vetoed.

The Supreme Court had ruled in 1989 that such executions were constitutional, at which time only two states had laws barring the death penalty for mentally retarded killers. Now, the Court said it would look at the practice again, agreeing to hear a North Carolina case with a defendant considered to be mentally retarded.

Perry had signed a bill, however, that was designed to improve the quality of court-appointed attorneys for indigent defendants. That bill, according to lawmakers, came as a result of the intense criticism of Texas's indigent defense system during George Bush's presidential campaign in 2000. Other measures, including several aimed at reducing executions, were considered this year, although they failed to pass.

Several state representatives told Jeanette they would have to be patient, educate the public and other lawmakers during the coming two years and try again in the next session, in 2003.

Patience was not one of Jeanette's virtues, but she gave it her best shot while continuing her torrid pace, trying to reach as many people with her message as she could.

Jeanette was both heartened and saddened when she heard of the United States Supreme Court's 2002 ruling concerning mentally retarded inmates. True to the promise they made in 2001, the justices banned capital punishment for the moderately mentally retarded, saying that it constitutes cruel and unusual punishment in violation of the Eighth Amendment to the United States Constitution.

Texas state representatives kept their word, preparing legislation for the 2003 legislative session. Even before the session began, Jeanette and TMN members knew it was going to be a long, rocky road over the next six months. In the November 2002 elections, Republicans picked up a substantial number of seats in both the Texas House and the Senate. In the House for the 2003 legislature, Republicans outnumbered Democrats eighty-eight to sixty-two and in the Senate, nineteen to twelve. Jeanette knew that the new Speaker of the House would be a Republican, which meant there undoubtedly would be a Republican chair of the House Criminal Jurisprudence Committee.

Many of the anti-death penalty group's strongest supporters did retain their seats, however. And even before the session began, Representative Lon Burnam of Fort Worth immediately filed a bill to end the execution of juvenile offenders in Texas, a change that would bring the state more into line with international law and a change which a majority of Texans supported. Also, in a historic first, a bill to completely abolish the death penalty in Texas was introduced. Even though she had been advocating it all these months, it was almost unimaginable to Jeanette that anyone would actually file a death penalty abolition bill in Texas.

The theme of the year for TMN was, "We can be successful this time around; we will just have to work harder."

In March, Representative Harold Dutton, who had long been a supporter of the anti-death penalty movement, announced the first ever "Day of Innocence" in the state of Texas to recognize all exonerated individuals from across Texas and the nation. It was a huge event with Barry Scheck as the keynote speaker. Jeanette and Chris Ochoa also were on the platform. Dutton also announced that he had introduced both a moratorium bill and a bill to abolish the death penalty in Texas. Representative Dutton said he did so because "the increasing number of factually innocent persons who were previously found legally guilty should shake the conscience of all free people. There should be no disagreement that our justice system's inability to get at truth undermines public confidence and provides a drumbeat for a march toward anarchy. All reasonable and fair-minded persons must act now to bring needed reforms to our justice system."

Representative Dutton also noted that since the reinstatement of the death penalty in 1976, Texas had led the nation with 299 executions, with the 300th scheduled on March 20. In 2002, Texas executed thirty-three persons, which was almost one half of all executions in the United States for the same period of time.

Dutton concluded that clearly Texas's use of the death machine should be halted while the much needed reforms were investigated, debated and implemented. To continue Texas's flawed system of justice while ignoring the cautions expressed recently by those closest to the process would be unconscionable.

To Jeanette's dismay, in spite of the best efforts of a few legislators, little was accomplished in the way of reforms during the 2003 session.

It seemed to Jeanette that all her effort, all her talking, all her traveling had accomplished too little except growing frustration—and a mountain of debt. For three years, she had paid her own expenses everywhere she went, to anti-death penalty rallies, for hundreds of trips to cities and towns across the state—and her credit cards were maxed out. She and Jim had started on this mission as partners and he had supported and encouraged her all the way. He was earning good money, until he lost the job where he had worked for more than a decade. It became obvious that they could no longer continue as they had been. Jeanette would have to go back to work. She might have to give up her life as a full time activist, but she wasn't ready to quit. Not just yet.

"There must be a better way to reach these people," she told Jim. She thought about it until her head hurt, looked at the challenge from every perspective she could imagine, but at the end of every day, she felt depressed and dejected. Suddenly a new idea came to her.

"There is one thing I haven't tried," she told him. "If the legislature won't listen to an outsider, maybe I should try getting *inside*. Maybe I will run for state representative." The more she thought about the idea, the better she liked it. And Jim, as always, encouraged her. Deep inside, Jeanette knew she had little chance. They were living in Azle, located in District 99, which was comprised of a dozen suburbs of Fort Worth, but not including the city. She would be running against a popular three-term incumbent, a Fort Worth businessman who had been an active city leader for many years. He had access to scads of money.

Jeanette Popp, on the other hand, could spend only five thousand dollars on her campaign, which meant virtually no advertising. Her money would have to be spent on gasoline and person to person campaigning. Nevertheless, just as she dedicated herself to bringing her anti-death penalty cause to all she could, she now resolved to knock on every door in District 99 if she had to, in order to get her message across.

Even if, by some miracle, she won, it wouldn't solve her money problems. The Texas legislature meets biannually, from January through May, and representatives are paid seven hundred dollars a month. When the legislature is in session or members are in Austin on state business, such as committee meetings and preparation of bills, they get a per diem. Occasionally an extra, thirty-day session will be called to address urgent legislation. The rest of the time, most of the members are busily engaged in making a living, in professions such as the law and business, with some exceptions.

Though Jeanette knew her uphill battle had little chance to succeed, she hoped to call attention one more time to what she saw as critical flaws in the way the criminal justice system worked and to persuade people to join her in pleading for the death penalty to be outlawed.

Since she had no experience in waging a campaign, her first step was to seek the advice of one of the state representatives she had gotten to know and respect through her TMN activities. She met him for lunch and peppered him with questions.

Finally, he said, "Jeanette, you just can't go around telling the voters you're against the death penalty."

"Why not? That's why I'm getting into the race."

He shook his head. "Because, if you do that, you'll never get elected. *First,* you get elected. *Then* you try to do what you want to do."

She stared at him incredulously. "You mean I've got to go all over this district lying to the people from day one? I can't do that."

"It isn't lying. Just don't tell them. It is the only way you have any chance at all of winning this election."

"I just can't do that," she said. "Besides," she pointed out, "Harold Dutton has been supporting anti-death penalty groups ever since I can remember and he keeps getting elected." Dutton was a Houston Democrat who had been in the legislature for years.

So she started her campaign the way she had started her presentations for the last three year: "Hi. My name is Jeanette Popp and I'm against the death penalty." She figured honesty was always the best policy. She was determined to stand up and tell the truth. Tell voters what she believed.

She said it in public forums where she and her opponent shared the platform. She said it in the doorways and on the front steps of thousands of homes in her district. She said it in stores, gas stations and medical offices.

She was delighted when she was invited to a Dennis Kucinich fundraiser. When it was her turn to speak, she rose, looked around the room and said, "There's something you people need to know about me. I'm against the death penalty."

She got a standing ovation.

Other state representatives took note of what she was doing and told her privately that they too were against the death penalty. But most of them were not about to say so where the voters could hear. They too, like the friend she'd first queried, believed that was no way to get elected to the Texas legislature.

She posted an endorsement on her website from Bill Allison, who had been Chris Ochoa's attorney.

Allison wrote, "I have worked with Jeanette Popp for the last three years, resolving the wrongful convictions of the two men who spent twelve years in the Texas prison system for her daughter's murder. She is the toughest, sweetest woman I have ever met. She has taken tragedies which in most people's lives would simply destroy them and turned it into a strength that cannot be defeated. When the going got tough, and it continued to get tougher and tougher, she just dug deeper. Jeanette Popp is a straight-shooter who can be trusted from her first word to her last. If you are looking for someone who is going to do what she says she is going to do, you want Jeanette Popp. *Wouldn't that be refreshing—a politician you could trust.*"

At gatherings and in the media, she told the story of a trip she had made to Montreal for the World Conference Against the Death Penalty. A French-speaking Canadian sitting next to her asked, "Where are you from?"

"I'm from Texas," she said.

"Aahhh," he said. "The killing state."

Jeanette was aghast. She didn't realize the reputation of her home state had spread so far, but she just laughed. "Yeah. That's us. Good old boy attitude. We're still playing Judge Roy Bean—hang 'em all and let God sort 'em out."

Sadly, that trip, as well as contacts with leaders in other states, made her realize that Texas still has a long way to go as far as social conscience goes.

Jeanette didn't win the election, but she was thrilled and amazed when she got 35 percent of the vote. She felt she truly had opened some eyes about the harm the death penalty was doing, not only to individuals and families, but also to the image of Texas, in the United States and abroad.

# Chapter 30

# Progress
# Inch by Inch

Although Texas lawmakers didn't enact the reforms Jeanette had hoped for, finally the United States Supreme Court took control of reforms she felt most needed to be made, absent a total ban on executions. In 2004, the high Court agreed to consider a case that would decide whether the execution of juvenile defendants is a violation of the Eighth Amendment. The case in question involved a Missouri Supreme Court Case, heard in 2003. In addition to the defendant's brief, amicus briefs were submitted by such notables as former president Jimmy Carter, the American Medical Association, the European Union and the United States Conference of Catholic Bishops.

In March of 2005, the nation's highest Court handed down its decision. By a 5-4 vote, the Court held that the Eighth and Fourteenth Amendments forbid the execution of offenders who were under the age of eighteen when their crimes were committed.

On the day the ruling came down, twenty states permitted the death penalty for offenders younger than eighteen, which is five fewer than allowed it in 1989. In those twenty states, seventy-nine people who had been under the age of eighteen when their crimes were committed were awaiting execution. Texas led the list with twenty-nine.

Justice Arthur Kennedy, writing for the majority, concluded that the death penalty for minors is cruel and unusual punishment, citing "a national consensus" against the practice, as well as medical and social-science evidence that teenagers are too immature to be held accountable for their crimes to the same extent as adults.

The court's judgment, which overturned a 1989 ruling that had upheld the death penalty for sixteen and seventeen-year-old offenders, was influenced by a desire to end this country's international isolation on the issue.

"From a moral standpoint, it would be misguided to equate the failings of a minor with those of an adult, for a greater possibility exists that a minor's character deficiencies will be reformed," Justice Kennedy wrote. "Our determination finds confirmation in the stark reality that the United States is the only country in the world that continues to give official sanction to the juvenile death penalty."

The court affirmed the necessity of referring to "the evolving standards of decency that mark the progress of a maturing society" to determine which punishments are so disproportionate as to be cruel and unusual. The Court reasoned that the rejection of the juvenile death penalty in the majority of states, the infrequent use of the punishment even where it remains on the books and the consistent trend toward abolition of the juvenile death penalty demonstrated a national consensus against the practice.

Jeanette was pleased that the Court had ruled as it had, but she was still angry and frustrated at the lack of action on the part of too many Texas lawmakers.

Now, though, she had to get on with her life. Jim had found a wonderful new job and they were moving back to Graham, Texas, which had been her home for much of her life. She had gotten a job, and they were working to create their lives in a different environment, in a new home, with new goals and ambitions.

Though her work to abolish the death penalty was no longer full time, Jeanette kept researching and advocating for the cause she had led for so long. She was deeply saddened and ultimately furious when she learned that in August of 2007, Texas would execute its 400th person since 1976—actually since 1982, because the state didn't resume executions for six years after the act was reinstituted—by far the most of any other state. The European Union, which opposes capital punishment and bans it in its twenty-seven nations, urged Governor Rick Perry to stop the execution and impose a death penalty moratorium.

Perry's spokesman Robert Black said the state would decline the call for a moratorium.

Another death row inmate was scheduled to be executed the following week.

When, a few weeks later, the Supreme Court agreed to hear another case concerning the death penalty, Jeanette's satisfaction was tinged with skepticism. The Court's willingness to consider the case was encouraging, but she thought she already knew what the outcome would be. Two Kentucky death row inmates were arguing that the current lethal injection method violates the constitutional ban on cruel and unusual punishment by inflicting needless pain and suffering. One of the points in the case was that the three-drug cocktail currently being used could, if given at too low a dose, cause extraordinary pain for the person, who would have no way to let anyone know he was suffering. There was evidence of botched executions in which inmates had taken more than thirty minutes to die.

Most states had decided to postpone any planned executions until the Supreme Court had issued a ruling. So, for a while, at least, no one else would die in Texas's death house.

In April of 2008, on a beautiful day, the President of the United States was host to Pope Benedict, an avowed opponent of the death penalty, when the Court announced it had rejected the challenge by the Kentucky inmates. The justices had decided that the present three-drug formula used in executions did not violate the Eighth Amendment.

The Court did leave open the possibility of future changes to lethal injection practices if another method were discovered that could be proven to significantly reduce the risk of severe pain. Any alternative execution method must be feasible, readily implemented and significantly reduce a substantial risk of severe pain for the death row inmate, according to the announcement.

When she heard the decision, Jeanette turned to Jim to release her frustration, as she had so often over the years. "Because of that ruling, they will be running people through the death house like cattle," she fumed. "They will start executing people just as fast as they can. Texas will be the first to execute someone and they'll do it just as fast as they can."

In fact, the nation's busiest death chamber reopened in June 1, 2008, after a nearly nine-month hiatus, and the first execution scheduled would be the fourth in the nation since the Court ruling. By June 23, however, about two dozen had been scheduled from June through October, although several had been stayed or postponed, one because the Supreme Court had agreed to review it.

On December 15, 2007, Ronnie Earle, who had been Travis County District Attorney for thirty-two years, announced that he would not seek re-election. He planned to retire in January of 2009. Jeanette watched with interest to see who might be succeeding him. She hoped they would get a commitment from someone against the death penalty.

Even before Earle's announcement, his staff and others in the Austin legal community had seen signs of his impending exit and were considering running, including three members of his staff. Also expressing interest were a county attorney, a retired district judge and one of Earle's Assistant District Attorneys, Rosemary Lehmberg.

The Texas Moratorium scheduled a press conference to be held in downtown Austin on January 12, 2008, urging all the candidates for District Attorney to impose a moratorium on the death penalty in

Travis County by not seeking the death penalty in any capital trials and instead, using life without parole as an alternative to the death penalty. Jeanette Popp and the mother of another murder victim were invited to speak at the event. Scott Cobb of TMN also spoke and his talk was posted on a blog site. "The death penalty system in Texas is broken," he reminded his listeners. "The next DA in Travis County should reflect how the Travis County community's views on the death penalty have evolved in recent years and pledge that for now, the death penalty is off the table within Travis County."

Cobb said that people know the Texas death penalty system is flawed from start to finish, from the initial investigation and arrest, to the process used to decide whether to seek the death penalty, to the actual prosecution and defense of a capital trial, to the appeals process and the manner in which an execution is finally carried out.

The most fundamental problem, he told them, is perhaps an inability to distinguish with certainty whether a person is guilty or innocent. If a system cannot ensure that the guilty are convicted and the innocent protected, then the death penalty should not be an option. The need for local prosecutors to impose a moratorium on death penalty prosecutions is particularly great because of the failure of state leaders to enact a moratorium and create a commission to study the death penalty. In fact, the state legislature would not even create an innocence commission.

Cobb suggested that the people of Travis County were comfortable with life without parole as an alternative to the death penalty. "Any candidate who seeks to become District Attorney in Travis County should pledge not to seek the death penalty. Life without parole is a valid alternative. In a contested Democratic primary, a candidate who acknowledges that the death penalty system in Texas is riddled with problems and puts innocent people at risk of execution is likely to be rewarded with votes. If we want to slow down the number of executions in Texas and reduce the risk of executing an innocent person, we need to elect a District Attorney who will pledge to impose a moratorium on seeking new death sentences and a moratorium on setting execution dates for cases with existing execution death sentences. Certainly, a DA candidate in Travis County who makes such a pledge will find a rich reward of votes in the Democratic primary," Cobb said.

Cobb speculated that the conscience of the Austin community had changed enough that any person seeking the Democratic nomination for Travis County District Attorney in 2008 was going to have to seek the support of voters within a community whose conscience does not include support for the Texas death penalty.

By that time, the field of candidates stood at four, all Democrats, all members of Earle's staff and none of them had made any statements concerning their position on the death penalty or a moratorium. Whoever won the primary would be the next District Attorney of Travis County.

The primary was held in March and turned out to be a close race between Rosemary Lehmberg and Mindy Montford, who faced a runoff. In the runoff, Lehmberg took 65 percent of the vote and became the new District Attorney of Travis County.

Jeanette hoped and prayed that Lehmberg would prove to be an advocate for life without parole in capital cases.

Jeanette wished she could see the changes Scott Cobb had advocated, but she wasn't as optimistic as he was. It wasn't over, she knew. And she knew that whenever and wherever she could, she would continue to support and fight for her convictions.

# Chapter 31

# Postscript

Jeanette opens her eyes and can tell by the quality of the light filtering through her bedroom windows that it is going to be another warm sunny day in Graham, Texas. Jim has already gone to work, around 3:30 A.M., as he usually does. She will get up and get ready to go to her job in a little while. First, though, as she does every morning of her life, she says a prayer for Nancy. On her way to the kitchen, she detours to the hall where the portrait of Nancy hangs and tells her daughter good morning. As she looks into Nancy's smiling blue eyes, she reflects on the past twenty years: the terrible, almost insurmountable grief; the recurrent nightmare vision of Nancy at the hands of her killer—a dream that almost never visits her now; the satisfaction she felt when Chris Ochoa and Richard Danziger were set free; the vicarious grief she experienced when she met other mothers of murdered children; the anger and frustration that had consumed her for years, because people seemed not to see the flaws inherent in the current criminal justice system, nor to hear that there is a better way to deal with people who commit crimes.

She thinks of Chris Ochoa and his confession to Nancy's murder, an act that altered a number of lives directly, and who knows how many lives indirectly through his and Jeanette's work to raise awareness of the need to abolish the death penalty. That confession was almost incomprehensible to her when she first discovered it was false and it is still difficult to pinpoint any single reason for Chris— or anyone else—to make such a statement, knowing he is innocent.

The occurrence of false confessions is not as uncommon as Jeanette assumed in the beginning. Although it is almost impossible to estimate the number of false confessions that have been given nationwide, the Chicago Tribune conducted an investigation into ten years' worth of murder cases in one Illinois county. That investigation found 247 instances in which the defendants' self-incriminating statements were either thrown out by the court or a jury found them to be unconvincing and refused to convict.

The most devastating fact to Jeanette is that sometimes the goal of every law enforcement officer, including prosecutors and courts, is to properly solve a case. Unfortunately, the quickest and easiest way to convicting a suspect is through gaining a confession. It is estimated that 80 percent of all solved cases rely on a defendant's confession. For centuries, physical abuse and torture were used to elicit confessions, resulting in an unknown number of false statements, because confession was tantamount to conviction. As the United States began to demonstrate a more highly developed social conscience, the use of physical and psychological abuse to gain confessions was prohibited by law.

In 1936, the U. S. Supreme Court heard the case of Brown v. Mississippi, in which three black men were arrested for murder. The men were not allowed to talk to a lawyer and during their interrogations they were threatened, beaten and tortured. Finally, each of them signed a statement, written by the police, in which they confessed to the murder. All three were convicted and sentenced to death. The Supreme Court reversed their convictions, ruling that evidence gained through physical torture and brutality could not be presented in trials. The Court stated that a trial "is a mere pretense where the state authorities have continued a conviction resting solely upon confessions obtained by violence." Since that landmark ruling, the admissibility of confessions is subject to the requirement that statements must be made voluntarily; they must be given freely and knowingly, without physical or psychological coercion.

That decree has not deterred the use of psychological manipulation of suspects to achieve the desired goal: getting them to confess to the crime so the detectives can move on to other cases. Unfortunately, some suspects are unable to prevail against the tactics practiced by the interrogators, so they confess even when they know they are innocent.

Law enforcement interrogators have learned, through experience or through training manuals written by psychologists, methods by which a suspect can be led to confess to a crime. Sometimes even when he or she is not guilty of that crime. Interrogators resort to the use of tactics such as prolonging questioning over many hours or even days, refusing to let the suspect go until he has confessed. No one confesses falsely—or truthfully—in an hour. But investigators know that everyone has a breaking point and if they can control the conditions of the interrogation, including time, they can more easily prevail.

Isolating the suspect is commonly used, putting him into a small room furnished only with a table and one or two chairs, with no windows. Throughout the long hours of grilling, the suspect sees only one or two detectives and no one else. Some interrogators go so far as to refuse to let the suspect contact his family or an attorney—although he has a right, by law, to talk to an attorney whenever he wishes—but imply that these privileges might be granted as soon as he makes a statement.

Introduction of false interrogation evidence is common in nearly every false confession case. For example, the interrogator may tell the suspect his fingerprints are on the gun used in the murder. Although this may be patently untrue, U. S. courts have upheld the practice.

Often, police tell a suspect that if he tells them the "truth", he can go home. Thus, the false confession becomes an escape hatch and may seem rational. If he tells them what they want to hear, they will let him go.

Or some interrogators tell the suspect a confession will be rewarded with lenient sentencing, and the suspect may confess to a murder, hoping to win a prison term rather than a death sentence.

Some suspects are more vulnerable to the pressures of police interrogation than others. Those with low IQs, for example, are less likely to understand the charges against them. They may not realize the consequences of falsely incriminating themselves.

People with normal-to-higher IQs are not invulnerable to the pressure, however. Suspects with suggestible personalities and/or anxiety disorders may not be able to withstand an interrogation.

On occasion, people confess to crimes of which they are innocent, because they have deep-seated guilt issues. They are guilty of "something", even if that something is ill-defined.

In many cases, an innocent suspect being grilled by detectives will confess, because he thinks he can recant when he gets an attorney. He just wants—needs—to get out of that box where they have questioned him for all those hours. Then, he knows he can call an attorney or have one appointed for him and he can tell the truth, that he is innocent. Unfortunately, most of the time it is too late. No one will believe him.

And at times, Jeanette thinks, suspects confess for reasons unknown to themselves and unknown to all the psychologists and psychiatrists and all those who seek the answers to the disquieting subject of false confessions. Although she may not understand what motivated Chris Ochoa's confession, she remembers the answer he gave to all who questioned him after his release. "I don't know," he said. "I was so scared. If you've never been in that situation, you don't know what you're going to do. You can sit there and say, 'I would never

ever confess to something I didn't do.' But you just don't know."

If Chris doesn't know why he did it, then neither can she or anyone else know, unless they have been there.

Then Jeanette remembers: There have been victories—small and few—but victories nonetheless. Texas no longer executes juveniles or mentally retarded individuals. The consciousness of people has been raised over the past half dozen years, so that more and more, the citizens of Texas and around the nation are developing a social conscience, leaning toward more humane treatment of their fellow humans.

Nancy has been dead twenty years now and people tell Jeanette, "It should be over. You should forget. With all that you have experienced, all that you have accomplished since 2001, you should have closure."

For Jeanette, however, there's no such thing as closure. In order to close a chapter of your life, you have to close out the person you've lost. If she were seeking closure, she would have to close the door on Nancy. That is unthinkable. "You can't just close the door on one period of your life," she says. The sum of your life, all that you have been, creates who you are today, and today, Jeanette is still a mother who loves her daughter dearly and doesn't want to lose a single memory of her.

Sometimes, when Jeanette is outside, she looks up at the blue sky and the sun and talks to Nancy. "What a beautiful day we're having! We could go swimming. Are you raining or shining on me today?"

Somewhere, she is sure her daughter is listening, maybe laughing with her. And Jeanette is thankful.

# About the Authors

Jeanette Popp is the mother of the victim and advocated actively for the release of her daughter's wrongly convicted murderers. Jeanette went on to run for the Texas Legislature and has been active as a motivational speaker on the topics of wrongful imprisonment and the abolishment of the death penalty. She lives in Graham, Texas with her husband, Jim.

Wanda Evans, an accomplished journalist, author and speaker, has been published in many venues, including the notable true crime book *Trail of Blood* and magazines such as *Reader's Digest*, *Good Housekeeping* and *Southern Living*. A former columnist for the *Lubbock Avalanche-Journal*, she lives in Lubbock, Texas.

The Innocence Project commends Jeanette Popp, Chris Ochoa, Richard Danziger and their families for enduring years of injustice with courage and determination.

The Innocence Project, which is affiliated with Benjamin N. Cardozo School of Law, assists prisoners who could be proven innocent through DNA testing and brings substantive reform to the system responsible for their unjust imprisonment. Over 225 people in the United States have been exonerated through DNA evidence, including 17 who served time on death row.

You can help. To learn more, visit www.innocenceproject.org.

# INNOCENCE PROJECT